FACILITATING PLAY

Sara Smilansky, Leah Shefatya

FACILITATING PLAY:

A Medium for Promoting Cognitive, Socio-Emotional and Academic Development in Young Children

Psychosocial & Educational Publications
Gaithersburg, MD

Printed in the United States of America

Published by:

Psychosocial & Educational Publications
P.O. Box 2146
Gaithersburg, Maryland 20886

Library of Congress Catalog Card Number: 90-60170

To our children:

Jonathan and Saul,
Avital, Noah, Ofra and Livnat

With many thanks for involving us in their
sociodramatic play

Contents

Introduction

Sociodramatic play is one of the most fascinating phenomena of early childhood. It consists of complex behavior, characterized by joyful concentration, intensity and expressive fluency.

We began to be interested in this form of play when we realized that entire groups of children either did not develop this type of play behavior or did so in a most limited way. We were in the middle of a period when Israeli preschool educators and researchers were looking for methods to promote cognitive development in preschoolers whose parents had minimal or no formal education. While working in the kindergartens we were puzzled to discover that the majority of these children did not take advantage of the equipment provided for pretend play (the doll or hospital corners, etc.), despite the fact that they had been coming to preschool classes daily from the age of three or four. Those few who did go into the play corners engaged mainly in solitary manipulation of the toys for short periods of time. This behavior was in such sharp contrast to the sociodramatic play of children from higher socioeconomic backgrounds that it could not be overlooked. This behavioral distinction posed an educational challenge as well as a theoretical problem and so we embarked on a series of observational studies in nursery school and kindergarten classes as well as in the children's homes. Following these studies, we carried out an intervention study—the first of its kind—in which we engaged in activity which would foster development of sociodramatic play specifically in children whose parents had little formal education. The findings of the observational and experimental studies, as well as the theoretical formulations related to the findings, were presented in our first book, published in 1968.

Since then a large body of research has accumulated, conducted by us and others in the United States, the United Kingdom and in Israel. These research studies provide cross-cultural support for our contentions about the existence of differences in sociodramatic play behavior with regard to socioeconomic background; they also support our suggestions about the relevance of such play for school-related behavior and achievement and about the feasibility of "teaching" social make-believe play by means of short-term adult intervention using a variety of methods. Moreover, it has been demonstrated that there is transfer from such intervention to a variety of cognitive, creative, socio-emotional and academic skills.

Since publishing our first work on sociodramatic play, we have deepened our understanding at the conceptual level. I was visiting professor at Ohio State University from 1971-1972 and conducted a graduate seminar on sociodramatic play with ten experienced preschool educators and psychologists. This seminar broadened my understanding of sociodramatic play as it occurs in the culture of another country. It led to an elaboration of my original scale for evaluating sociodramatic play. Moreover, the dissertations of several of the seminar participants have become important empirical works in the field. Subsequently, my position as professor of psychology at Tel Aviv University also provided me with opportunities to learn a great deal about sociodramatic play from my graduate students' research.

During my stay in Columbus, Ohio, I had the privilege and the pleasure to work with and learn a great deal about sociodramatic play from our dear friend, the late Professor Ross Mooney of Ohio State University. The lengthy consultations and discussions with him were an important experience for me and contributed many new insights about the essence and significance of sociodramatic play as an expression of the child's world as well as a vehicle for further growth and development.

This book incorporates the new understanding gained as well as the relevant empirical work that has been gathered and that underscores the importance of including differential training for sociodramatic play as an integral part of the preschool curriculum. We present our past findings together with the more recent research findings as an integrated whole. This book also suggests an instrument for the evaluation of sociodramatic play that assesses the major categories of make-believe play as perceived and defined in the body of this work. The instrument's usefulness, reliability and validity was established with Israeli as well as children from the United States. Make-believe play deserves to be observed, diagnosed, fostered and evaluated. This book is meant to provide the theoretical rationale and the empirical basis for this purpose, for all concerned with early childhood education and development of young children: college and university teachers, developmental psychologists, researchers, nursery and kindergarten teachers and parents.

In addition, we hope that the information and questions raised in this book will stimulate further research; we draw your attention to some particularly important issues which are pointed out in the summary chapter sections.

It is hoped that this book will be a step towards recognizing sociodramatic play as an enjoyable and useful activity per se, as well as a means for enhancing the young child's socio-emotional and cognitive development and academic achievement.

Sara Smilansky

Chapter One: The Nature of Dramatic and Sociodramatic Play

In this chapter the characteristics of dramatic and sociodramatic play are described and criteria for determining and evaluating the level of such play is determined.

1. Sociodramatic Play: A Unique Form of Play Behavior

In order to delineate the characteristics of sociodramatic play, it is convenient to view it as a distinct type of behavior among other forms of play. There is a basic difference between dramatic and sociodramatic play and other play varieties, in regard to the focus of interest and activity. Dramatic (symbolic) play focuses mainly on social roles and interaction; other types of play focus on bodily activation and/or the exploration and utilization of objects and materials.

There are four general types of play behavior: functional play, constructive play, dramatic (also known as symbolic or pretend) play and games with rules. Children from three years of age up to school age can be observed alternating between the different types of play at different levels of elaboration. Essential features of each of the types are as follows:

Functional Play

It is the first form of play to appear and continues in some form throughout early childhood. It is characterized by simple muscular or sensory-motor activities and is based on the child's need to activate his physical organism. The games played are "naturally" functional; the child repeats his actions and manipulations, imitates himself, tries new actions, imitates them, repeats them, etc. The child also makes utterances and plays at repeating and imitating them, laying the foundations for speech. Manipulation of toys and materials provides experience which reveals the material environment to the child; functional play thus affords the child practice of his physical capabilities and the chance to explore and experience the material environment.

Constructive Play

Appears in early childhood and lasts quite often right into adulthood. It also focuses around sensory-motor activity, but with the important addition of a preconceived plan. This form of play introduces the child to creative activity and thereby to the personal joy of creating. The child learns the different uses of play materials: he moves from functional activity to activity that results in a "creation." He is now able to sustain his play and concentrate for a longer period of time and organize the use of materials according to a plan. The child who is able to achieve play goals he has set for himself is also able to achieve, to some degree, play goals set by others. Development from functional play to constructive play is a progression from *manipulation of a form to formation*; from *sporadic handling* of sand and bricks to *building* something which will remain even after he has finished playing. The child expresses his activity through these "creations" and recognizes himself as "creator."

Games with Rules

Another route leading from random functionalism to elaborated play is "Games with Rules." Two broad categories of games with rules are: table games (dominos, cards, dice and board games, checkers, etc.) and physical games (hide and seek, jumprope, ball games of various types, etc.) Both categories of games with rules require the child to accept prearranged rules and adjust to them. He must learn to control his behavior, actions and reactions within the given limits. This form of play also remains with the child into his adult life.

Dramatic Play

This plus its more mature form, *sociodramatic play* expresses the child's growing awareness of his social surroundings. Acts of pretend behavior have been observed in children from approximately the second year, paralleling other play behavior development. The child consciously imitates certain gestures and acts out an "as if" situation. Dramatic or symbolic play allows the child to experience human relationships actively by means of symbolic representation. Sociodramatic play, allows the child to be an actor, observer and interactor simultaneously, using his abilities in a common enterprise with other children. Dramatic and sociodramatic play differs from the three other types of play* in that it is *person-oriented* and not material and/ or object oriented.

The subject of this book is dramatic play behavior in its most developed form: sociodramatic play.

2. A Sample of a Sociodramatic Play Episode

The following dialogue represents a play episode of kindergarten children in a modern, suburban school in Jerusalem. On this particular day three girls, Sarah, Ruth and Tamar get together at the corner of the kindergarten room which contains toys and objects suggesting a doctor's office. There are both hospitals and neighborhood community clinics which offer medical services to the families in Jerusalem; as the dialogue proceeds, it will become clear that the girls are assuming that they are in a hospital clinic.

(1) SARAH   (picks up two dolls and gives one to Ruth): Ruth, that is your baby.

---

*See in Chapters Two and Four, more on the differences between these four types of play.

(2) RUTH	Let's pretend both have the measles.
(3) SARAH	(noticing that Tamar is already busy with the doctor's medicine bag) Tamar, why are you taking that?
(4) RUTH	(joining Sarah and speaking to Tamar) You can't take that; that's the doctor's bag.
(5)	(Observing and accepting Tamar's evident desire to be the "doctor") Tamar, okay!
(6)	(As mother, looking at her own baby) You know, she *is* sick; she has the measles. No, no, she has the flu!
(7) TAMAR	(as the doctor) If she has the measles, she shouldn't have cough syrup!
(8) RUTH	But she has the flu! My mommy has the flu, too, really!
(9) SARAH	It is my turn now; I have number 65.[1]
(10)	(looking at Ruth) You have number 66.
(11)	(looking at Tamar) Doctor, are you going to give her (Sarah's baby) a shot?
(12) TAMAR	There's no need for a shot. I will examine her.
(13) SARAH	There, there darling; the doctor is only examining you. Don't cry.
(14) TAMAR	(giving a shot with a long object) I just did it; I finished giving her a shot.
(15) RUTH	You did it already?
(16) SARAH	Yes, she did a good job.
(17)	(turning to her own baby) Don't cry, sweetie, sweetie; it's all right.
(18) TAMAR	(speaking to Sarah) Give me some cotton; she is bleeding!
(19) SARAH	(taking red cotton out of the doctor's bag) Oh, poor baby, she is bleeding! Sit nicely, I will change your clothes.
(20) DAVID	(comes by and asks) What's going on here?
(21) SARAH	It's a hospital.
(22) DAVID	What, a shot in a hospital?!

---

[1]There are no appointments in these clinics, but you are given a number when you arrive.

(23) SARAH   Let's pretend it was a blood test.

(24) RUTH   (watching Tamar) A blood test is taken from the finger!

(25) TAMAR   I did it from the foot.

(26) RUTH   Excuse me, but a blood test is taken from the finger. My grandma works at the clinic and she takes blood tests from the finger; I know better!

(27)   (speaking to David as a "man") Isn't that right?

(28) DAVID   (responding as a "man") Ruth is right!

(29) SARAH   I have to go shopping now. Oh! She took all my money (referring to her baby)! She is a bad girl!

(30) RUTH   My baby is good. I buy her all kinds of candy and ice cream and she is quiet.

(31) SARAH   I buy [things] for her too and [still] she goes on screaming.

(32)   (turning to David) Do you know what her name is? Nitzan.

(33) DAVID   That's a boy's name!

(34)   (turning to Ruth) Where is your baby?

(35) RUTH   At home.

(36)   (turning to David) Let's pretend you are a dog.

(37) DAVID   Good, then you feed me.

(38) TAMAR   Who's next?

(39) SARAH   I open the curtain; now I must put a bandage on my baby's head; she fell and hurt herself.

(40) RUTH   Mine too! She went by a tree and got a bad scratch!

(41) SARAH   (referring to her baby) Lie down now, darling. Oh, she is crying so much. She probably swallowed a stone.

(42) RUTH   Mine swallowed a board! (laughing)

(43) TAMAR   (leaving the role of doctor for the sake of the joke) Mine swallowed a whole house! (all laugh)

(44) DAVID   (on all fours, barking) Bow wow! Bow wow!

(45) RUTH	(accepting role of caretaker for the dog, throwing a piece of cotton to David) There, now you have a bone!
(46) DAVID	Bow wow!
(47)	(replacing the cotton with a piece of rubber which was nearby) Let's pretend that this is my bone.
(48) RUTH	(turning to David) Now come, dear puppy; let's go home.
(49) TAMAR	(taking a call on an imaginary phone, pretending to hold the receiver) I am coming home soon. I will finish with the last patient soon; it'll be all right.
(50)	(turning to the others) Let's pretend we are closing the clinic. Now I am not the doctor any more.
(51)	(speaking to Sarah) I will be your baby.
(52) SARAH	No, you are my big girl in the Army.
(53) TAMAR	(accepting the role of the older girl in the Army) Yes, but now I am on leave.
(54) ESTHER	(approaches holding a case, pretending she is selling things) Candy? Cookies? Chewing gum? Who wants to buy something?
(55) RUTH	(as caretaker for the dog and as a customer, gives Esther an imaginary coin) Here, for the dog.
(56) DAVID	Let's pretend that dogs like chewing gum.
(57) RUTH	No, only candy! Here (offers imaginary candy to David).
(58) TAMAR	(as customer for Esther, as older daughter in the Army for Sarah and as big sister to Sarah's doll) I will take some ice cream for my baby sister.

(The episode continues)

3. Analysis of the Dialogue

The dialogue begins when one child, Sarah, takes the initiative to set up the preconditions for the episode. She moves to a corner which contains the props (toys, equipment, playthings) necessary to suggest the setting of a family medical clinic, a commonly occurring setting in the environs of Jerusalem.

Entries 1–2. Sarah assumes a theme and provides herself and her partner, Ruth, with roles to play and toys to use. The theme is that of mothers with sick babies at the medical clinic; dolls represent the babies and Sarah and Ruth are the mothers. *The children gather together in order to play of their own initiative and free choice; their play is voluntary, cooperative activity.*

Entries 3–8. A third child, Tamar, is admitted into the play group, but not until it is clear to Sarah and Ruth that she is willing to take on a role which complements their own and is important to the construction of their play episode. Tamar takes the role of doctor and the play episode begins.

Each player generates her own speech and action, but she must adjust what she does to fit what the others do. When Ruth stipulates that her baby "has the measles. No, no; she has the flu!" the doctor, Tamar, replies from her role perspective, pointing out the differences that doctors would make in treating measles as opposed to flu. Tamar structures her thought and action according to what input Ruth has supplied. Thus, the dynamic moves from one player to another to generate the sequence that makes up the course of the play episode. *Sociodramatic play is thus a social medium and a social creation although each step depends on individual initiative. The speech/action of the players is spontaneous, created on the spot for the moment. Play episodes include theme definition and role declaration.*

Explanations are also sometimes necessary. Tamar, as doctor, explains why she needs to do one thing if the baby has the measles and another (implied) if the baby has the flu. Her explanation is offered in the form of an "if . . . then" construction: "If she has the measles, then. . ." *Rationality is usable and exercised.*

Entries 9–12. Explanation, speech and action all refer back to the child's past experience under other circumstances; in this case, what they experienced or observed happening around them the previous time(s) they had gone to the clinic with their mothers and the play reflects what they or others had undergone in their contacts with doctors. Sarah's reference to the number system for making appointments reflects her personal experience of having a number in order to get into see the doctor as does her suggestion of giving a shot. When Tamar makes specific responses concerning the proper treatment, it also reflects personal past experience while at the doctor. *Past experience constitutes the children's reality and authority for what they say and do within the play episodes.* Further, *when past experience is the source for action and justification for actions, memory is more than a handy tool; children are exercising their memories and depending on them.*

The roles taken by the players are also significant; they are no longer simply the recipients of someone else's activity; they are the actors; they are no longer the helpless, but the helping; they are not acted upon by the surroundings, they initiate action to alter the surroundings; they are no longer the baby being cared for by the mother, but the mother caring for her baby, not the patient being doctored, but the doctor treating a patient, not a little person, but a grown-up. The transition from being a child to being an adult carries a great deal of weight: they behave like "big people" and relate to "little people" as adults. *The play episode allows the children to seek the reality of adulthood, as it were, from within; they thus gain experience and understanding which is important for their eventual maturity.*

Entries 13, 17, 19. Taking on a role calls for feeling as well as action. Sarah expresses concern, sympathy, caring and understanding for her baby.

When a child takes on a role, he not only projects himself into the role-person, but also acts toward other persons from within the role-person and according to their relationship to the role-person. Sarah not only feels and acts like a mother (her role-person), but also imagines as a mother would, what it would be like to be getting a shot. Sarah is living out as well as acting out the mother-child relationship. *Sociodramatic play offers the opportunity to children to be (to feel and experience) and not only to act (to do and behave). Being and acting interflow as mutually formed and forming.*

Entry 14. Objects (toys, playthings) do not have to be exact duplicates (replicas, miniatures) of what they represent. Tamar gives a shot "with a long object"; similarly, Ruth uses a piece of cotton for a bone (entry 45) and David exchanges it for a piece of rubber (entry 47).

The same is true for actions; they need not be exact duplicates (strict imitations) of the acts they represent. They can be quick, suggestive gestures, sometimes backed by verbal explanation. Thus, Tamar administers the injection quickly and explains, "I just did it; I finished giving her a shot." *Objects and actions are used symbolically. They can be merely suggestions in the most general sense and, if necessary, interpreted verbally to co-players.*

Entries 15–17. Ruth's question to Tamar, referring to the shot, "You did it already?" This question is understood by Sarah as a cue that there might be a disagreement between Tamar and Ruth and a potential break in the play episode. She enters into the conversation to smooth things over before such a break could occur by saying, with reference to Tamar's quickly gestured "shot" "Yes, she did a good job." and proceeds to soothe her baby. This backs up Tamar's actions and enables Ruth to continue with the play, content that a shot had indeed been given. Sarah's action here fits in with her other acts which ensured the appropriate preconditions for engaging in the play episode: Sarah initiated the play episode (Entry 1), she provided a role for Ruth (Entry 1) and Tamar (Entry 3), she pushed the action along (Entries 9–11), and now she acts to see that there will be no break in the course of the developing episode. Similarly, Ruth senses that David's challenging remarks (Entries 22, 33) are not parallel with the play theme and so she defines a role for him which will fit into the course of the play episode (Entry 36). *Continuity of meaningful action is a necessity in sociodramatic play which demands internal discipline; the children reinforce one another in adhering to a central discipline.*

Entries 18–19. Although there is no objective condition which can represent it, Tamar remarks that the baby is bleeding. Sarah accepts the statement as a suitable fact on which she bases her next act: to get a piece of red cotton, which suggests it is bloody, out of the doctor's bag. Words and then symbolic objects are substitutes for facts. *Symbolic acts and verbal declarations are utilized as substitutes for complex conditions, situations and events which occur in real life.* (See also Entries 21, 23, 29, 31, 40, 50) *Verbal statements are accepted as valid grounds for further elaborations of the play theme.*

Entries 20–23. David, a newcomer, arrives on the scene. He sees himself as a potential participant in the play episode. Since he is experienced in the central discipline of sociodramatic play behavior, he knows he will not be admitted by the current participants unless he finds a way to fit into the setting and theme in an appropriate role. Therefore, his opening questions is "What's going on here?" Sarah, functioning once more as leader, takes on the responsibility for responding. She was involved in admitting Ruth and Tamar into the play episode and therefore takes action when it is possible that David will join the group and responds with the definition "It's a hospital." David then responds, "What, a shot in a hospital?!" indicating two things: his acceptance of the theme and *h*is personal knowledge that shots are given in neighborhood clinics and not in hospitals. Sarah quickly catches on to his inference and reacts to save the situation: "Let's pretend it was a blood test." This satisfies their sense of reality which has declared that the hospital clinic is for diagnostic activities including blood tests, whereas the neighborhood clinics are for treatment and do not commonly include blood tests. Through this suggestion Sarah acts to save the dignity of the girls' play and definitions and also informs David that she accepts him into the game in the role of "the man who knows." David is now "in." Thus, the leader acts not only as a guardian of the gates to get into the play, but also initiates a rational, realistic way for including an outsider in the episode. *Subtleties of knowledge, control and feeling are involved; sociodramatic play is a complicated human art played by the children at quite advanced levels of human understanding and behavior. Real leadership roles evolve within the context of the make-believe play.*

Sarah's solution: "Let's pretend it was a blood test" begins with the stock phrase "let's pretend. . ." This phrase recurs throughout the dialogue. It is a contraction of the words "let us" and signifies a basic condition for sociodramatic play: agreement between the "us," the participants. When it occurs at the beginning of a sentence, it is a flag and a warning to the players that the speaker is introducing something as "real" which can affect everybody's play. It is a plea for acceptance of what the speaker sees as a good way to construct the play episode. It asks implicitly for agreement from the others for some sort of precondition:

the kind of sickness to be treated (Entry 2), the kind of activity which will be considered appropriate (Entry 23), the role to be taken by a player (Entry 36), the quality to be attributed to a toy (Entry 47), the time sequence to be assumed (Entry 50), an unreality to be agreed upon as real (Entry 56). *The function of pretending is to establish an imaginary context, which is agreed on by the co-players, within which the action can take place.*

Entries 24–28. Ruth responds to Sarah's acceptance of David as "man-who-knows" and proceeds to show that she also is "one who knows." She watches Tamar and observes, "A blood test is taken from the finger!" Tamar had just "done it" from the foot and states it, apparently hoping she might get by. However, Ruth does not let it go and declares, "Excuse me, but a blood test is taken from the finger. My grandma works at the clinic and she takes blood tests from the finger; I know better!" Ruth marshals the authority of her personal experience buttressed by that of her grandmother who is both grandmother and a worker in an official clinic. If that weren't sufficient, she turns to David in his role as "man-who-knows" and asks for his confirmation, "Isn't that right?" David responds, "Ruth is right!" Thus, Ruth "teaches" and Tamar "learns" supported by all the authorities including David. *Sociodramatic play functions as a teaching-learning medium. Children teach each other and learn from each other.*

The central discipline of the play itself makes the teaching-learning dimension possible. Each act must fit what the children know to be a fact. Knowledge is the base and he who has the knowledge has the right to shape his actions accordingly. He is entitled, in the play, to judge the actions of others in the light of what he knows to be the case, to challenge others when their actions don't fit their knowledge of reality, and to have his knowledge accepted by the group if he can proffer suitable authority and proof for his knowledge: personal experience in situations or observation of the actual acts in question or the experience of others accepted by the members of the group as appropriate and experienced authorities.

What adults are observed to do determines what is "right" for children to do; Ruth saw her grandmother take blood tests from the finger and that procedure is what she calls "right" when she asks David, "Isn't that right?" David's reply repeats the term "right." "Right" and, implicitly, "wrong" are concepts consciously employed within the play to arrive at peer agreement and to determine what is appropriate to do next. David provides support for Ruth if David's data supports Ruth's data on the way blood tests have been observed to be performed. This places a premium of "getting the data" and on "getting to know," for which children seek one another's support and presence. *Social support is based on data support. Sociodramatic play encourages the children to grow cognitively.*

What is observed as "right" turns into a moral "right" when the behavior to be determined is "what is right for people to do." By its very nature *sociodramatic play involves experience and exercise in questions that have moral as well as intellectual relevance.*

Entries 29–31. The situation has developed where David supports Ruth and both Sarah and Ruth are supporting David as "man-who-knows;" therefore, Tamar finds her position as doctor has become precarious. She has been proven incompetent by peers. Sarah senses that a break could be coming in the play if she doesn't do something to change the focus and direction of attention and action. Remaining in her role as mother, she announces that she is going shopping and turns the attention to her baby's "bad" behavior, opening a door into a new course of events. The strength of the central discipline of the play is such that transitions rather than breaks are used *within* the rational reality of the episode. The clinic scene is going bad and the leader, rather than breaking up the game, provides a transition while staying in her role as mother, making it reasonable to leave the clinic in order to go buy something in a store. The transition proceeds smoothly.

Although there is only one acceptable way to perform blood tests, more than one way of behaving can be approved when it is reasonable to assume that different personalities and individuals do things differently. Sarah is free to call her baby "bad" and Ruth is free to call her baby "good." Sarah and Ruth have undoubtedly observed "bad" and "good" babies. The variation is allowable since reality allows it. The crunch of "only one right choice"occurs when reality itself is observed to offer no alternatives.

When differences are emphasized, as they are in the dialogue between Sarah and Ruth about the goodness/badness of their babies, explanations for the differences are offered within the dialogue. Sarah explains that her baby is "bad" because she took Sarah's money; Ruth explains that her baby is "good" because she gave her candy that she had bought for her. Such phrases show the players are acquainted with cause-and-effect as an operative principle in understanding the world and explaining people's behavior.

The reaction of the group serves to test the adequacy of the explanations offered. Thus Sarah responds to Ruth's assertion: "I buy [things] for her too and [still] she goes on screaming." This is a subtle way to let Ruth know that Sarah knows that candy may not be enough to quiet babies down; candy may not bee a sufficient "cause" for the "effect" of quietness. Thus, one child's knowledge becomes available to another, expanding the range of knowing from everything a single child knows to everything every child in the group knows. *Children have a chance to exercise their rationality and test the adequacy of what they say by what their peers accept. Sociodramatic play functions as a group teaching instrument.*

Entries 32–37. When David's role begins to peter out, Sarah brings him back into the action: she refers to her baby and says to David, "Do you know what her name is? Nitzan." Sarah must have known that Nitzan is a boy's name. Her assertion is an invitation to David to reenter the action in his role of "man-who-knows" and he replies satisfactorily: "That's a boy's name!" back in action once again. Ruth follows Sarah's lead in taking care of David's participation and offers him a new and entirely different role: "Let's pretend you are a dog." which David accepts readily: "Good, then you feed me." This could be a way for Ruth to get David under her control as a dog rather than having him remain in competition as an authority, as the "man-who-knows." However, David appears to welcome the opportunity for more action. These passages demonstrate once again the awareness of each player for the role, place, and action of the other players, and the foresight of the leaders in arranging promising and productive roles.

Since the dynamics of sociodramatic play depend on each player utilizing the possibilities suggested by the action and speech of the other players, it is important to have all players active and productive. Experiencing such interdependence contributes to the development of social skills and sensitivity.

Entry 38. Once being admitted into the play episode, players who have been left out of the stream of action may need to take the initiative in order to get the action to include them again. Tamar has been neglected as doctor in the clinic while David entered more actively into the play. She now breaks into the dialogue to remind Sarah and Ruth of the clinic and asks, "Who's next?" Similar initiative is shown by David after Tamar takes center stage before he can be active in his new role as dog when he speaks up with, "Bow wow! Bow wow!" (Entry 44). In both instances it is Sarah and/or Ruth who respond as key actors to hold the players together and keep the course of the play moving smoothly. *Individual initiative is necessary to make the social system work.*

Entries 39–43. Sarah notes as an explanation for her baby's crying, "She probably swallowed a stone." and Ruth adds, "Mine swallowed a board! She laughs while saying that and Tamar could not resist joining in the fun. She steps out of her role as doctor in order to deliver her one-liner, in the role of "mother of a sick baby": "Mine swallowed a whole house!" Tamar's joke caps the progressive series of humorous absurdities with an even greater one, which provides everyone with a good laugh. Tamar breaks out of her role and also out of the range of reality with her remark. However, the children recognized what Tamar's motives were and were able to reap the benefit of the moment without losing discipline or continuity. Tamar reenters her role and the other players return to theirs. There is no criticism of Tamar for getting "out of line" and acting inappropriately. *Humor is possible and permissible.*

Entry 44. Although roles generally are those of "big people" occasionally other roles are adopted; in David's case, he accepted the role of the dog which Ruth suggested. Preschool children are waking up to life as it appears in all its varied forms. They can become deeply attached to their pets, considering them as playmates. They would not feel close attachment if they were not projecting part of themselves into their pets, trying to feel what life might be like to the pet, within the pet's response system. When taking the role of dog, David limits his speech and action to that which a dog would say and do (Entries 44, 46, 47). Thus he can remain within the role and sense what happens as the dog would sense it; what does living feel like when in the "paws" of the dog. Tamar's wish to take a baby role (Entry 51) could have expressed both her wish to behave in a babyish fashion and her wish to be close to Sarah, the leader.

Whether roles are those of animals or of big and/or little people, they lead to the appreciation of life. Enacting a variety of roles allows for experiential variation and flexibility, in both doing and feeling.

Entries 45–50. Tamar observes the course of events centering around David and his new role; it would seem that Ruth and Sarah may leave the clinic scene altogether and her role as doctor has run its course. Tamar stays within her role and arranges a rational way to close the clinic and thus leave the role she is stuck with. She uses an imaginary telephone and receives a call from her family to come home. She notes that she is finishing up the last patient and announces to the others: "Let's pretend we are closing the clinic. Now I am not the doctor any more." The ending of themes and roles must be rational and evident to all the other actors, just as the beginnings do.

Since sociodramatic play is dependent on a course of events which is imaginary rather than obvious in a sensory fashion, the progress must depend on the actors making what they have in mind clear to themselves and to the others. *The players become accustomed to explaining what ideas, images, hypotheses and assumptions they have in mind as background for what they do—a very useful habit for later on in both school and life.*

Entries 51–53. Other participants may turn down a role a participant proposes. Tamar proposes to be Sarah's baby; Sarah rejects the proposal by making a counter-assignment: "No, you are my big girl in the Army." Tamar accepts the suggestion and then makes an explanation which would make it rationally possible for her, a big girl in the Army, to be at home with Sarah: "Yes, but now I am on leave." Tamar recognizes Sarah's leadership and adjusts to her assignment, making a useful reality-reference which will allow her to get on with the action.

This illustrates both the control characterizing good sociodramatic play and also the quick flexibility that it promotes.

Entries 54–58. If an outsider appears in a role to which the players in the group can respond without moving out of their present roles, the outsider has relatively easy access to being included in the group's sociodramatic play. Esther comes along as a candy peddler and is accepted readily as a player since Ruth, David and Tamar can all immediately find a way in which to relate to her role. There is no break in the discipline and a smooth transition is effected once again.

The question of dogs and candy vs. gum is another reality test. If dogs do not chew gum, but eat candy, David, as a dog, cannot be given chewing gum even though he clearly wants it. Even though David suggests, "Let's pretend that dogs like chewing gum." Ruth will not allow it and offers candy instead. As a mother and caretaker for the dog, Ruth has the position and authority to instruct David on what he can and cannot have, according to reality, despite the invitation to "pretend."

The dialogue ends at Entry 58 with Tamar fulfilling a variety of roles: she is a customer for Esther, the older daughter in the Army for Sarah and the big sister to the doll-baby. Although the recorded dialogue ends, the play continues, growing in subtlety and complexity. In fact, the play continued for 40 minutes, until the teacher announced that time for free-play was over.

Good sociodramatic play usually continues for long periods of time (sometimes up to two hours), when allowed to, often taking new directions, changing co-players and roles and moving from one corner to another.

Another point which is important in the analysis of the play episode and which may not be fully felt in the verbatim description is the sense of real enjoyment, evident in direct observation of the children's busy activity.

Sociodramatic play is characterized by a joyous cooperative working atmosphere.

The sample episode, presented here, is typical of many other play-scenes recorded by us in our study and by others in other studies. It contains most of the characteristics of sociodramatic play and the generalizations derived from its analysis are valid for other play-activity as well. It illustrates most of the points that will be discussed in the succeeding paragraphs, centering around three issues:

1. The flexible nature of sociodramatic play
2. The descriptive definition of sociodramatic play
3. Sociodramatic play as contributing to cognitive, social and emotional development.

4. The Dynamic Nature of Sociodramatic Play

Sociodramatic play is one of the most manifold of human phenomena, as manifold as life itself. In fact, it is intended as a representation of life and human behavior in all its complexity. Therefore, it is many things at the same time; the dynamics of play can be characterized as an array of many pairs of antithetical propositions. The most dominant and obvious are described below.

The Dimension of Freedom-Control in the Environment

—Good sociodramatic play develops where there are certain preconditions[2] (time, space, evocative objects). However, it remains *spontaneous and voluntary*.

—It is a *cooperative group enterprise*, requiring social sensitivity, but at the same time it is geared toward *individual* expression and creativity. The development of the play themes depends wholly on individual preferences, knowledge and skill.

—It is characterized by *personal freedom* of action, but there is an intrinsic *discipline* which is imposed by the themes and roles chosen. The child is free to choose and create, but has to keep in mind self- and group-imposed limits.

—An initiating *leader* is easily discernible and leadership is exercised throughout the course of the game. However,

---

[2]See Chapters III and V for elaboration of this point.

the same leader acts as a *follower* with the evolution of secondary leaders; leader ship is flexible and others may take initiative, suggest new directions and take over the leadership role.

—The play develops according to a *predefined theme* and is controlled by it; yet the play is *flexible* enough to allow for *shifts* of themes, introduction of new story-line directions, the expansion or transformation of the original theme, etc. These shifts are usually smooth and develop as spin-offs, arising naturally out of the original play theme.

—It is expressive of a world of make-believe, of imagination, yet it is *reality-bound*. Although themes and roles are developed within an "as if" consciousness and are symbolic and pretended, the frames of reference for developing the action are real events and real characters. Make-believe is structured to fit real life.[3]

—The child enacts his experiences as perceived *subjectively*, yet their acceptance, social support and approval is conditioned on their match to *objective reality*. Each player's action has to be understood by the others in order that they can carry on the continuity of activities. Idiosyncratic behavior has to be explained and defended on rational grounds. There are often lively discussions about *right* and *wrong*, *true* and *false*, with the context being *reality*. Appropriateness of role-enaction is analyzed and tested according to what holds true in real-life situations. Sociodramatic play is a teaching-learning medium.

—Participants are *teachers* and *learners* at the same time. Expertise and knowledge are communicated and shared.

—The *private* is brought in and fitted to the *public*; the conceptual movement is from the *"in"* to the *"out,"* from within the reality of the the play episode or from the outside objective reality of the "real world." Play episodes are considered *seriously*, a work of art; yet, *humor* is permissible and welcomed. It seems to serve as a catalyst for releasing

---

[3]Fictitious characters and themes, mostly borrowed from television, are very rarely enacted in sociodramatic play; if they are included, it is usually only for short periods of time.

tensions and fatigue; care is taken that humorous asides do not disrupt the current of the play episodes.

Intra-personal Processes during Sociodramatic Play

—Although the child takes on a *role*, he continues to act as a real *person*. Even when acting out his play-role, trying to be some other person, the nature of his interaction with the co-players depends on both the role he took and the person they know him to be. The feedback he receives mirrors both dimensions.

—Sociodramatic play behavior includes chains of *action* and *speech*, complementing each other.

—The role includes simultaneous *acting* and *being*, *behaving* and *feeling*. Children bring understanding and empathy into their role. They act as if they were someone else and experience what it means to *be* someone else.

—Sociodramatic play means *cognitive* as well as *affective* learning. While *playing* the child learns by forming his own actions or *by observing* other children's behavior.

Time and Space Perspectives in Play

—The play episode is organized along *space* and *time* continuum. The definition of the theme and roles includes a definition of the site of the unfolding drama, sometimes *static* and sometimes *changing*. Similarly, the play events take place in a time-sequence, sometimes *continuous* and sometimes with *large leaps*. Verbal declarations are crucial for locating the play in space and time and for making changes when desired.

—The raw material upon which the child's role-play rests is based on *past* experiences, both personal and observed; when he translates this part of his past to the immediate *present*, he must be cognizant of the adaptation required in order to make his behavior fit that of his co-players. At the same time he must organize his play to fit *future* developments. Thus the entire gamut of behavior is geared to sustain the play, to enrich it, to facilitate further activity-chains of his peers and of himself. The play episodes are past and future oriented with present as a link between the two.

—The life-cycle is also represented in the play. The most popular roles are those of *adults*, the grown-ups, the people who are actively doing "real" things. Often child roles may be chosen as well, although rarely children who are the same age as the child. The child can choose to be a *baby* or a *grown-up child* and even a *grandparent*. Thus he experiences and learns about the unique aspects of each period within one's life-span. The time sequence is also expressed in another dimension: that of the immediate (home and family) and the remote (school, world).

—Future orientation within play has other educational and intellectual implications as expressed within time and space dimensions, especially while playing school. Often play episodes are moving between *home* and *school*. *Mommies"* bring their children to school; *"teachers"* teach and *"students"* learn and go back home. Through the group experience and group learning, notions are formed and tested about what school is like and how it feels to study. In many ways sociodramatic play means direct preparation of school behavior. This point will be elaborated more in the next two chapters.

5. A Descriptive Definition of Sociodramatic Play

It is clear from the analysis of the play episode and the description of the manifold quality of sociodramatic play, that no formal definition can reflect the richness and complexity of this play phenomenon.

Nevertheless, it is clear that sociodramatic play is substantially different from solitary dramatic play. Most of the components and characteristics are specific to this type of play behavior and are not present when a child engages in make-believe by himself. Although sociodramatic play contains all the ingredients of dramatic play, the need for cooperation and coordination within the framework of a play theme alters the entire behavior of the individual child. It is social interaction which makes the difference; it facilitates exchanges of ideas and collective elaboration of the play theme in flexible, open-ended ways.

At this point it is important to have an operational definition of sociodramatic play such that we can derive criteria for it's systematic observation of its existence and for its evaluation.

Sociodramatic play, as we refer to it in this study, *is a form of voluntary social play activity in which young children participate.*

In dramatic play, the child takes on a role; he pretends to be somebody else. While doing this he draws on his first- or secondhand experience with the other person in different situations. He imitates the person, in action and speech, and uses real or imagined objects. The verbalization of the child during play is imitative speech or declarations that serve as substitutes for objects, actions and situations. The play becomes sociodramatic if the theme is elaborated in cooperation with at least one other role-player; then the participants interact with each other in both action and speech. Some of the verbal interaction is imitation of adult speech or of other role figures and is an integral part of the role-playing; some of the verbal interaction is verbal substitution for objects, actions and situations directed to co-players; some of the verbal interaction constitutes discussions necessary to plan and sustain the cooperative play activity.

There are two main elements in this description. The central element is that of imitation, which can be regarded, paradoxically, as the "reality element." The child tries to act, talk and look like some real person or role figure and creates situation that are like real-life ones. In most cases, he tries to reproduce the world of adults as well as other situations and realities. Because the child's reality, identity and surroundings limit the possibility of exact imitation, another element enters the play behavior: the element of non-reality, of make-believe, of imagination.

Make-believe serves as an aid to imitation. It is a technique by which the limitations of the child-reality in time and space can be overcome and by which a richer reproduction of real-life events is made possible. It allows the child to project himself into activities and situations that cannot be actually reproduced but only represented. Satisfaction, however, is derived not only from the imitative element but also from the imaginative, make-believe element, which broadens the limits of the play world and enables the child to enter the exciting world of adults.

The imitative element finds expression in both imitative actions and imitative speech. A diminutive bus driver moves the steering wheel, makes hand-signals, makes hand movements of taking money and giving bus tickets, just like a real bus driver. He also tries to talk like a real bus driver: "Watch your step, please!" A pint-size Mommy undresses her doll, puts it down on a toy bed and says, "Now, darling, you must go to bed."

The imaginative element relies heavily on verbalization. Words take the place of reality and broadens the scope of imitation. This takes place in four forms:

a. Verbal declarations serve to change personal identity, to take on make-believe roles: "I am the Daddy, you are the Mommy and the doll is our baby."

b. The identity of objects is changed by verbal declaration or action: "I am drinking from the bottle" while the child is making motions of drinking from his fist; the drinking motion is imitative but pretending that his fist is a bottle is make-believe.

c. Speech is substituted for action: "Let's pretend I already returned from work, I cooked the food and now I am setting the table" when only the last activity is actually imitated.

d. Language is used to describe situations: "Let's pretend that the doctor is sick, so the nurse does the operation" or "Let's pretend that this is a hospital and there are a lot of sick children in it" or "Let's pretend we are very rich. . ."

In all these instances make-believe serves not to escape out of the real world, but to extend the scope of imitative activities and speech and to provide a comprehensive context so that the activities will seem more like real life. It serves to fill the gaps imposed by circumstances.

Both imitative and imaginative verbalization appear in egocentric form when children are playing alone; however, they are much more developed in sociodramatic play. Here the imitative speech takes the patterns and content of adult verbal interaction. The make-believe speech is essential to interpret situations to each other, to make the behavior understandable for the co-players and to elaborate the play theme collectively.

Speech in sociodramatic play has an additional function: planning, developing and maintaining the play requiring cooperation which is reached by verbal explanations, discussions, commands, etc. "We don't need two bus drivers; no bus has two drivers! You sell the tickets." "We cannot go on like this, we need another player. Go ask Tammy if she wants to be the baby." This type of speech is completely reality oriented. It is not imitative or substitutive, but serves to manage the play and to expedite problem-solving as part of the child-reality and the child-interaction during the play episodes.

Although we have tried to differentiate between the various elements of play and the different functions of actions and speech, all of these appear in quick succession and interaction within the play process. Not every sociodramatic play episode includes all of the above behavior, but without some manifestation of imitative behavior, some sort of imaginative or make-believe behavior and some sort of play-related interaction, there is no sociodramatic play.

6. Quantitative Assessment of Dramatic and Sociodramatic Play

The description of dramatic and sociodramatic play elements brings us toward a formal definition of criteria and categories for evaluating play behavior. The development of tools for assessing sociodramatic play is essential for furthering research as well as educational aims in this field. Singer stresses this point when he notes (1973, page 26): "What we most seriously lack are large bodies of formal data, collected under conditions specified in sufficient detail that they can be replicated by others. In addition, we need a set of categories and formal tools for measurement of play behavior." Singer's book includes several important studies that utilize various evaluation categories for pretend play. However, assessment categories are mostly in terms of a specific element of symbolism like imaginativeness (Singer, 1973; Tower, 1979), transcendence (Pulasky, 1973) or in terms of behavioral characteristics expressed during play, but not an integral element of that play, such as affect, mood, aggression, concentration, etc. (Singer, 1973; Freyberg, 1973). Similar categories were utilized by other researchers of sociodramatic play as well. Marshall & Hahn (1967) included dramatic play language, imaginativeness and aggressive language as evaluation categories.

Our aim was to establish criteria for assessment of those elements that define the uniqueness of sociodramatic play behavior. The descriptive definition of dramatic and sociodramatic play behavior discussed in the previous paragraph provided the basis for deriving our measurement categories. Six elements which we believe reflect the essence of sociodramatic play served as criteria for its evaluation in our first study (Smilansky 1968). They are:

a. *Imitative role-play*. The child undertakes a make-believe role and expresses it in imitative action and/or verbalization.

b. *Make-believe with regard to objects*. Movements or verbal declarations and/or materials or toys that are not replicas of the object itself are substituted for real objects.

c. *Verbal make-believe with regard to actions and situations*. Verbal descriptions or declarations are substituted for actions and situations.

d. *Persistence in role-play*. The child continues within a role or play theme for a period of time at least 10 minutes long.

e. *Interaction*. At least two players interact within the context of a play episode.

f. *Verbal communication*. There is some verbal interaction related to the play episode.

The first four criteria apply generally to dramatic play, but the last two define only sociodramatic play.

According to these criteria it is clear that when we see a little girl, dressed up as a "lady" with a shopping basket in one hand, announcing to no one in particular: "Pretend that I'm Mommy and I'm going shopping" we could not define this enactment as sociodramatic play but as dramatic play. Only elements a and c are clearly present. When two girls are in the "House" corner, one ironing and the other dressing a doll and "feeding" it with a bottle, and the only interaction between them consists of remarks like "Give me that dress, I want it for my doll"; "You go over there, I have to get by with the doll buggy"; "I got the best block in this kindergarten!" etc., it is clear that there is no interaction going on and no communication within the context of the play episode. There is imitation, but no make-believe. Thus, only element a is present (imitative role-play), which is the most basic element of dramatic play, but not sufficient for the imaginative elaboration of a play theme. If two boys are sitting on a bench with wheels in their hands, turning them, beeping, pushing the bench, but not communicating with each other, only elements a and e are present: the lowest level of sociodramatic play.

We have not determined an order of importance in the above elements. It would seem that each one of them is essential for play to develop and they seem to be interdependent to a certain extent. The richness of the play, however, depends not only on the presence of the above elements, but also on the extent to which they are utilized and elaborated. For example, it is different if a child cooperates with a whole group or with only one other child; or if he only occasionally uses make-believe in order to create and describe a nonexisting situation or if his play is full of such imaginative creations.

In the first Smilansky study (1968) sociodramatic play was evaluated in a global way, just by checking whether each of the six elements were present or absent; i.e., whether there was evidence that the child has the basic skills necessary for developing dramatic and sociodramatic play at its disposal. For the purpose of quantitative evaluation, a checklist was used and filled in during the observation periods (see Chapter five) as well as for posterior analyses of the detailed play records by the observer and by a non-observer.

A more elaborate measure which allowed for precise differentiation, was first developed during a "seminar on sociodramatic play" with a group of preschool and kindergarten supervisors in an inservice course (1967–1969) at the School of Education, Tel Aviv University, and then continued to develop during the Ohio Seminar (1970–1971) with a group of graduate students working under the guidance of Sarah Smilansky. The same scale was reevaluated and used during graduate seminars in the Department of Psychology, Tel Aviv University (1977–1979).

Each of the six elements was defined in more detail as a four-level scale, ranging from absence of the element (0) to full integration (3). There were only slight variations between the participants of the Ohio Seminar on some details of the definition of each element. The version presented in this book in the Appendix is recommended by us on the grounds of its match with our conceptualization of sociodramatic play and its usefulness as established in the United States as well as in Israel.

A detailed description of the scale and its psychometric properties appears in the Appendix. The Smilansky Scale is a criterion-referenced assessment tool since its purpose is to serve preschool educators and to facilitate research and intervention studies. It is assumed that every child can be helped to develop his play skills to their highest level of elaboration.

Thus, it seems that by devising and using the six element evaluation instrument an important step was made toward quantification of play behavior, for research as well as diagnostic and teaching purposes. The studies described in this book testify to this.

7. A Note on Terminology

In order to avoid confusion due to terminology, it seems worthwhile to define not only what we mean by the terms "dramatic play" and "sociodramatic play" but also why we prefer this term and how it differs from alternative terms often used to describe the same or similar play behavior.

Two terms often used, "symbolic play" and "representational play" stress the mental processes involved and not the manifest behavior. They are from the point of view of the cognitive and developmental psychologist, rather than the performer or the onlooker. The terms "symbolism" and "representation" describe the necessary condition for the emergence of the type of behavior we are discussing. However, representational thought and symbolic play include a wide variety of behavior that cannot be defined as dramatic play as we use the term. At the same time they do not convey all the basic elements of thought and behavior which are present in dramatic and sociodramatic play; i.e., they are over-inclusive and not adequately encompassing at one and the same time.

Two other common terms come closer to what we mean: "make-believe" and "pretend" play. They express accurately what the child consciously intends to do while engaging in dramatic or sociodramatic play. They are based on the manifest behavior and even on the child's verbal expression during play: "Let's pretend/make believe that. . ." They also convey the awareness of reality despite its transformation into make-believe. However, these terms are often used to designate behavior that we would not define as dramatic play, like enacting a plot with puppets, pipe-cleaners, etc. where the task of the performers is delegated to objects while the child acts more as a stage manager.

The term "role-play" which is also used quite often, is too narrow a description of what children are actually involved in when engaged in dramatic or sociodramatic play activities. It relates to just one element: taking on a role. As already stressed before, there is much more to dramatic and sociodramatic play than just taking on a role.

Our preference for the terms "dramatic" and "sociodramatic play" is based on the following reasons:

1. We deal with the more mature forms of this type of play: that of children from the age of three years and up. At these stages the play progressively tends to be social if the opportunity is provided and it is strikingly like a dramatic performance (see Chapter three). The children are at a developmental stage where they usually possess the tools needed for decentralized, decontextualized and sequential pretense and they have adequate language ability at their disposal.

2. Well developed sociodramatic play involves a wide variety of mental processes and behavioral characteristics that cannot be conveyed by the alternative terms used. It involves not only representation and pretense, but also reality orientation, organizational skills, reasoning and argumentation, social skills, etc. The spontaneous integration of all these elements into sequential and meaningful activity is

the essence of sociodramatic play. The complex nature of this type of play is one of its main characteristics.[4]

3. There is one shortcoming in the term "dramatic:" it obscures the element of spontaneity, of ongoing improvisation. It implies fixed roles and plots by association with "drama" and "dramatics." Therefore, we would like to make clear that we do not include dramatization of stories under this definition or sociodrama.[5] We deal with the spontaneous choice of roles and enactment of an improvised plot. The addition of the word "play" to the term "dramatic" should correct for this shortcoming; the addition of the word "dramatic" to the word "play" implies the consciousness of the child that he is willingly transforming reality for the sake of fun and not getting lost in fantasy.

Certainly we don't intend to challenge the legitimacy of other terms. As long as the specific behavior implied is made explicit, terminology is mainly a matter of preference or of the point of emphasis.

---

[4]It is possible that this explains the large variety of dependent variables affected by intervention in play. See Chapter V.

[5]We tried enactment of a story as a teaching technique in the context of an experiment, but it was not successful. This failure was an additional reason for making a clear distinction between dramatization and spontaneous sociodramatic play.

Chapter Two: The Relevance of Sociodramatic Play for School Related Behavior

As may be seen from the previous chapter, sociodramatic play is a very complex activity that necessarily utilizes many of the child's emotional, social, and intellectual resources. In our theoretical discussion (Chapter IV) we present our view on the prerequisites for well developed sociodramatic play. At this point we wish to elaborate the contention that the activation of resources in the sociodramatic play situation stimulates emotional, social and intellectual growth which contribute to success in school.

1. Theoretical remarks, based on observations

Observation of sociodramatic play demonstrated the great similarity between patterns of behavior inherent in successful participation in sociodramatic play and patterns of behavior necessary for successful integration into the school situation or full entry into the "school game".

School subject problem-solving requires the activation of representational processes (e.g., visualizing how Eskimos live; reading dramatic stories; imagining a story to write; solving problems in arithmetic): geography, history, literature—all are conceptual constructions that the child has not directly experienced.

"Problems" are conceptual conditions a child must project himself into in order to solve them. Having learned that conceptual conditions are satisfying grounds for action, the child can accept a teacher's setting the limits of the conceptualized forms and operate within them. He has then internalized a condition in which he can "learn" more readily and from which he derives a certain satisfaction.

The following school-related behavior, activated, learned and practiced in the context of well-developed sociodramatic play, illustrates the relevance of this type of play behavior for school adjustment and success.

—*Gathering scattered experiences and combining them in new ways.*
Everything the child does and says while playing his role are imaginative combinations of many details and not an exact imitation of any single observed behavior.

—*Selective drawing on experiences and knowledge according to a fixed frame of reference.*
Playing a role demands intellectual discipline. He may only include behavior that characterizes the role he is enacting. He must judge and select.

—*Discerning and enacting the main characteristics of roles and themes; grasping the essence of things.*
If the child does not project the essence of his role, he is criticized by his peers and the role may be taken from him. When a child is given the role of kindergarten teacher, for example, it is not enough that he imitate the activities of the teacher, he must also project the "teacher attitude" as broadly as possible. Detail, as such, is not insisted on, but the main feeling of the theme is definitely required. This means that the child must:

(a) understand the theme;

(b) imagine the role as he intends to perform it;

(c) compare the role as he imagines it with the role as he has observed it in the real world; and

(d) limit and select his actions in order to clearly portray the main characteristics of the role. He cannot let it become diffused with a clutter of detail or distorted through irrelevant excursions.

—*Concentrating around a given theme.*
Participation in sociodramatic play means the child must keep himself "centered in the togetherness" offered by the given limits of the play episode. When a child loses his

concentration he loses his grip on and his relation to the play episode; the other children then demand his ejection on the grounds of his deviation from the agreed play presumptions. Concentration is enforced by the child's peers, not by a parent, teacher, or other adult. Because other children seem able to concentrate in this way, the child has cause to believe that he can do the same. Discipline is therefore "natural" in sociodramatic play. The concentration essential to sociodramatic play encourages the development of concentration in a general sense.

—*Controlling himself in relation to an internalized sense of evolving order.*

Playing a role means receiving cues from the environment, reforming them into a personalized vision of action, then acting. By performing within this feedback system the child senses himself as central to the ordering of his own world, and his ability to control his behavior develops accordingly.

—*Controlling himself and disciplining his own actions within a context.*

A child playing at being a pilot, may fall and hurt himself. He wants to cry, but he knows that a pilot would not cry, so he controls his impulsive reaction in order to remain within the role and thereby sustain the play episode. This self-discipline grows out of his own understanding and is of his own choice. It is also a social discipline, as he leans to adjust himself to the requirements of a social setting.

—*Flexibility in approaching various situations.*

Other children in a sociodramatic play situation tend to use approaches that differ from his, but still prove relevant to the play episode. Sociodramatic play channels attention to the inner world of others who form their actions from their own frame of reference within the limits of the play episode. As an actor himself, each child needs to learn to respond to the various forms of experiencing of the other actors. This is basic to sociodramatic play: flexibility is a requirement.

—*Respect for the individuality of others.*

In participating in sociodramatic play the child learns that he sets his own standards for his actions; that other children do the same; and that satisfaction comes when each one adheres to his own standards, with subsequent reinforcement of the others' standards. In other words, the individuality of each is to be respected, and individual fulfillment depends on a common operation in which all can participate and be rewarded. Sociodramatic play is a form of individual responsiveness, and an effort to blend into a mutual meaning each individual's contribution.

—*The intrinsic satisfaction and extrinsic reward for being creative.* Participating in sociodramatic play enables the child to be a creator. He experiences himself as a creative being, formulating a personal response to the world from his position in it and experiencing the world as a place responsive to, and inviting of, his creation.

—*Developing the child from being predominantly egocentric into being capable of cooperation and social interaction.* When several children play together progress in their work depends on constant interaction and mutual help; thus, they do not remain at the same level of self-expression but are constantly learning to expand and exploit their individual possibilities.

—*Observing reality (the surroundings) with a view to utilizing these observations in relation to himself.* The environment has active value for him. Successful sociodramatic play calls for meaningful interaction with the environment, both as an observer of it and as an actor affecting it. This heightened perception continues as a need even when the sociodramatic play is at an end, for the child knows that he must be able to draw on his observations of the adult world as his source of authority when he wants to convince the others of the validity of his performance.

—*Moving from the particular and limited to general and more inclusive concepts.* A child participating in a role soon realizes that the concept of "father", for example, may include behavior patterns not necessarily part of his own father's behavior pattern. The concept of "father", therefore, expands and re-forms. The role is generously enough proportioned to invite many inclusions, re-formations, and enrichment.

—*Developing the use of abstract thought.*
He may begin using a toy to relate him securely to his role and be wholly dependent on it. After a while (because of the rapidity of spontaneous play and its growing complexity) he is able to pretend that he has the toy in hand and act accordingly. Still later, he is able to substitute words for both action and toy.

—*Vicarious learning utilizing the experience and knowledge of other children.* A child playing the role of a "policeman" refuses to help a "mother" cross the road on the grounds that he is a prison policeman whose job is at a jail and not on the street as a traffic policeman. The girl had not previously known that policemen also worked in jails!

The child gets better at sociodramatic play as his experience in it accumulates. As he undertakes different roles in different settings he grows in his capacity to respond. As he plays with different actors he becomes acquainted with different interpretations that different actors give the "same role". As he plays the same role with the same actors on different occasions each play episode is spontaneously re-formed and therefore new in some respects. The form of sociodramatic play allows him to absorb these fresh inclusions, which enrich his capacity to sense the main themes and the range of possible variations on them.

It is our opinion that children denied the opportunity to their ability for sociodramatic play will have less chance to learn how to accept a problem-centered world, for they will be unable to sense the relevance or value of problems and will be less prepared for taking hold of what schooling offers. When such a child does get a start in grasping a problem, he will lack sustaining power, not knowing how to hold his "role in the play", his place in the conceptual structure, and he will make "mistakes". "Mistakes" are items taken amiss, that is, outside the provisions offered by the problem (outside the role); as a result he will see himself as less able to do what seems rewarded than others.

Lacking reward and repeatedly lacking reward, he will come to the conclusion that he is unable to "play the game", and he will be correct. He lacks the generalized capacity to reach for conceptual structures and to operate from within their implicit limits.

It is our contention, which deserves further exploration and research, that the more a child engages in sociodramatic play, the readier he is to participate in the "school game". Empirical studies that lend support to this contention, are presented in the next part of this chapter.

In conclusion we can state that the child participating in socio-dramatic play profits simultaneously by being actor, observer, and inter-actor. As an actor he is motivated to utilize his resources and create; but, within the limiting framework of the role and the theme, he learns intellectual discipline and self-control. The play induces him to observe his co-actors and real-life persons, and these observations widen his conceptual world; the interaction with his peers requires tolerance and sensitivity to demands, and these prepare him for positive social interaction in school and in life in general.

Because learning takes place in a play activity that is in itself rewarding, reinforcement for the learned behavior is inherent in the situation. It should be added that language has a pre-eminent role in all the learning processes described above, taking place while the child engages in sociodramatic play. Numerous modes of action and interaction are involved in play (mimicry, gesticulation, motor activities, movement, etc.), but language is by far the most central. This fact cannot be overlooked when considering the value of sociodramatic play for schooling.

In view of the above, it is amazing that there is so little recognition of the importance of sociodramatic play as preparation for school, while games-with-rules are widely used for this purpose. Although we don't want to deny the merit of games-with-rules and their possible contribution to school, it seems to us that the complex and flexible nature of sociodramatic play offers very promising possibilities for preparing the child for the social and intellectual demands of schooling.

We assume that sociodramatic play and games-with-rules are two distinct behavioral systems. Each may be learned as a system without significant transfer in learning from one to the other. Both play forms provide satisfaction to their participants (intrinsic) and both are guided in their operation by reference to "rules" (extrinsic). However, the rules, the activities, the satisfaction provided, and the social situation differ in the two kinds of play.

(a) *In games-with-rules, the rules are relatively specific and relatively arbitrary.* They are based on agreement between the children as to specific acts that are allowable (five steps left, five steps right, touch the ground, etc.; or the only allowable answer is "yes" or "no", etc.), and must be known and understood before the game begins. In most cases the rules are fixed by tradition and rarely modified by the children. Even if the game is an original construction (which is seldom), the rules are settled before the game starts, and from then on behavior is completely controlled by them.

In sociodramatic play, too, activities are guided by rules, but they appear in the form of principles as to what is allowable and what is not; imitation and make-believe must comply to real-life behavior. *The behavior of children in sociodramatic play is not constrained by arbitrary rules, but by norms provided by life itself.* Although adherence to the main principles must be strictly observed, the more specific "rules" emerge and change constantly during the play, according to the ever-changing situation. (The children object to a little girl who is ironing. Little girls don't iron, only Mommy does. But when the girl changes the situation by claiming, "I already grew up and am now big," no more objections are raised to her behavior.)

Games-with-rules force children to concentrate on the skills necessary to operate under the rules. Sociodramatic play demands that a child concentrate on the selection and formation of the external reference (planning and creating the role), and then on selection and elaboration of behavior relevant to the self-imposed reference (enacting and sustaining the role).

(b) *Activities in games-with-rules emphasize one specific skill at a time.* At a young age such skills are mostly motor (running, jumping, throwing, etc.). Games that are of an intellectual nature emphasize some specific ability (attention, memory, or knowledge in some specific area). *Activities in sociodramatic play are manifold, however, and utilize and develop almost all areas of children's ability.*

(c) *Most games-with-rules are competitive rather than cooperative.* The only cooperative aspect in games with rules is in the mutual honoring of the rules. There is seldom interaction in the sense of give-and-take, mutual influence, and so on. Some interaction is present in team games, but then it is strictly regulated by the rules of the game. *Sociodramatic play is by definition a cooperative enterprise.*

(d) *The satisfaction derived from games-with-rules is determined by two factors.* The two factors being: (1) the nature of the specific activity and the enjoyment of it; (2) "winning", reaching the goal, the end. Satisfactin in games-with-rules is rarely derived from creative activity, as it is in sociodramatic play.

(e) *Games-with-rules demand a minimum of verbalization.* (Verbal games-with-rules are seldom played by young children.) The little verbalization present is either standard and part of the rules or is to discuss the game. *Verbalization is an integral part of sociodramatic play.*

We may conclude by stating that, even though games-with-rules are widely used in teaching specific skills or content, and are valuable as such, it seems to us that sociodramatic play might be more relevant to the over-all social and intellectual preparation of the children for the problems encountered in school and the behavior patterns necessary for successful schooling.

2. Empirical Findings

Our assertion that sociodramatic play is relevant to school-behavior (that was raised intuitively already in a previous book—Smilansky, 1968), has gained considerable empirical support from several studies conducted in Israel and the United States. Some of these studies were based on our conceptual framework, while others were pursued independently. We will describe the issues studied and the central findings.

A. Sociodramatic play and cognitive-verbal abilities

We found three studies especially designed to assess the relationship between sociodramatic play performance and cognitive tasks.

—One study was conducted by Helen Lewis (1972), who took part in the Smilansky seminar at Ohio State Univeristy, 1970–1971.

The subjects in the Lewis study were 78 Appalachian children (40 girls and 38 boys), from families of low socioeconomic status. The age range was five years 8 months to six years and 9 months.

The I.Q. range as measured by the Goodenough-Harris D-A-M test was from 70 to 127. The underlying assumption of the study was that the child who demonstrates a high level of organized thought through action and language in the framework of sociodramatic play will show organized thought in response to an image-representation, as revealed in a picture-reading task.

Play was assessed with the "Smilansky scale for evaluation of sociodramatic play." For picture-reading the child was presented 3 pictures, the stimulus being: "What do you see in the picture?" "Do you see anything else?" "What do you think about what you see in the picture?" "What is happening in the picture?"

The child's responses served two purposes:

a) To evaluate his ability to organize picture stimuli and to comprehend the general idea of the picture;

b) To elicit a language sample which could be analyzed for symbolic maturity.

Table 1 presents findings on the relationship between sociodramatic play and several indices of picture-reading performance: *General meaning*—scored on a five point scale for level of organization of picture content, from naming and enumeration of objects, to evaluation in terms of generalization or drawing conclusions about the event in the picture; *Language output and expressiveness*—rated on a five point scale by fluency of response to stimulus questions; *Percentage of words in garbles*—garbles defined as false starts, redundant subjects and word tangles; *Mean length of T-units*—minimal terminable syntatic units, audible pauses and garbles excluded; and *Total words*—including garbles.

As can bee seen from the correlation presented in Table 1, there is a significant relationship between the child's ability to pursue a theme in the framework of sociodramatic play and his

Table 1: Pearson correlation coefficients between children's Sociodramatic Play Performance and variables in picture reading

| | PLAY VARIABLES | | | | | |
COGNITIVE VARIABLES	Total play	Role play	Persis-tence	Make-believe with objects	Make-believe w/ situa-tions	Verbal commu-nication within a role
General meaning	.33*	.35**	.37**	.28*	.15	.08
Language output	.28*	.31**	.35**	.22*	.14	.10
% of words in garbles	−.19	−.20	−.23*	−.20	.04	.08
Mean length of T-units	.25*	.29**	.25*	.20	.28*	.25*
Total words	.28*	.23*	.24*	.23*	.17	.01

*p<.05   **p<.01

ability to relate to picture content, organize it and describe it verbally.

The child who can take a role and carry out a theme in socio-dramatic play is apparently more adept at the interpretation of pictures than the child who does not engage in role play. Role play and persistence in it correlates with most of the picture variables.

The child who can symbolize in his play, (make believe with objects only) can go beyond the literal level of picture interpreta-tion, imaging and inferring missing details. The child who plays at the highest level of symbolic play, representing actions and situations by verbal means (make believe with situations & verbal comunication within a role), has a higher level of syntactic maturity (mean length of T-units) than the child who does not play or only reaches the level of dramatic play.

It is interesting that verbalization during play—especially ver-bal substitution of actions and situations—is not related to the quantity of verbal output when interpreting picture content, but rather to syntactic maturity as revealed in length of T units.

The relationship between sociodramatic play and the ability to interpret the meaning of picture content was also evaluated through analyses of variance. There was a significant effect of level of picture interpretation on total play scores, and also on some of the subscores: Role-play, persistence and make-believe with objects.

—In a Canadian study on play behavior with 16 middle-class four-year-olds, *Rubin & Maioni (1975)* tested the hypothesis that there is a positive relationship between the incidence of dramatic play, measures of role-taking skills (empathy) and classification ability. Their expectation was based on the contention that all of the above involve understanding of reciprocal relations.

Each child was observed during free play for one minute during 20 consecutive school days and his behavior was classified on a checklist according to four play categories (functional, constructive, dramatic and game-with-rules) and an additional category of unoccupied or onlooker behavior.

The authors report a small (r = .20), nonsignificant relationship between dramatic play and empathic role-taking as measured with procedures from Borke (1971). The authors did not differentiate between dramatic and sociodramatic play.

However, dramatic play was found to correlate .49 (p<.06) with classification tasks. There was also correlation of .55 (p<.05) with spatial role-taking (spatial perspective taking or egocentrism) evaluated with an adaptation of Piaget & Inhelder's (1956) three-mountain test.

—In work reported by *Johnson (1976)* the relationship between make-believe play and tests of cognition and divergent thinking was studied with a sample of 63 children from various social and ethnic groups enrolled in a Detroit poverty area preschool program.

Fantasy play was categorized as social or nonsocial, total scores reflecting the frequency of play units in each category added across 10 samples of 5 minute observations for each child.

The cognitive measures were the Peabody Picture Vocabulary Test (PPVT), and the picture completion subtest (PC) from the WPPSI intelligence scales.

Divergent thinking was assessed by the uses task adopted from Guilford, and a story completion task devised especially for this study (two stories) to be completed by the child. The responses were evaluated for non-repetitious statements and interpretable gestures judged to add meaningful content to the stories.

While the correlations between nonsocial dramatic play and the other measures were very low (not exceeding .15), sociodramatic play was found to be highly related to three of the four divergent thinking measures: $r = .35$ with picture completion; There is no significant correlation with the fourth subscore, common uses.

Correlations of sociodramatic play are somewhat lower with the cognitive tests, but still significant at the .05 level: .25 with the PPVT and also .25 with the PC subtest of the WPPSI.

The author interprets the findings with the remark that intelligence is apparently necessary, but not sufficient for make-believe play. Divergent thinking ability is also a component.

Since both intelligence and divergent thinking are important for school, and in view of the evidence presented here from three different sources, we conclude that sociodramatic play either utilizes relevant learning capacities or contributes to their development, a question that will be further discussed later.

It is important to point out that the relationship between language development and symbolic play probably starts at a very early age. McCune-Nicolich (1981, page 791) points out that, "Children use language to try out various representational equivalences and so learn about the range of acceptable symbolic transformations." She cites correlational findings from several studies with children as young as 12 months of age, presenting her own findings on the developmental correspondence between symbolic play and early language. She is probably correct in stating that intervention studies in particular can provide evidence for the underlying relationship between skills in these two domains (see chapter V).

B. *Sociodramatic play and social-emotional adjustment*

Cognition and achievement may be the most important elements in adjustment to the school situations, but they are not the only relevant dimensions. Social adjustment also plays a very central role in the school-game as well as in the game of life. The child's happiness and success in school will depend to a very large degree on his ability to interact positively with his peers and teachers on a one to one basis as well as in group situations. This is also true for the adult's functioning in life in the framework of family, work and society. Evaluation of the relevance of sociodramatic play behavior for the school situation should therefore include an evaluation of the relationship between play behavior and social adjustment. Such an investigation would be carried out by a longitudinal study. Currently we have only cross-sectional data in one study conducted in Israel and two in the U.S.A.

—The earliest study reporting a relationship between imaginative play and social skills was conducted in the U.S. by *Marshall (1961)* with a sample of 108 children aged 2½–6½ years from high SES families. Frequency of language use during sociodramatic play was found to be highly correlated with acceptance by peers, number of friendly interactions and independence of teachers during play (see also Marshall & Dashi, 1967).

—Another American study *(Tower et al., 1979)*, designed to evaluate the effect of two television programs on subsequent behavior of children, also yielded significant correlational data between various pre- and post-test measures, including imaginativeness of play during free-play sessions. The 58 subjects were middle-class Caucasian nursery-school children. The pretest correlations of imaginativeness (extent of pretend behavior) were .70 with positive affect; .65 with concentration (persistence with activities during free-play); −.51 with fear, −.40 with sadness and −.41 with signs of fatigue. All correlations are highly significant.

Similar correlations are also reported on posttest measures, except for the negative affect measures (fear, sadness, fatigue) which were nonsignificant.

—In Israel, Taler (1976) studied the relationship between sociodramatic play performance (as measured with the Smilansky scale, see appendix), and two measures of social adjustment: Teacher rating on a standardized rating scale, and sociometric ratings by peers in the kindergarten class, in response to two questions: "Which of the children in your class would you like to play with? Who else? (three choices). Which of the children in your class do you not want to play with? (also three choices). Four sociometric scores were derived for each child; weighted scores for choices (First Choice = 3, Second Choice = 2, Third Choice = 1); no. of choices; salience (no. of choices plus no. of rejections) and no. of rejections.

The sample consisted of 96 children, 12 children from each of 8 kindergarten classes: four from poor neighborhoods and four from middle-class neighborhoods.

In each class the children were selected according to their scores on the social-adjustment rating by the teacher: four children (two boys and two girls) were randomly drawn from among each of three levels of social-adjustment: low, middle and high. At least one child from each level was represented in the play group of four children, and invited to play together (see procedures and equipment with the Smilansky scale in appendix).

Sociometric data was obtained from all children in the class by means of individual interviews, (while the child had a view of all his peers), several days before the play sessions took place.

As expected, Taler found significant correlations between both measures of social adjustment and total score for sociodramatic play (Table 2).

There seems to be a significant relationship between sociodramatic play performance, as measured by total sociodramatic play-scores and teacher ratings of social adjustment, as well as with all sociometric measures, except the rejection scores.

Table 2: Pearson product-moment correlations between sociodramatic play scores and social adjustment

Social adjustment measures	Correlation coefficients	Significance
Teacher ratings	.23	.02
Sociometric ratings		
Weighted scores	.31	.002
No. of choices	.28	.006
Salience	.22	.028
No. of rejections	.03	N.S.

Choices seem to be better related to play-behavior than rejections, with weighted scores for choices yielding the highest correlations with play.

The same tendency was found with socioeconomic subgroups*. While correlations were of similar magnitude, they did not reach significance because of smaller number of subjects.

Taler also tested the hypothesis that the relationship found between sociodramatic play and social adjustment were due mainly to those subscores of sociodramatic play that reflect the degree of sociability in the play situation: Element 5—interaction, and Element 6—verbal communication.

This hypothesis was not supported by her findings. Correlations of teacher ratings with these measures were lower than with total play scores, and nonsignificant. Also, correlations of elements 5 and 6 with sociometric ratings were lower but still significant on weighted score for choices ($r = .24$, $p < .02$) and for no. of choices ($r = .21$, $p < .05$).

Taler concludes that the total play score gives a more accurate picture of the children's performance than the subscores, and therefore correlations are higher. The fact that solitary as well as social make-believe play was found to be related to social skills in different cultural groups lends support to our contention that sociodramatic play has importance for social adjustment, which, in turn, facilitates school adjustment.

---

*Both high and low socioeconomic groups were very heterogeneous in their play performance. The range of total play scores was 0–13 for the low S.E.S. and 1–16 for the high S.E.S. groups.

Although the studies described here did not examine causal relationships between play and social adjustment, the relationships that were found are supported by experimental studies that assessed improvement in social skills as a result of experimental modification of sociodramatic play (see Chapter V).

C. Sociodramatic play and school achievement

The only research known to us that has investigated the relationship between sociodramatic play and school achievement was a longitudinal study based on the Taler data. The sociodramatic play scores obtained in kindergarten by Taler (1976) for her study on the relationship between social adjustment and play were utilized by Smilansky and Feldman (1980) to study the relationship between sociodramatic play and school achievement.

Smilansky & Feldman located part of Taler's sample in second grade: 17 children of middle and 32 of lower socioeconomic background*. They were tested with standardized tests for reading comprehension and arithmetic achievement.

Table 3 presents Pearson product-moment correlations between play score and achievement in reading and arithmetic.

The correlations between the total sociodramatic play score in kindergarten and achievement both in reading and arithmetic are astonishingly high. Surprisingly, the correlation with reading is even higher than what was found in another study (Smilansky and Shephatiah, 1976) between Stanford-Binet I.Q. in kindergarten and reading achievement (with the same reading test) at the end of first grade ($r = .36$).

Looking at correlations with subscores of play, it seems that the ability to make-believe with objects, as well as with pretend actions and situations in the framework of imitative role play are most highly related to second grade test scores. That is, the

---

*The follow up groups were compared to the other part of Taler's sample, and no difference was found on total play scores, neither for the middle nor for the low class sample.

Table 3: Correlations between sociodramatic play scores in kindergarten and achievement in reading comprhension and arithmetic scores in second grade.

SCORES	READING	ARITHMETIC
Total play score	.40**	.45**
Imitative role play	.38**	.34**
Make-believe with objects	.41**	.41**
Make-believe with actions and situations	.32**	.38**
Persistence in role play	.22	.33**
Interaction with coplayers	.31*	.34**
Verbal communication with a role	.27*	.30*

*p<.05   **p<.01

imaginative-representational abilities of the children in kindergarten are the most relevant to school achievement. But the three other ingredients of sociodramatic play also yield high correlations. (All but one are statistically significant.)

In multiple regression analysis of reading scores on the six subscores of sociodramatic play it was found again, that two—make-believe with objects and make-believe with actions and situations—explains 23% of reading variance, while the other subscores do not add significantly to prediction.

Findings were similar with arithmetic scores. The two make-believe subscores explain 26% of the variance in second grade arithmetic, while the rest do not add significantly.

It is interesting to note that when the sample is divided by socioeconomic level, significant correlations between total play scores and achievement are also obtained. In the lower class group $r = .27$ with reading ($p<.05$) and .34 with arithmetic, while in the middle class group correlations are somewhat higher and significant, despite the small N.

These findings seem to indicate that the abilities mobilized in the framework of sociodramatic play are highly relevant for schoolwork. Findings of such magnitude over a three year period are rare, and therefore it is important that this study be replicated cross-culturally.

3. Summary

The relevance of sociodramatic play for school adjustment in various areas was stressed, and empirical evidence was presented to support this point. Table 4 summarizes the major findings.

The studies described here show a positive relationship between the level of sociodramatic play and cognitive verbal abilities, as well as social ability measures. One study also found a high relationship between sociodramatic play in kindergarten and achievement in second grade.

All the studies presented in this chapter are correlative and therefore do not provide information on the direction of the relationship. Chapter V deals with experimental studies that were designed to estimate the effect of sociodramatic play training on a variety of cognitive, creative and social abilities.

In conclusion it seems important to point out that the relationship between school-relevant behavior and dramatic and sociodramatic play were obtained with a variety of evaluation tools

Table 4: Studies of the Relationship Between Dramatic and Sociodramatic Play Activities and School-Related Variables

Investigators	Subjects	Variables Related to Play
Marshall (1961)	2.6 – 6.6 Middle SES	Acceptance of peers, friendly interaction with and independence from teachers
Lewis (1972)	5.8 – 6.9 Low SES	Picture reading—language output and meaning
Rubin & Maioni (1975)	4 year Middle SES	Classification tasks, spatial perspective taking
Johnson (1976)	Preschool, Mixed SES	IQ and other cognitive tests; Divergent thinking
Taler (1976)	5 – 6 Low & Middle SES	Sociometric ratings; teacher ratings of adjustment
Tower et al (1979)	Nursery, Middle SES	Positive affect, concentration and persistence; Interaction and cooperation; emotional indices
Smilansky & Feldman (1980)	2nd Grade, Low & Middle SES	Reading comprehension, arithmetic

and across various cultural and socio-economic groups, a fact that lends strong empirical support to the significance of this form of play behavior for the child's present and future school adjustment.

Chapter Three: Socioeconomic Differences in Sociodramatic Play Behavior

The evidence concerning the relationship between sociodramatic play and school-relevant behavior raises important questions: What is the nature of sociodramatic play for children who are known to have difficulties adjusting to school? Are socioeconomic differences reflected in sociodramatic play? If so, what are the parameters of such differences?

1. Descriptions based on nonstructured observation

We observed sociodramatic play initially in various kindergartens and noted the existence of such differences. Aware of the possible relationship between the level of play and school functions, we conducted a large scale observational study of socioeconomic differences in sociodramatic play.

Lacking evaluation tools at the time, the material gathered in this study was analyzed post-factum and summarized in an informal, descriptive fashion. The formal categories for evaluating sociodramatic play are based on material and insights gained from this study.

Children were observed during free-play in 36 kindergarten and nursery classes by five workers. The children ranged in age from 3 to 6 years; in half of these classes the population came primarily from the mid to high socioeconomic levels, and in the other half the children were mainly from a low socioeconomic background.

When the study was conducted, there was a strong correlation between parent's education, country of origin and economic status. Parents with European background had more formal education and were higher on the vocational ladder. Most parents from a Middle East or North African background had little or no formal education and were mainly non-skilled, blue collar laborers. There were also European-born parents with little formal education who were generally Holocaust survivors that had been deprived of formal education in their home countries, but none were illiterate.

Subsequent studies on sociodramatic play with other subjects and with different groups, point to parent's education rather than the country of origin as the major factor that accounts for the bulk of the socioeconomic differences in Israel (Smilansky, Shephatiah, and Frenkel, 1976). Later studies also show some relationship between educational level and country of origin; however, the number of illiterate mothers are fewer and a considerable proportion of parents with a Middle Eastern or North African background are now found in the higher socioeconomic group.

Nevertheless, this study dealt with two culturally distinct groups, according to various criteria.

At least 20 observation sessions were recorded for each of the five play settings: the brick-laying corner, the hospital corner, the kitchen and home corner, the doll's corner and free time in the playground for each of the two cultural groups. Detailed records included the play content, form and process of the play activity, the number of children participating, toys, tools or other objects used, the length of time of each play episode, and a word-for-word record of verbalizations.

A. Differences by Behavioral Categories

Findings will be presented and discussed according to the following categories:
a. Level of Participation
b. Play Themes
c. Role Enactment
d. Toy Utilization

e. The Function of Verbalization
f. Leadership Activity
g. Coping with Difficulties; Problem-solving

a. Level of Participation

In classes composed mainly of children from higher socioeconomic levels, the observers found most of the children organized into small groups (from 2–6 children). There was so much activity that the observers had to limit themselves arbitrarily, randomly, to one group from among the many. In classes composed of children from low socioeconomic levels, there were generally only one or two small groups involved in sociodramatic play and the play itself was quite short-lived. The bulk of these children did not participate in such play. At that point the observers had a problem obtaining sufficient evidence for analysis. The play episodes collected in these groups disclose the behaviors of those LSES that did try to play make-believe. Thus an important factor to keep in mind is that play behavior observed in children from higher socioeconomic levels are a sample of many rich and well sustained games, whereas the play recorded for the other group was exceptional and produced by a very small proportion of the group. Some 80% of lower socioeconomic level children did not participate at all in sociodramatic play.

b. Play Themes

Play themes and roles were similar for both groups despite the different cultural backgrounds. The themes included four main types:
- *Family and Home*: members of the immediate family at home in day-to-day life; parents' social life; family outings and visits; parents and other adult family members at work; relationships with neighbors; secular, religious, and family celebrations; occasionally, pets.

- *Occupations*: doctor, nurse, policeman, fireman, teacher, drivers for various vehicles, pilot, sailor, shopkeeper, etc. These were roles the children had personally observed, and did not include roles they had heard about. Although those parents whose children had not directly observed them at work may have described what they did, the children lacked sufficient experience to be able to play out the role. They said, "Let's pretend I work in an office and I'm going to work." The children made reference to the occupation but did not act it out.

- *Dramatizations*: circus, zoo, theater, movie, exhibition, etc. Such themes appeared mostly as episodes in the course of acting out one of the themes in the other categories.

- *Kindergarten and Nursery School*: birthday parties in class, walks and field trips, other common class activities

Except in the case of the last category, the children chose themes and roles in which adults were prominent. They preferred to take adult roles, but would be children in order to further adult themes as part of playing House, going to the Hospital, etc.. In the latter cases they generally played children older or younger than themselves. They did not play themselves or someone of their own age.

Children from the higher socioeconomic levels preferred themes which were well-defined episodes from family and neighborhood life. Not one child based his sociodramatic play solely on the theme of a movie or story which may have been read to him; nor was sociodramatic play based purely on the children's fantasy. Nevertheless, the themes often included parts of stories and references to details outside the immediate environment. It is possible to say that while these children know about the "bigger world out there" and can make reference to it, even as they have observed others referring to it, they do not tend to undertake roles they have not internalized from their own direct experience.

c. Role Enactment

Although the themes were the same for children from lower and higher socioeconomic levels, differences showed up in terms of play dynamics, content complexity and persistence in playing. For example, a girl from the lower socioeconomic group might announce, "Let's play mommies and daddies," take on the role of Mother, pick up a doll-baby, rock it for a while, put it down and go look for another game to play. Her play was limited to the rocking activity and she elaborated it no further. In contrast a child from the higher socioeconomic group in a similar situation, playing the role of Mother, would pick up the doll-baby, rock it, feed it, put it to sleep, go shopping, invite friends in for a chat, greet daddy when he comes home from work, prepare a meal, talk with grandma, go visiting an aunt, take part in a family argument, etc., adding more episodes to broaden and deepen the theme. Her play involved complex content structure and included many different activities, as well as lasting for an extended period of time.

In the first example, the child could go no further into the role-play than imitate a specific activity which she had observed a mother doing. In the second case the child could enter into the theme so completely that she could focus on how it felt to *be* a mother. It is possible to say the children from lower socioeconomic levels were limited to focusing on *things to do*, whereas children from higher socioeconomic levels were free to focus on *persons to be*. The latter includes the stages of the former and continues to a higher developmental stage; the behavioristic yields to the experiential; doing yields to being.

d. Toy Utilization

We noted a progressive development of using toys and objects.

Level One, *manipulation*—a child handles a toy over and over, learning how it feels and responds to his handling (piling up small boxes in the hospital corner; wheeling an empty baby carriage around, etc.).

Level Two, *imitating actions*—a child selects toys which are replicas of tools and instruments used by adults and his play with these toys is an imitation of adults' use: a child picks up a small knife and "cuts bread," often with the statement "Now I'm cutting bread" or picking up a doll, undressing it and giving it a bath. The latter is imitating adult activity; however, without explicit indications it is unclear if it is also role enactment.

Level Three, *imitating role behavior*—this stage is reached when there is a clear link between imitative use of toys and role enactment. Thus, while cutting bread the child declares, "I am preparing a meal for my baby" or while washing the doll, the child imitates adult facial expressions, smiling at the baby or looking angrily at it, or makes statements such as "Don't cry, the water isn't hot!"

Level Four, *supplementation*—the toy use is supplemented with verbalizations and gestures explaining what they are and what is being done. At this stage non-structured materials are more useful than replicas since they are potentially more flexible. A child says to his playmates: "Pretend that this [a round box top] is a steering wheel for a fire engine and I'm turning it really fast because I'm hurrying to a fire. I have to get there as fast as I can or else everything will burn up and then where will the children live!" When he finishes with the box top, another child picks it up and turns it into a plate and then a placemat for the table. The use of both gestures and words may completely replace a toy; e.g., a child says "Pretend I'm a driver and I'm driving" while he turns an imaginary wheel.

Level Five, *substitution*—there are only words, no toys, no gestures to carry out the activity. A child says, "Let's pretend I'm Mommy and let's pretend that I cut the bread with a knife and feed Baby and now I really must go and lie down because we're having guests tonight" with no toys and no gestures accompanying the tale.

The developmental progression depicted in the above descriptions shows movement from the present to the represented, from the concrete to the imagined, from the literal to the symbolic, from objectively defined to subjectively created, from privately used to socially shared, from non-verbal to verbal and from indispensable to the dispensable.

Children from the upper socioeconomic groups played mainly at Level Three or above. Children from the lower socioeconomic groups played, for the most part, at Level One and Two and some reached Level Three.

Children from higher socioeconomic backgrounds tend to form groups for sociodramatic play, decide among themselves on a theme and then look for toys to help them act out the game. The primary interest was in acting out the theme and toys were seen as instrumental and secondary. Children from lower socioeconomic backgrounds, however, would go to the toys first (a truck replica) and choose a theme that fits the toy (play truck driver). They would imitate the appropriate actions, act by themselves, and stop when tired of the toy or when another child takes it away. Toys were primary important for initiating, controlling and ending the play episode.

Children from the upper level groups paid little attention to the amount, quality, size or color of the toys. Often they used the toys symbolically: "Let's pretend that this is a steering wheel" (the object is round); "That can be a bed" (a rectangular box). They did not usually use a toy for a purpose which was contrary to its usage in the adult world. For example, they would not use a cup as a steering wheel although the cup was round. A stick with no defined shape may serve as a fork, knife, spoon, garden tool, etc.

If a toy was snatched away from a child in the higher socioeconomic groups, he rarely chased after it or even looked for a replacement. He would rather switch to an imaginary object so that the game would not be disrupted. The object and the action connected to it would be brief and suggestive; the player was intent on getting on with the theme. Sometimes neither the object nor the action would be used and words would be substituted entirely: "Let's pretend that I've finished washing the dishes and they're ready to be put on the table and we can start eating." There was also a tendency to explain the function of the toy and the reason for using it: "I'm telephoning now" while using a toy telephone.

Not too surprisingly, the child from the higher socioeconomic levels seemed to prefer less well-defined play objects which could serve several purposes within the context of the play theme. He tended to choose symbolic play objects rather than miniature copies of adult life. When a toy was used as a symbol (a stick for a horse), the child's motor activity was reduced to just those actions sketching out a bare outline of his function; words explained the rest of the activity.

We found no significant difference in the frequency or standard of play among the higher socioeconomic children when they were on the playground, where very few toys were available, and when they were in the classroom. The children did not run from the playground into the classroom in order to fetch toys, nor did they search for play objects outdoors. A minimal amount of play materials was necessary since symbolization extended the usefulness of everything that was available. One moment a child used the finger of one hand as a pencil, the next moment he closed his fist and it became a cup from which to drink; then he opened his hand and the palm became a plate from which he ate with a spoon (a finger from the other hand). Sometimes such children preferred the imaginary creation to a suitable replica which was available close at hand: using a rubber tube as a telephone instead of the toy lying on the ground nearby.

Toys took on much more importance for the play of the children from the lower socioeconomic levels. If a toy was taken away, the child would usually chase the snatcher, shout and call for help. If the toy was returned, he would then repeat the same motor activity with it until bored. At that point he would abandon that toy and pick up another, engaging in a different motor activity. He would move from one toy to another in a sequence of disconnected play activities with no thematic continuity.

Such children were possessive about their toys while playing with them and were inclined to see other children as threats rather than potential collaborators. Several children might undertake the same role simultaneously if there were sufficient toys, e.g., four steering wheels, one for each of four children. All players would then become drivers, each individually engaged with his own wheel, with no planned interactivity and no further elaboration of the theme, either by individual drivers or by the group as a whole. When there were no toys, no dramatic or sociodramatic play ensued.

Toy usage took a rigid form: when a child wished to feed a doll, she needed a miniature bottle or plate. If these items were unavailable, she would not feed the doll. She might continue playing with the doll, but only by making use of such toys which were available to support her activity. Thus, she would bathe the doll only if a bathtub was available. Furthermore, her play activity was repetitious and she would repeat the activity over and over.

Toys which were replicas were particularly important to children from lower socioeconomic backgrounds. Their use suggested play activity and provided quick identification with the adult who uses the real item. It is emotionally satisfying to be able to do exactly as the adult does: to use a toy telephone just like father does it, imitating his tone of voice, his stance, his gestures and his vocabulary. The child can feel he is acting exactly like his father when he uses "exactly" the same item. However, in the long run the replica is limiting because the child feels free to use it only for a specific purpose. Thus, children from the higher socioeconomic groups preferred the greater freedom of imagination and action that less well-defined toys allowed.

We can summarize by stating that toys and the activities immediately connected with them constituted the core of play activity for children from lower socioeconomic backgrounds. On the other hand, for children from higher socioeconomic levels toys had a secondary role and they used imagination to supplement the toys or substituted verbal declarations and descriptions of attendant activities.

Perhaps the difference in toy utilization reflected a lack of toys in the homes of the children from lower socioeconomic groups as compared to ample supplies in homes of children from the higher groups. Thus, the attachment of the former to their toys could arise from their unsatisfied hunger to have such toys, whereas the freedom of the latter would reflect the fact that their need to have toys has been satisfied. Investigation of the children's homes revealed that children in the former group did have toys in most cases. The number and variety of toys were not as great as those of children from higher socioeconomic background, but the quantity and types were sufficient to invalidate "blind deprivation" as a "cause" of toy attachment. In addition, the kindergarten and nursery classrooms were fully equipped with sufficient toys for both groups and it would have been expected that eventually the children from a lower socioeconomic background would have become used to the toys and have lost their attachment to them. Most of the children attended well-equipped nursery and kindergarten classes daily from the age of three; there were many opportunities to move toward higher stages of toy utilization, but it did not happen.

It would seem that the difference in toy utilization stems from different sources of satisfaction. The satisfaction for a child from a lower socioeconomic level comes from imitative activities, *from doing what adults do*. The closer his actions are to an adult's activities as the child perceives them, the more he enjoys them, which makes toys indispensable.

Imitation is a source of satisfaction for a child from a high socioeconomic background as well; however, imitative activities are extended by imitative speech and make-believe. They move from experiencing what adults do to *experiencing what adults are like and feel like*. There is no need for an object or toy for imitative speech. The technique of make-believe, representation, enables substitution for objects and activities, and, thus, the child may imitate using more things in more ways in a shorter time. Thus the child may ignore the actual limitations of his material environment.

The difference in sources of satisfaction are directly related to the differences in role perceptions. The child from lower socioeconomic backgrounds tends to perceive of the role in terms of specific actions, while the child from higher socioeconomic background tends to perceive in terms of a conceptual scheme of adult behavior at an experiential level. Behaving like another will bring the child through Stages One and Two (Manipulation and Imitating Actions), but in order to reach the other stages it is necessary to reach *experiencing like another*— imitating role behavior, supplementation and substitution.

e. The Function of Verbalization

Talking is necessary for good sociodramatic play—for its development and progression. Each participant takes his cues from the lines spoken by the other participants, supplying new, verbal cues in his turn. Constant talking back and forth is essential to carrying out the theme.

We observed that both groups talked a great deal, although children from the higher group tended to verbalize more. The most essential difference was, however, in the quality and function of the talking rather than in the quantity. Children from higher socioeconomic backgrounds used speech for three functions: management, role enactment and dialogue. When children from lower socioeconomic background participated in sociodramatic play at all, they limited their speaking mainly to management and the announcement of roles.

Verbal expression seemed to be one of the most important attractions of the play for children from higher socioeconomic levels. They kept up a constant flow of chatter related to the roles being enacted. Their talking facilitated their identification with the role and intensified their enjoyment. They "fed" on the words of others, gaining cues from them which aided them in further creating and elaborating their play with more verbal responses. There was satisfaction in knowing that others were listening similarly to their words and responding to them. Words became a basic, creative medium for the sociodramatic game.

Children from the lower socioeconomic levels, involved primarily with their toys, would make sounds or say words associated with the toy manipulation (a bus driver making the sound of the motor revving up) but would not try to imitate the way bus drivers might talk or engage another child in being a customer on his bus. If such a child did engage another child in a dialogue, it was primarily a case of giving orders on what to do: "Bring me that. . ." "Take that away. . . ." There was no back-and-forth exchange of verbal makebelieve; the speech content was focused on actions to perform rather than experiences to share. Speech functioned primarily for management.

In summary, comparing the language usage between the two groups of children revealed a "concept and word" orientation among higher socioeconomic level children and a "act and object" orientation among lower socioeconomic level children. Experience generated more experience for the higher level group whereas behavior generated more behavior for the lower level.

We arrived at the following observations about the role of speech in sociodramatic play and child development over the course of dealing with language in play activities.

- A child needs to make use of what he imagines or his imagination becomes of little use to him; fluent, rich language helps the child express what he imagines; sociodramatic play is an instrument to give speech such use and thus will give the child a better chance to realize the existence and value of his imagination and creativity.

- The use of speech enables a child to realize himself as a creative being, becomes valuable as a means for the child to recognize how to use speech itself creatively; he will begin to pay attention to language as a medium in its own right; in advanced stages of sociodramatic play the children play with language as they play with each other; this approach prepares them for the next stage of language development, in school, where they must confront language as a means to learn to read and write.

- When a child speaks out during a dialogue, he has two focuses of awareness and development:
  a. he can hear himself as he speaks within his role and gains insights from what he hears into his relationship with the role he has created;
  b. he hears himself-in-role communicating with other players who react to him in turn from their selves-in-roles, forming a context of relationships in the environment. The child perceives himself both from an inside point of view (himself with others) and from an outside point of view (himself within the environment). Speech serves as a transactional connection between inside and outside and is thus a medium for self-and-other development.

- The act of talking is another form of kinesthetic expression. This is clear when children talk in conjunction with gesturing and moving their bodies to express what they want enacted in a role. Speech serves as a catalyst to physiological as well as psychological activity, which expresses more than what speech alone can say.
- Children cull new words and concepts from the vocabularies and experiences of other participants while they search their own memories for special words appropriate for the role they wish to take. Vocabulary growth and enriched oral styles increase the chance of school success greatly since words are the primary medium of future school activity.

Success in school, success in sociodramatic play and success in language usage are all dependent on the same process: using experience cooperatively for the mutual benefit and development of the participants.

f. Leadership Activity

Leadership among children from lower socioeconomic levels was most often taken by the child who initiated the game. He would procure the necessary toys, turn to a second child, announce the theme he wished to play and invite the second child to join him: "Do you want to play House?" "Let's build a [something]." If the second child agrees, the leader would begin to give orders: "Give me that block, bring me another one, put it here. . ." As long as the second child obeyed these orders, things would proceed smoothly; but the moment the second child refused to obey or criticized or made any remarks about how the leader was doing things, a quarrel would break out. The leader would usually shout and swear. If, despite this outburst, the second child was still unwilling to follow the leader, there was usually a fight and the game would end. If a third child were to join in the game and was willing to obey the leader, everything would proceed smoothly until he tried to give advice or make a suggestion, even only to the second child. At that point he would be ejected from the game by the leader. The leader took on the role of authority and maintained it, making use of any means to maintain his power. He perceived his playmate(s) as foils and subordinates. Leadership meant dominance, often with an overtly aggressive tone.

It was often difficult to spot who was the leader in many of the higher socioeconomic level groups. One could identify who held the most important role or who was most active, but neither role importance nor degree of activity was a necessary clue to the identity of the child taking a leadership role. In fact, in many groups, leadership seemed to be shared between two players and the role was a cooperative one. If there was a conflict between the two leaders (usually with regard to questions of how the episode should unfold, how the role should be enacted or whether to allow a new player to join), the leaders would review the situation together with the rest of the participants and resolve the conflict through discussion.

Even in groups with a single leader, we often noticed a democratic approach. He was willing, in most cases, to listen to advice and opinions of the other participants and to use argument and explanation as his main lever. The unbroken continuity of the play episode and theme holds great importance; leaders would sacrifice their own opinions and even their own roles to enable theme continuity. Leaders focused on the play as the source of discipline, maintaining its primacy for themselves as well as over the others. Shouting and swearing seldom occurred; fighting was rare. An introverted, shy child would and could be leader if he had a lot of exciting ideas. Such a child would have no chance at a leadership role among lower socioeconomic level children.

It is possible to explain the difference in leadership styles between the two groups as a function of their culture base. A higher socioeconomic level child comes from a more democratic home environment; his parents tend to talk things over more often, argue the pro's and con's of their opinions, rarely ending up shouting and swearing at each other or fighting. Indeed, if there was a tendency in that direction, such parents generally take care that their violent disagreements do not take place in front of the children. Parents ordinarily do not give orders to each other, to their friends or even to their children. They tend to explain reasons behind their actions; even if the child's wishes are not met, the child would nevertheless know that there are reasons and reasoning behind his parents' decision. Thus, when a leader in a high socioeconomic level group exercises a leadership role using discussion, explanation, reasoning, reality references, etc., he is following his cultural orientation. This is echoed by the responses of the other participants, who reply appropriately: "I suggest. . ." "Do we agree that. . .?"

It is also possible that parents of higher socioeconomic level children teach a wider acquaintanceship with behavioral roles. Thus, such a child would know that there are various kinds of Daddies and they may all act differently; he might be more flexible in what would be acceptable as "Daddy" activity and would not need to enforce strict compliance with specific activity patterns of his own father. When he comes up against a very different Daddy role played by another child, he would have the tools to accept such a difference if it were convincingly reported and explained. Roles have variety and resilience in their conduct, and democratic leadership has a wider range within which to accommodate the progress of the play activity.

In homes of lower socioeconomic level children, parents tend to give instructions and exact demands without offering reasons or explanations: "Take your sister's hand and see her across the street. If she lets go of your hand, you'll be sorry. . ." Reasons are rarely provided for such strictures. Questions and discussion seldom form part of such a child's environment: "Do what your father tells you and don't ask questions." "Do as you're told." "It's none of your business; just do as you're told and don't ask questions." The parents themselves rarely engage in mutual discussion. Each states an opinion and then each reaches a decision. This is the immediate adult reality for many children from lower socioeconomic backgrounds.

The play of such children is most likely an imitation of the actual adult environment in which he lives. As "Mommy" or "Daddy" he gives orders, does not heed advice or answer questions, which would be inconsistent with reality as he knows it, and if he is not obeyed, he often shouts, hits, swears. In addition, having had no explanations, he often has only a limited understanding of adult behavior, particularly that of his father and mother. This limited understanding is reinforced by the daily recurring parental behavior patterns that the child perceives as parental functioning, and even as the only parental functioning possible. Therefore, not only does such a child find it difficult to understand the motivations behind parental behavior, but he also does not learn to "construct" an adult role by gradual evolution. Daddy did what he does like this and always will; and so when the child tries to play Daddy, he, too, does what he always does just like this. There is little flexibility.

In sum, there could be two main reasons for the difference in leadership patterns of the two groups:

—Children from higher socioeconomic backgrounds tend to have a more generalized conception of the roles being enacted and are, therefore, ready to accept their peers' role play even if it represents experiences different from their own. Children from lower socioeconomic backgrounds, on the other hand, tend to conceive roles in terms of observed activities and therefore have difficulty accepting errant behavior.

—Each group reflects the leadership image of its own environment: children from higher socioeconomic background imitate the more democratic behavior patterns of their parents and children from lower socioeconomic background imitate the more authoritative behavior patterns observed in their homes. Language usage also reflects this pattern difference: language is used to command.

g. Coping with Difficulties; Problem-solving

Sociodramatic play generates many problems for the participants: in the planning stage suggestions may be contradictory; during the play period new players may wish to be admitted or present players may wish to leave or change roles; it may be necessary to adjust to outside demands, such as acceding to the teacher's request to move to a different place or to abandon the activity for something she wishes the children to start doing, or dealing with overcrowding where the groups may interfere with one another and interrupt each other's game; particular toys and materials must be planned and procured for specific episodes (a kitchen, a platform on which to hold a circus) and alternatives decided upon when nothing suitable is to be found in the classroom. Such play can be a difficult undertaking; it requires concentrated activity, discipline, foresight, compromise, coordination, making choices, problem-solving, patience, imagination, good will, quick thinking, etc. Children must have ways to deal with difficulties as they arise.

Our observations of sociodramatic play revealed it to be a continual process of problem-raising and problem-solving. The fact that the actions of the children was accompanied by running verbal commentary enabled us to see the problems as the children themselves perceived them and to understand how they dealt with them. The verbal commentary was often sufficient to allow us to depend upon it alone, without necessarily watching the actual activity.

Most of the difficulties which children from lower socioeconomic backgrounds had to deal with centered around toys and attempts to force another child to obey orders: "How long has he been playing with that toy?" "Too long!" "What is he doing with that toy again?" "Why didn't you put the blocks where I told you?" Most problems which arose bore no relation to the content of the play episode; the problems remained the same no matter what the thematic content.

The major arena of problems for both groups was that of the social grouping: how to ensure cooperation and coordination during the play activity; how to handle deviation. Our observations pointed up three areas of differences between the two groups: the use of and response to humor, to criticism and to aggression.

—Humor

Children from higher socioeconomic levels tended to laugh *with* one another rather than *at* one another. Often a player would make a statement which struck the others as funny because of its absurdity: "Mother swallowed a stick" and they would all enter into a dialogue to extend the absurdity: "Mother swallowed a desk" "Mother swallowed a house," ending with everyone laughing uproariously. When the uproar subsided, the children would return to their roles and continue playing. Humor relieved the tension caused by the constant, intense concentration required by creating the theme; in addition, humor was shared along with other affective elements in the play: joy, sympathy, alarm, disgust, etc. Such children generally did not import jokes or humor from outside the world of their own make-believe, but created their own humor in their own terms.

Children from lower socioeconomic levels tended more to laugh *at* one another. They clearly felt proper behavior was prescribed behavior; deviation from prescribed behavior was either funny or wrong. Those who behaved deviantly were often laughed at and sometimes ridiculed and shamed into appropriate behavior. Laughter was an instrument of social control and not a means for the release of tension.

—*Criticism*

Whenever children from higher socioeconomic backgrounds criticized each other, they rarely focused on the personality involved; such criticism referred to the interpretation of a role according to the speaker's experience. Most of the time the child on the receiving end of the criticism was allowed to counter with his own experience (and criticism) in return, and did so. The grounds for the exchange tended to be conceptual rather than personal and the common aim was to continue playing according to mutually agreed-upon "reality." Compromises were reached when the child initially criticized was able to convince the others that his actions were legitimate according to *his* experience; otherwise the critic's view would prevail.

Criticism among children from lower socioeconomic backgrounds tended to be personally directed. A wrong act was identified with a wrong actor, the two being considered inseparable. Blame was, therefore, personal. Attention focused on prescribed behavior not on carrying out a theme; the vindictiveness of the personal criticism leveled by such children at one another did not seem to have a severe effect. The children criticized or excluded seldom looked hurt or sad. Since the focus of such children was on the extrinsic object, activity or standard and not on shared experiences, criticism and exclusion was probably felt less acutely, whereas such criticism would probably signify desertion, operating outside the rules and deviation from the entire game rather than just a part to a child from a higher socioeconomic level. Once again, the behavior pattern current in the children's adult world probably reinforced the form that criticism took. Adults from a lower socioeconomic community tend to look for complete obedience and acceptance of authority; children imitating such adults would expect the same obedience from those over whom they presumed authority.

—*Aggression*

There was very little overt aggression during the sociodramatic play of children from higher socioeconomic backgrounds. We rarely observed hitting, cursing, biting, tantrums or other outward displays of anger. Even the "spoiled" children in these groups seldom showed signs of aggressive behavior during sociodramatic play.

However, aggressive behavior was fairly common among the children from lower socioeconomic backgrounds. They often hit, cursed, threatened and willfully interfered with one another. Left to their own devices, they were rarely able to generate good sociodramatic play and sustain it with any degree of success.

The marked difference in aggressive behavior observed raises the following question: Why does sociodramatic play arouse aggressive feelings in children from lower socioeconomic levels while it seems to minimize such behavior among children from higher socioeconomic levels? We have observed aggression among children from higher socioeconomic levels, during and between various other activities although less than among children from the lower socioeconomic levels.

The paragraphs describing the differences in leadership roles and function of toys and objects can partially explain this phenomenon. In addition we propose the following possible explanations:

—Lower socioeconomic group leaders pursue goals that do not invite cooperation and follow practices which are frustrating to themselves and to their playmates. Conflicts flare up easily and in such an atmosphere are not amenable to a positive denouement.

—Toys serve as the main underpinning of roles undertaken by children from lower socioeconomic groups. Since toys are objects representing the "real" world and it is possible to fight over their possession, the children struggle competitively with each other over those toys which are available. Children from the higher socioeconomic groups adhere to the major purpose of the game: carrying through the play episode, a concept which is contained in their minds and is not subject to the same type of competition.

—Children from the lower groups do not find satisfaction in the repetitious motor activities in which they engage. They succumb easily to feelings of aggression directed against a world which denies them satisfaction.

—Children from the lower groups are, moreover, bored by their unfulfilling activity and could become jealous of children who do show signs of satisfaction at what they are doing; therefore, they attempt to destroy that child's sense of fulfillment.

—Memory seems to be the focus of activities of children from lower socioeconomic groups rather than imagination. They attempt to copy adult behavior through recall rather than projecting fresh possibilities of activity into a role. This very activity will arouse conflicts since the role of mother refers to the specific behavior of the actor's mother which inevitably will not be the same as the mothers of the other players.

If sociodramatic play develops to the level present in the higher groups, various positive forces come into play even when problems or conflicts arise.

—enjoyment is so pervasive that moods of anger and aggression have little to feed on

—the importance of continuing the theme is so strong, breaking off from the play to indulge in a dispute is not considered worthwhile

—thematic and role flexibility becomes broad enough to include amicably differences which would have been disruptive in lower socioeconomic groups

—the players are concentrating so hard on following the course of the theme during the episode and finding suitable ways to enact it, they are inclined to disregard things which could have been grounds for conflict

—the constant give and take of the game process allows the players to feel the support they receive as well as that which they give to each other; breaking off the game in anger would be felt as a personal loss

—imagination opens up possibilities; anger and aggression closes them down; the dynamics of the two processes are antithetical so that play behavior based on imagination tends to exclude anger and aggression

—when conflict does emerge, children use rational methods to deal with the difficulty; the emphasis is on mutual understanding rather than on power plays

—sociodramatic play allows for the expression of many emotions and provides a vehicle for containing them in reasonable proportions; if related to a theme, anger has a place and can be expressed. It is, however, held under control and thus the children experience practice in such control.

Summary of Differences

In terms of the topics discussed above, the major differences observed between preschool children from lower socioeconomic groups and those from higher socioeconomic groups were as follows:

Referent	Higher SES Group	Lower SES Group
Participation	Nearly all children	Very few of total group
Themes & Roles	Primarily home and work themes adult roles well elaborated	Same themes and roles less elaborated
Toys	Toys not of primary importance; non-structured materials or verbal substitution often preferred	Toys of primary importance; replicas preferred
Talking	For management, imitative speech and verbal make-believe	Mainly for management; some imitation and almost no verbal make-believe.

Referent	Higher SES Group	Lower SES Group
Leadership	Democratic; discipline integral to requirements of the medium	Authoritarian; discipline pertains to status
Problems	Dealt with by shared control, humor; criticisms focused on process of fulfilling theme; deviations accepted when based on reality perception	Dealt with by means of leader's control; criticism focused on personalities; overt aggression directed at deviating individuals

B. Sociodramatic Play Viewed as a Dramatic Performance

Separate descriptions of each characteristic of sociodramatic play do not project a whole, integrated picture. The essential difference between sociodramatic play of children from higher socioeconomic backgrounds and that of those from lower socioeconomic backgrounds becomes more apparent when sociodramatic play is considered from the viewpoint of a dramatic performance.

The following elements of drama were clearly discerned in the sociodramatic play of children from higher socioeconomic groups. The description which follows is based entirely on observation of children from the higher socioeconomic level groups.

a. Direction (management of the whole)
b. Dramatic role
c. Theme
d. Scene and props

a. Direction

The direction of a play episode is usually accomplished by means of the verbal participation of all the players. The leader of the group could be called the "chief director" and the others in the group are his co-directors, helping him plan the entire episode. Each one contributes his ideas, creative or functional, so that the planning of the game and the division of roles is the result of the full cooperation of the group as a whole. The leader is "democratic" for the most part; he generally does not impose his will on the others, but does try to influence them: "But little children don't do ironing!" He often turns to the others for support. The teacher rarely has to arbitrate differences of opinion; the group usually manages to settle them on their own.

The creative planning stage of sociodramatic play represents a large portion of the time spent in the game as well as of the enjoyment of the game. Frequently, the planning stage becomes so important and so satisfying to the children that the actual play episode dwindles to insignificance. The planning stage does not end when the children actually enter into the game, for there are frequent role changes as well as thematic changes.

Planning is verbal and characterized by such expressions as "Let's pretend that. . ." and "Let's say that. . ." These expressions are also an important aid in solving problems that arise during the game: situation on a playground—there is only one little girl and she wants to be the baby; who will be Mommy? solution—"Let's pretend that your Mommy is dead and you live with your uncles." They are in a "car" and the little girl wants to "eat". "Eat! I want to eat!" The others say, "Let's pretend that we brought food for the baby from home" and they offer her a curled up leaf to represent a bottle. Flexibility during the planning is reflected during the course of the game by all the participants and avoids group conflict while sustaining the game. The withdrawal of a child from a game in the middle need not disturb or beak up the story: situation on a playground—"Let's say that Daddy's gone to work"; a train game—"I'm going on a holiday. I'm not here any more; I've gone away. I'm not coming back, I'm going to stay there all day and all night."

b. Dramatic Role

Children tend to identify themselves fully with their dramatic roles. This identification is often expressed through verbalization in the dramatic script. Manipulation of materials and play objects are not terribly significant. Mommy speaks the language of Mothers; Baby lisps like babies do; Drivers and Mechanics all use the language of Drivers and Mechanics. The child plays the part with his whole being: he imitates the tones and gestures; he spoils his babies and is spoiled; he shouts in mock anger and speaks pompously. Not only does each one act out his dramatic role, but each participant also reacts dramatically to the dramatic images projected by his fellow players from within the context of his own role; thus, each calls the other by role-appropriate terms: Madam, Mommy, Dollykins, Honey, etc.

At the same time the child remains aware of the "real" world around him while he is playing. The identification with his role is the result of a conscious act and can therefore be cut short. If he changes roles, for example, if Doctor becomes Daddy, he easily exchanges one identity image for another, one dramatic script for another suitable to the new role. Children tend to slip in and out of roles with little difficulty.

c. Theme

Sociodramatic play usually involves a complex, imaginative plot. Something is happening although it may not necessarily be made clear from any specific action on the part of the children, but rather from the verbal planning that accompanies the game. The explanatory commentary on roles and theme keeps the observers fully informed about what the children are thinking during the game process, including: characteristics, attitudes, actions of the personalities being portrayed, the unifying theme, what has already happened and what is yet to happen between the characters.

d. Scene and Props

Flexibility characterizes this aspect as well. Children sometimes construct the scene using props and sometimes conjure it up by verbal description alone: situation on playground— "Pretend that that's a car. . ." (pointing to tree trunk). Play objects, as such, have little importance for the game. Any handy object may be used in several ways: situation in the Doll Corner—a piece of rubber tubing is used first as a dog's bone and then as a telephone although a toy telephone is available nearby; a bit of play-dough is used as a bone; a situation on the playground—a leaf is used as a baby bottle. The child makes little effort to procure the most suitable play object (like the telephone), but is content if the object simply stimulates some sort of association with the specific use he intends. Such an object is even preferred, on occasion, to an exact replica, because it may be able to fill various uses. The course of a game is seldom suspended for the lack of the toy; any object is picked up, the formula is recited: "Let's pretend that this is. . ." and the game goes on.

Two block-building games were observed where the buildings themselves were very poor architecturally; they were, however, not buildings, but scenery, authentic background for sociodramatic play of the children: one was for "circus" and the other for "garage."

The fact that play objects take secondary place in the game process together with the ability of the children to conjure up any prop they might need through their imagination, explains why sociodramatic play episodes are so varied, covering a tremendous variety of subjects and experiences and are performed both in the classroom and on the playground.

Sociodramatic play of children from lower socioeconomic backgrounds takes place only inside the classroom and only in those "Corners" designated and equipped for such play. Because it lacks the prerequisites for dramatic performance described above, it is impossible to evaluate it along the same lines. There is no planning stage or discussion of assigning roles, but begins with the immediate manipulation of play objects. The roles and themes are revealed through the activities or through verbal pronouncements, such as "I'm Mommy" "I'm going to work" or "I made a party." There are no negotiations between the children over the roles to be played or about the aim and direction of a game. Each child decides for himself and plays his own game. When there is a leader with creative and imaginative ability, he is almost always an authoritarian leader. The other children either agree with his decisions and do as they are told or they withdraw from the game.

In most cases there is no evidence of a dramatic script, of verbal identification of the child with his role or other signs, gestures etc. of dramatic involvement: situation in the Dolls' Corner—"Make the doll's food" rather than "Make Baby's food." The child is not playing a part; she is feeding a doll, not a baby (doll). There is almost no verbal mimicry in any of the roles and it is obvious that the children would not react to each other's pseudo-dramatic impersonations. Role identification, when there is any, is expressed through toy manipulation. The doll is undressed and put to bed; the driver turns the steering wheel; the doctor arranges medicine bottles or examines the doll. Role-typed activities rather than real imitation are the major means of conveying the role play. Thus, while it was sufficient to record the verbalization of children from the higher socioeconomic groups in order to understand the unfolding of the theme during the game, in games of children from the lower socioeconomic groups, it was necessary to keep a detailed record of all the movements and actions of the children in order to reveal the roles and themes of the play.

2. Quantitative Findings on SES Differences in Sociodramatic Play

The differences between lower and higher socioeconomic groups of children engaging in sociodramatic play which emerged from our observations and analyses of play records led us to search for quantitative research data on the subject. At the time we could not find any empirical evidence in the professional literature. Freiberg pointed out several years later (1973, p. 129) "There is little information of a systematic nature regarding cultural or social class differences in make-believe play."

It seemed to be taken for granted, on the basis of observations of middle-class European or American children, that this form of play was a *universal type* of early childhood experience. The major theories of play—whether the early instinct theory of Grooss, the surplus energy approach of Schiller, the developmental theory of Piaget or the psychoanalytic theories—all seem to make this assumption.

However, there were some suggestions from several sources in the United States that make-believe play of young children from lower socioeconomic strata was different (Murphy, 1956, Siegel and McBane, 1956). It tends to be fragmental and lacking in imaginative and symbolic content when compared with make-believe play of middle class children.

Measurement problems might explain the complete lack of systematic research on the subject. Singer observed (1973): "What we most seriously lack are large bodies of formal data, collected under specified conditions in sufficient details that they can be replicated by others. In addition, we need a set of categories and formal tools for measurement of play behavior."

In our first work in Israel, in search of quantifiable dimensions of sociodramatic play, we tried two directions. One direction assessed differences in several linguistic dimensions of the children's verbal output during play; the other addressed itself to comparing the level of play itself, as expressed in role-taking and verbal behavior.

A. Quantitative Analyses of Speech During Play

We expected the differences observed in the play of children from lower and higher socioeconomic groups, especially in terms of the different function of verbalization during sociodramatic play to be mirrored in several quantitative speech measures. The verbal material has been taken from three parallel situations of play episodes with children from both groups. It represents verbalization during sociodramatic play around the House and Hospital and the Blocks Corners plus verbal interaction in the Drawing and Painting Corner. Including the third Corner provided us with a larger sample of speech participation for children with lower socioeconomic background than if we had concentrated solely on sociodramatic play episodes.

We used the following criteria for comparison purposes:

1. Word Count—the number of words uttered during the 45 minute period (15 minutes in each of the three Corners)

2. Utterance Length—the average number of words in 90 utterances (30 from each play situation). When play episodes were longer, we took ten utterances from the beginning, ten

from the middle and ten from the end. An utterance included any uninterrupted sequence of speech from a child, even if it was not a coherent unit. The sample used here is not identical with that used for measuring the word count.

3. Sentence Length—the average number of words in 90 sentences (30 from each play situation). The sample was drawn randomly from the one used for measuring utterance length.

4. Parts-of-speech Analysis—approximately 735 words (245 from each play situation) were broken down into parts-of-speech. For this purpose we used the speech samples which served to calculate word count and supplemented them with those used for calculation of utterance length.

5. Vocabulary Range in Parts-of-Speech—all repetitions in the total sample of words used for parts-of-speech were deleted to get the vocabulary range.

6. Vocabulary Overlap between the two groups—the vocabulary of each group was divided into two: the words shared by both groups of children and the words used by each group separately.

It is important at this point to note that every word uttered by the participants was included whether it was relevant to the play activity or not. It is likely that if only play-related speech were analyzed, the differences would be even greater.

Results

We found marked differences between the higher and lower socioeconomic groups in all areas measured.

1. *Word Count*. Children from higher socioeconomic groups speak considerably more than those from the lower groups. During 45 minutes of play, they uttered 698 words as compared with 425 spoken by children from the lower socioeconomic levels (Table 5). This situation obtained in each of the three corners as well.

Note: We tried to equalize the number of children participating in the play episodes from which we drew our speech samples. Because this was not completely feasible, we preferred to have a larger number of children in the Lower SES group to exclude bias due to more

Table 5: Word Count During 45 Minutes by SES Groups and Play Corners

	Higher SES		Lower SES	
Corners	Number of Words	Number of Children	Number of Words	Number of Children
Drawing and Painting	185	5	110	7
Blocks	268	2	135	3
Hospital	245	4	180	4
45 Minute Total	698	11	425	14

children participating in sociodramatic play in the higher SES group.

2. *Utterance Length*. Children from the higher socioeconomic groups have longer utterances than those from the lower groups. Their average utterance was 5.4 words as compared with 4.1 words for those from the lower socioeconomic level groups (Table 6). The average utterance length was shorter for children from the lower groups in all play situations.

3. *Sentence Length*. Children from higher socioeconomic levels speak in longer sentences than do children from lower socioeconomic levels. The average sentence length was 3.4 words as compared to 2.9 words for children from the lower groups (Table 7). Shorter sentence length for children from the lower groups was consistent in all play Corners.

4. *Parts-of-speech Analysis*. 735 words were broken down into parts of speech (Table 8) and the following differences emerged:
   a. Children from the higher socioeconomic groups use a larger percentage of nouns, both abstract and concrete, numbers and adverbs.
   b. Children from the lower socioeconomic groups use a larger percentage of adjectives, conjunctions and pronouns.

5. *Vocabulary Range in Parts-of-Speech*. Children from the higher socioeconomic groups display a larger range of vocabulary than those from the lower groups (Table 9). The 716 words analyzed for the first group (names and expletives were excluded) included 238 different words. The 721 words of the second group included 200 different words. The speech sample of the

Table 6: Utterance Length by SES Groups and Play Corners

Corner	Higher SES			Lower SES		
	Number of Words in 30 Utterances	Average Number of Words in Utterances	Number of Children	Number of Words in 30 Utterances	Average Number of Words in Utterances	Number of Children
Drawing and Painting	144	4.8	5	133	3.4	11
Blocks	156	5.2	6	142	4.7	4
House and Hospital	186	6.2	5	130	4.3	3
Total	486	5.4	16	375	4.1	18

Table 7: Sentence Length by Groups and Play Corners

Corner	Higher SES			Lower SES		
	Number of Words in 30 Sentences	Average Number of Words in Sentences	Number of Children	Number of Words in 30 Sentences	Average Number of Words in Sentences	Number of Children
Drawing and Painting	103	3.4	5	83	2.8	11
Blocks	111	3.7	6	90	3.0	4
House and Hospital	96	3.2	5	91	3.0	3
Total	310	3.4	16	264	2.9	18

Table 8: Breakdown of Words Uttered During Play By Parts of Speech According to Groups

Parts of Speech	Higher SES		Lower SES	
	Number of Words	Per Cent	Number of Words	Per Cent
Verbs	167	22.7	168	22.8
Nouns—Concrete	118	16.0	99	13.4
Nouns—Abstract	39	5.3	21	2.8
Adverbs	144	19.5	112	15.2
Adjectives	44	6.0	63	8.5
Numbers	23	3.1	9	1.2
Conjunctions	59	8.0	95	12.8
Pronouns	93	12.6	115	15.5
Prepositions	12	1.6	16	2.2
Names	17	2.3	23	3.2
Exclamations, Expletives	21	2.8	17	2.3
Total	737	100.0	738	100.0

higher socioeconomic group contained 66.7% repetitions and that of the lower group 72.3%.

Table 8 indicates that children from the higher socioeconomic groups used a larger vocabulary in all parts of speech except adjectives and pronouns.

6. *Vocabulary Overlap between Higher and Lower Socioeconomic Groups.* Both groups used the same 105 words. For children in the higher socioeconomic group, this constituted 44.1% of their actual vocabulary of 238 words and for children in the lower socioeconomic groups, this constituted 52.5% of their actual vocabulary of 200 words (see Table 9).

Examining the total conversation of the two groups, including repetitions, we can see that the use of overlapping vocabulary is more extensive for children from the lower group: out of 721 words 521, or 72.3% of the total sample, were repetitions (excluding expletives). The total sample of the vocabulary used by children from the higher group included only 461 words, or 64.4% of the 716 word total, drawn from the overlapping vocabulary. Thus it seems clear that children from the lower socioeconomic group make greater use of common vocabulary

Table 9: Vocabulary Range by Parts of Speech According to Groups

Parts of Speech	Higher SES			Lower SES		
	Total Number of Words	Repetition	Number of Words Without Repetition	Total Number of Words	Repetition	Number of Words Without Repetition
Verbs	167	113	54	168	119	49
Nouns—Concrete	118	61	57	99	55	44
Nouns—Abstract	39	20	19	21	11	10
Adverbs	144	110	34	112	82	30
Adverbs	144	110	34	112	82	30
Adjectives	23	20	24	63	37	26
Numbers	44	10	13	9	5	4
Conjunctions	59	46	13	95	83	12
Pronouns	93	81	12	115	101	14
Prepositions	12	7	5	16	11	5
Exclamations	17	10	7	23	17	6
Total	716	478	238	721	521	200

than do children from the higher group. This measure is somewhat dependent on the previous measure—range of vocabulary; a smaller range would necessarily contain a higher percentage of basic words which probably constitute the bulk of the overlapping vocabulary.

It is possible to summarize the speech analysis by stating that children from higher socioeconomic backgrounds speak more, in longer sentences, in longer utterances and use a higher percentage of nouns, adverbs, and numbers; they also use fewer adjectives, conjunctions and pronouns and have a richer vocabulary.

The study described above may be considered a preliminary study in the field of verbalization during sociodramatic play. It seems to us that further studies in this field are needed. Language assessment during play activity could take several possible directions: it could study the relevance of utterances to the play activity itself (see our analysis of Tables 5, 6 and 7); it could render a quantitative and qualitative evaluation of speech according to the possible imitative, substitutive (make-believe) and/or managerial functions within the context of play activity. Developing schemes for language evaluation and tools which are specifically aimed at sociodramatic play could contribute a great deal to the understanding of the reciprocal relationship between linguistic maturity and involvement in make-believe play.

B. Quantitative Differences in the Quality of Dramatic and Sociodramatic Play

Now we wished to assess the play activity itself in quantitative terms. A preliminary "Smilansky Scale" was constructed based on the observational data gathered previously. It used the following six categories of play behavior:
1. Imitative Role-Play
2. Make-Believe with Objects (Substitution)
3. Make-Believe with Actions and Situations
4. Persistence
5. Interaction with One Co-Player or More
6. Verbal Communication (Pertaining to the Play)

This scale was developed in order to assess the effectiveness of an experiment that explored ways to raise the level of play in kindergartens made up of children from lower socioeconomic backgrounds. Each element received a dichotomous score (present/absent) during the observation sessions (Smilansky, 1968). At the time the scores were utilized to indicate whether the child demonstrated some form of sociodramatic play behavior, solitary dramatic play behavior or neither. Table 10 presents the findings for both lower and higher socioeconomic groups.

Table 10: Proportion of Kindergarten Children (Age 3−6 years) Engaging in Dramatic and Sociodramatic Play

Groups	No Make-Believe Play		Dramatic Play Only		Sociodramatic Play		Total	
	N	%	N	%	N	%	N	%
Lower SES	250	69	72	20	40	11	362	100
Higher SES	13	3	81	19	333	78	427	100

The striking inter-group difference did not repeat itself in such magnitude in later studies. Hopefully, positive changes in parental education as well as greater awareness of the importance of play behavior on the part of kindergarten teachers helped narrow the gap during the years since this study. Later studies also applied more flexible criteria (persistence was reduced from 10 minutes to five minutes).

Nevertheless, there was still evidence of considerable differences in the study of Taler (1976) comparing the play of two socioeconomic groups[1] (48 low and 48 high SES) in order to examine the relationship between sociodramatic play and dimensions of social adjustment (N = 96). Statistically significant differences (P < .04) were found, using the final version of the Smilansky Scale, with a mean score of 8.8 for the higher socioeconomic group and 6.4 for the lower. Thus, a decade after our first study, differences by socioeconomic strata had not disappeared.

Even larger gaps between socioeconomic groups were found in the United States in a study by Griffing (1979). The study

---

[1]SES Criteria was determined by parents' occupation and education.

compared sociodramatic play of 169 black kindergarten children, about half of them low and half of them higher SES (5–6 year-olds), in nine schools from Columbus and Franklin counties. Socioeconomic groupings were determined by the occupation and education level of the Head of the Family (the one who provides the main financial support). Children were observed in groups of four (two boys, two girls) for a half hour period in a structured laboratory setting. One observer was assigned to each child and kept a specimen record of the child's verbal and non-verbal behavior. The records were evaluated by independent scorers using the final version of the Smilansky Scale (see Appendix). Table 11 presents the findings of this study according to sex and SES grouping.

The mean scores presented in Table 11 clearly indicate strong differences between socioeconomic groups for children of both sexes from the United States which is consistent in all of the six play categories as well as in the total play score. These differences are highly significant, viz. the analyses of variance of the play scores by SES and sex in Table 12. When all six play scores are processed together in a multi-variate analysis of variance, the F ratio for SES is very large. There is also a significant but considerably smaller F ratio for sex, while there is no interaction effect.

Highly significant findings are also obtained when the effects of SES and sex on the six play-criteria are evaluated separately. All F ratios for SES are very large. There are no significant findings for sex, but there are some slight SES and sex interaction effects in some play categories. The fairly large sample in the Griffing study seems to imply that differences in the nature of sociodramatic play behavior of preschool children according to socioeconomic level are a cross-cultural phenomenon.

Subsequent studies, using different child populations and a variety of evaluation procedures, all seem to support our conclusion. An overview of these studies, in chronological order, is presented below.

Rosen (1974) conducted an experiment in a small southern community in the United States comparing 58 children from five kindergarten classes, four classes of black, disadvantaged children and one of white, middle-class children. Demographic

Table 11: Mean Play Scores,[2] by Categories, by SES and by Sex

Sex	Play Variable	Lower SES	Higher SES
Boys	N =	43	42
	1. Imitative Role-Play	6.19	10.24
	2. Make-Believe with Objects	5.93	8.12
	3. Verbal Make-Believe with Actions and Situations	2.44	5.17
	4. Persistence	5.16	9.17
	5. Interaction within Context	3.93	7.95
	6. Verbal Communication within Context	3.40	6.76
	Total Play Scores	4.51	7.99
Girls	N =	44	40
	1. Imitative Role-Play	5.00	10.95
	2. Make-Believe with Objects	4.25	8.20
	3. Verbal Make-Believe with Actions and Situations	1.20	6.37
	4. Persistence	4.32	11.02
	5. Interaction within Context	2.59	9.70
	6. Verbal Communication within Context	2.25	8.40
	Total Play Scores	3.27	9.11
Total	N =	87	84
	1. Imitative Role-Play	5.59	10.59
	2. Make-Believe with Objects	5.08	8.16
	3. Verbal Make-Believe with Actions and Situations	1.82	5.46
	4. Persistence	4.74	10.35
	5. Interaction within Context	3.25	8.80
	6. Verbal Communication within Context	2.82	7.56
	Total Play Scores	3.88	8.54

[2]Mean sub-scores were derived from added scores on six five-minute observations (maximum 18).

data pertaining to individual children revealed that one of the black groups was middle-class or middle-class oriented. Both parents worked and the family was characterized by stable job income, whereas more than half of the lower-class children came from welfare homes.

Table 12: Results of Two-Way Analysis of Variance of Sociodramatic Play Scores by SES and Sex

Source	Degrees of Freedom	F Ratio	Probability
SES	(6.160)	15.06	0.001***
Sex	(6.160)	2.58	0.021*
SES × Sex	(6.160)	1.64	0.140

Univariate F Tests with Two Factors (SES and Sex)

Source	Degrees of Freedom	Play Variable	F Ratio	Probability
SES	(1,165)	1. Imitative Role-Play	54.36	0.001***
		2. Make-Believe with Objects	37.16	0.001***
		3. Verbal M.B. with Actions & Situations	47.65	0.001***
		4. Persistence	51.19	0.001***
		5. Interaction in Context	71.15	0.001***
		6. Verbal Communication in Context	51.55	0.001***
Sex	(1,165)	1. Imitative Role-Play	0.15	0.696
		2. Make-Believe with Objects	2.68	0.104
		3. Verbal M.B. with Actions & Situations	0.01	0.929
		4. Persistence	0.07	0.798
		5. Interaction in Context	0.06	0.810
		6. Verbal Communication in Context	0.10	0.757
SES × Sex	(1,165)	1. Imitative Role-Play	1.96	0.164
		2. Make-Believe with Objects	3.04	0.084
		3. Verbal M.B. with Actions & Situations	4.59	0.034*
		4. Persistence	1.88	0.172
		5. Interaction in Context	5.50	0.020*
		6. Verbal Communication in Context	4.43	0.037*

Using the Smilansky Scale to evaluate sociodramatic play during free-play, Rosen showed a highly significant difference between the amount of dramatic or sociodramatic play in which the white middle-class children engaged compared to that in which the lower-class black children engaged ($X^2(1) = 19.75$, $P<.001$). All the white, middle-class children were observed engaging in dramatic and sociodramatic play activities, whereas few of the lower-class, black children did. A very important point brought out was that the middle-class oriented black group displayed significantly more sociodramatic play behavior than the lower-class groups ($X^2(1) = 14.03$, $P<.001$). For more details about this study, see Chapter V.

Tizard et al. (1976) studied 109 3–4 year old children in three types of preschool centers in Great Britain: traditional English nursery schools staffed by trained teachers, similar nursery schools but with special emphasis on language programs and day-care nurseries without trained teachers, intended to provide care for children of working mothers. They reported large social class differences in the amount of symbolic play of any kind. Two additional findings are important: SES differences were smaller in the language-oriented schools and were even smaller in an additional sample of 23 low socioeconomic level children who were integrated into predominantly middle-class nurseries. It should be noted, however, that the study dealt with symbolic play as a general category and did not relate to sociodramatic play or the elements of make-believe.

Smith and Dodsworth (1978), another study done in Great Britain, focused more specifically on fantasy play criteria. They observed 64 children, aged 3–4 in a group equally divided by age, sex and social class. Each child's behavior was sampled during free play conditions over a five minute period on three separate occasions.

Social class differences were significant for all fantasy play criteria applied except for the mean length of episode per child: time spent in fantasy play per child, mean number of participants, elaboration beyond the properties of an object were all higher for children from higher socioeconomic strata; replica use of objects was higher, however, for children from lower socioeconomic levels. Nevertheless, the authors disagree with our conclusions about the cross-cultural quality of the effect of SES on sociodramatic play by stating that a majority of lower-class children did show some fantasy play.

It is possible that there are substantial differences between children from the lower socioeconomic levels in the United States and Israel and the England working-class children observed by Smith and Dodsworth. It would seem, however, there is also a considerable difference in the criteria applied, as pointed out by the authors. Criteria differences also explain contradictory findings cited by Fein (1981, page 1105) and Eiferman (1971, page 290). If fantasy play is defined as any imitative action or sound, or any imitative use of a toy replica, differences between socioeconomic groups are considerably smaller than with the Smilansky criteria. The question is if such criteria are sufficient. Truly symbolic play goes much beyond any imitative action or sound. Manipulating toy replicas in a rote imitation or running around making sounds of vehicles, even if the child declares "I am. . . ." is not the type of play leading to personal growth and enrichment. Such play is not much more than functional play and probably less than constructive play. For more on this point, see Chapters I and II.

Christman (1979) observed 48 MexicanAmerican children in the United States, aged 3–4, in a structured but familiar play setting over six five-minute sessions. Using the Smilansky Scale she finds low levels of play at both age levels and for both males and females. There was evidently no middle-class group for comparison.

Dansky (1980) found only six five-year old children engaging in sociodramatic play among 36 black and white children from lower socioeconomic backgrounds, observed in their familiar setting at a preschool center over six five-minute observation sessions. Further details about this study are in Chapter V.

Udwin and Shmukler (1981) conducted a more recent study in Israel and South Africa employing a sample of 15 children from the lower socioeconomic levels and 15 children from the higher socioeconomic levels in each of the two countries. The application of a two-way variance analysis in this study made it clear that socioeconomic status influenced the occurrence of imaginative play significantly, whereas the cultural differences (Israeli vs. South African) were nonsignificant. Application of a t test, however, obtained significant cultural difference for the middle-class samples.

Since the findings reported related to imaginative play, whether solitary or social, it is important to note that there was a significant effect caused by socioeconomic levels as well as culture in terms of interaction with peers. Middle-class children scored higher than lower-class children; Israeli children scored higher than South African children. The authors interpreted these findings in terms of environment stimulation and parental practices as well as opportunities for peer contact.

Table 13 summarizes the major details of the studies cited above.

Table 13: Studies on Cultural and SES Differences in Dramatic and Sociodramatic Play

Investigators	Subjects	Criteria
Smilansky (1968)	4 – 6.6 Israeli, Low and High SES	Preliminary Smilansky Scale
Rosen (1974)	5 – 6 American black low and middle and white middle-class	Adaptation of Smilansky Scale
Tizard et al. (1976)	3 – 4, British	Amount of Symbolic Play
Taler (1976)	5 – 6, Israeli, Low and High SES	Smilansky Scale
Smith & Dodsworth (1978)	3 – 4, British	Fantasy Play (time spent in, no. of participants, elaboration, etc.)
Griffing (1979)	5 – 6, American black, Low and High SES	Smilansky Scale
Christman (1979)	3 – 4, Mexican American	Smilansky Scale
Dansky (1980)	5, black and white low SES	Amount of sociodramatic play—5 behavior categories
Udwin & Shmukler (1981)	4 – 6, South African and Israeli, low and middle SES	Imaginativeness (Singer's Scale, 1973)

Summary

The empirical evidence from various sources presented here in addition to the lack of any findings to the contrary lead us to conclude that environmental factors have a powerful impact on the child's dramatic and sociodramatic play behavior. It seems that parental education is the single major background variable related to the level of make-believe play across the various cultures. Children whose parents have little formal education, in Israel, the United States and England, do not tend to develop the type of imaginative play that their peers, whose parents have more extensive formal education, so much enjoy to participate in.

The next chapter will discuss these findings from a theoretical point of view in order to facilitate a fuller understanding of the phenomenon.

Chapter Four: The Significance of Sociodramatic Play from a Theoretical Perspective

The phenomenon of play, especially spontaneous play of young children, fascinated many prominent observers of human behavior. It has been discussed from different points of view: its nature, its function, its significance in the developmental process, etc. We searched for a theoretical framework into which we could fit our observations of the characteristics of sociodramatic play and which would also allow for variations in amount and type of play related to sociocultural background.

1. Contribution of Existing Play Theories

Bio-philosophical theories of play dominated the period just before the end of World War I; these centered mainly about the work of Spencer and Groos and on the development of Freudian concepts and terminology. After 1917 most theoreticians concerned themselves with empirical examination in the field rather than developing new play theory.

Valentine, Buhler and Piaget, among others, conducted observational studies and experiments to examine developmental influences on children's play behavior. Many articles appeared dealing with children's reactions, preferences and choice of play materials when faced with a large variety and number of such materials in a permissive environment.

Special attention was paid to play as a means of personality projection. Much has been written about the clinical value of

91

play both as a diagnostic tool and a means of therapy. Freudian and neo-Freudian thinking sees play behavior, both spontaneous as well as induced, as symptomatic and mirroring the inner life of the child. Therefore, the therapist utilizes play behavior to help disturbed or maladjusted children in a therapeutic sense.

Until the 1970's there was little literature examining how dramatic play is related to and supportive of the child's social and intellectual development. There have been studies of the type and quality of learning that can be accomplished through play activities in kindergarten or primary grades. However, this work is based on "didactic games" and not on dramatic play episodes.

Since we are concerned with dramatic and sociodramatic play, we will only discuss theories and research related to such play behavior. In particular we are interested applying existing theoretical works and empirical studies in order to understand observed sociodramatic play performance of children from low socioeconomic levels.

An early theory of play, proposed by Schiller in 1795, sees play as a form of art. The child freely chooses the theme of his game from a fund of unlimited possibilities, and the choice is not seen as bound by practical or functional considerations. Play, like art, is not engaged in to fulfill certain positive or particular needs. According to Schiller, the child envisages imaginatively and moves in a dreamlike atmosphere, similar to an artist, poet or composer while immersed in his imaginative world. That world is, for him, reality. Man plays with beauty, says Schiller, as a child plays with his toys. These two activities meet on the common ground of "play drive" (Spieltrieb) where, through the act of artistic creation, man "turns reality into vision," that is, into a theme of "pure perception," not constrained by ulterior motives, without motivation toward positivistic goals, and not shackled by the chains binding him to objective reality. It is Schiller's opinion that the child, like the poet, turns the real objects with which he is playing into visionary or imaginary objects; he changes the meaning of his play objects according to his wishes; he involves them into and enwraps them with his experiences; the play objects take on a life of their own within the world that the child creates for them; they change their form, meaning, and function according to the dictates of the child's wishes and the child has no other motive than to enjoy the freedom and range of his own initiative and power of invention.

Schiller's theory does not account satisfactorily for the fact that "play drive," a phenomenon common to all children, does not apply to play behavior of children of low socioeconomic status as it does to children from high sociocultural backgrounds. According to Schiller, children manage through their "play drive" to free themselves from the shackles of reality. Yet, he does not explain why some, mainly those from low socioeconomic backgrounds, do not attain this freedom.

In 1872 Spencer expounded the theory that aesthetic feeling is related to creative play because neither play nor aesthetic activity is directly useful; neither is directly involved in the battle for survival. Spencer noted that nature has invested each living being with enough strength to satisfy its basic needs: hunger, self-preservation and propagation. The lower animals must spend all their available energy on fulfilling these fundamental needs. The more complex organisms, which function more efficiently, need not expend all their energy thus. They channel their excess energy into activities which are not motivated by necessity. Kittens, puppies, cubs, for example, run and jump and chase each other for no apparent reason except the pleasure of expending excess energy, which demands an outlet. Play is the "comedy of life"; it involves freedom of activity through which the child is able to disperse his excess energy. Spencer goes one step further and says that if one of the many sources of energy is bottled up over a certain period of time and finds no outlet, this energy will be turned into pretend behavior; pretend behavior or activity is what we call dramatic play.

When we apply Spencer's description and explanation of the term "excess energy" to observation of the behavior patterns of children from both higher and lower socioeconomic backgrounds, we find no confirmation of his claims. These children, ranging in age from three to seven years, did not expend their energies in fulfilling their basic needs of hunger, thirst and self-preservation to the degree that there was no "excess energy" left. All, or at least the greater part of their energy is readily and willingly expended in play activity. Yet, the children from lower socioeconomic backgrounds did not display "pretend behavior." Why did they not find an outlet for their "excess energy" in pretend behavior or imitation play? What makes children expend their "excess energy" in pretend behavior rather than some other behavior?

Stanley-Hall (1906) attempted to translate Haeckel's biogenetic law into psychological processes. Haeckel's law states that all creatures pass through all the developmental phases of their species (philogenesis) in their individual physical development (ontogenesis). Stanley-Hall asserts that the child passes through all the developmental phases of the entire human race in his psychic development and play reproduces the prehistoric periods through which the human race has evolved. In his play a child relives and recreates the life of the early wandering tribes, the traits and tricks of the hunter, the maneuvers of war, and, in fact, all those activities in which man had to become accomplished in his fight for existence. Through play the child channels his wild, primitive urges into a situation of social life acceptable to the social context.

Our observations of children playing, from Israel as well as the United States, from low as well as high socioeconomic background, did not reveal games played on themes of wandering tribes, hunters after prey, etc. The themes, as we have already described, were taken from the everyday life of the adults in these children's immediate surroundings.

Groos (1922) views play as a kind of preparation toward work. Play trains those mental and physical powers and skills that are necessary adjuncts to the adult in his working life. According to Groos, play is rooted in one's instincts. Instinctual behavior patterns are inherent in every animal, dormant in its very being and activated, although not necessarily perfected, during childhood. Such behavior patterns require training for their improvement, definition and final achievement. Baby animals do not know how to hunt or scratch a hole in the ground, build a nest, or defend and look after other young ones. They have a predisposition for such activities, but training is necessary in order to develop and strengthen natural tendencies.

Analyzing descriptive material dealing with play behavior of very young animals, Groos concludes that games of young animals are in every case similar to the activities of grown animals of their species, not because of imitation, but because of their inheritance of the basic instincts of the species. Play activities of very young animals achieve no practical results, according to Groos, because they lack physical strength. As they grow, slowly gaining such physical strength, their play more and more approximates the instinctual activities of their species. This process is a combination of natural physical growth and training.

Summarizing human play behavior Groos differentiates the term "instinct" from drives directing the individual toward physical and mental control and needs expressed through reactions to others. He theorizes both a causal and definitive explanation. The former describes the origin of play in instinct; that is, in latent needs and hereditary tendencies: play is characteristic of a particular developmental period and will disappear later in the growth process. The pith of Groos' theory is found in his definitive explanation: instinctual activity is clumsy and ill-defined at first and requires training through experience in order to attain its purpose. The newborn animal does not slip comfortably into a permissive environment, but is forced to train and strengthen its tendencies and abilities in order to survive the hazards of the environment. The question must arise: why do children from low socioeconomic background not actualize their instinctual tendencies through pretend play, as do other children? And, with this consideration in mind, how will such children acquire the necessary training to strengthen and support their chances of survival in adult life? Groos' concern with the parallel between play activity of the child and play behavior of young animals reflected the spirit and influence of Darwin. He emphasizes the "biological functionalism" of play and the common destiny of man and beast. Thus, he attributes instinctual behavior to human beings paralleling similar behavior in other species. He views psychological processes of the individual and society as secondary.

Buhler (1937) defines play as function training, emphasizing the functional enjoyment of play; that is, the special sense of

enjoyment that accompanies the fulfillment of functions characteristic of each stage of the child's development. She states
that play, unlike work, attaches primary importance to single,
isolated activities which are satisfying in themselves, rather than
to the end result or to the act of creating the activity. Children
may start any given activity in their play with a preconceived
purpose in mind, and suddenly, without accomplishing this
end purpose, they may switch to a new activity which is not at
all connected to the former activity. The results of the activity
are apparently unimportant to the child, whereas the functionalism—the actual activity in itself and for itself—seems to provide
him with satisfaction and enjoyment.

However, enjoyment of activity per se does not go far enough
to explain the reason behind the type and content of children's
play. The explanation of "he enjoys activity" to the question of
why a child plays "House" or "riding a horse" which is actually
a piece of wood, or why he plays with other children, sharing his
game with them, simply begs the question from a psychological
point of view. If all activity entails enjoyment, then how does
play differ from work? Why are motor activities involved in
work not enjoyable? What about physical and mental activities
which are unpleasant or even repugnant? To say that a child
enjoys play does not necessarily or logically mean that enjoyment is the ultimate cause of play. Buhler's definition is so broad
and abstract, it can encompass a variety of behavior patterns.
In this way we lose sight of qualities specific to play and cannot
perceive the motivation behind or variations and differentiations in observed play activities of children from low and high
sociocultural backgrounds.

Psychoanalytic theory sees child's play behavior as a mirror
of his impulses and as a means of controlling them (Erickson
1958). Play is an outlet, a means of expressing those drives that
control the child's life. Through play the child is able to release
experiences that have confused and blocked him emotionally
and left him in mental imbalance. According to psychoanalytical
theory, play is an imaginative rehearsal, anticipating traumatic
experiences that the child will probably meet in reality. Play
offers the child the possibility of turning his passive role as the
object of an experience into an active role, where he consciously

conducts and directs events according to his own desires. In play the child "digests" emotional pressures, becomes inured to them through familiarization so that they lose their sting and thus frees himself from them. Play brings the satisfaction of fulfilled desire that reality denies. It is impossible, for example, to satisfy fully the love of a child for his mother, for example, which suffers no competition and demands the exclusive attention of the love object (mother) every moment, in every situation, and forever. The child may release his feelings of bitter disappointment and denial through play, thereby gaining a certain measure of satisfaction and fulfillment—in the game the child can be with his mother to his heart's content.

Psychoanalytic theory describes the process of sublimation working through children's play. Play is the sublimated expression of various instincts. In this sense role-play is particularly significant. The child creates a role by projecting rich imaginative and emotional content into it. The role becomes a means of release and a regulator of the child's instincts.

Thus, we see, the emphasis of psychoanalytic theory is on the function of drives in play; the child expresses his inner state in play activity, projecting his emotional life into his play behavior. This theory attributes both diagnostic and therapeutic function to play. Playing out experiences and repeating them in play form weakens the impact of emotional pressure and furthers the child's emotional maturity by helping him to assimilate traumatic experiences. On the one hand, play helps the child absorb the inevitable emotional disturbances of life, and on the other hand, it alleviates the shock of those disturbances and helps check permanent traumatic damage.

Our observations did not find many manifestations of play behavior patterns described by psychoanalytic theoreticians. This could be explained by the fact that our observations were of normal children, whereas psychoanalytic principles grew out of observations of emotionally disturbed children. Therefore, for example, we did not find that the majority of children in the dozens of kindergartens and nursery schools used the play situation as a means of releasing traumatic experiences or expressing emotional shock. In addition, we have no reason to believe that children from higher socioeconomic backgrounds have more traumatic or frustrating experiences than those from low socioeconomic backgrounds, which would explain their higher use of dramatic play. How can we explain, then, the fact that most children from low socioeconomic background do not engage in dramatic play? Furthermore, among those children who did engage in dramatic play, we found no significant tendency or desire to channel games into themes or behavior patterns contrary to those accepted and customary among themselves or in their immediate surroundings. Another possible explanation for our not finding certain phenomena is the fact that our observations were focused on sociodramatic play episodes in which at least two children were involved. The observations of the psychoanalytical theoreticians were customarily of individual children playing alone or with a therapist.

There is no explanation in the literature of the psychoanalytical approach of why large numbers of normal children do not engage in dramatic play. Loewenfeld (1935) notes that spasmodic play or interspersed, disjointed play in children under the age of nine is symptomatic of intense emotional disturbance. This diagnosis, based on Dr. Loewenfeld's observations of institutionalized children, is, apparently, correct when generally applied to children so emotionally disturbed they have been institutionalized. However, it is difficult to accept the corollary that because the majority of children from low socioeconomic backgrounds do not engage in dramatic play, or do so in a disjointed manner, they are all emotionally disturbed.

Despite the differences in the behavior of normal children when compared to that of disturbed children in terms of dramatic play behavior, it is important to note the significance that psychoanalytic theory attaches to play for personality development. The child undergoes sublimation through play activities. The play situation offers him an opportunity to express and control creative impulses. It is possible that children of low socioeconomic background therefore do not have an opportunity for personality adjustment and development because they do not engage in dramatic play.

Susan Isaacs (1935), whose frame of reference is also psychoanalytic, realizes that the different types of play are an integral part of the orderly, genetic, intellectual, social and moral growth of the child. She believes that the reciprocal activities of the child with the physical world, with various play materials, with adults and with other children, characteristic of child play behavior during the growth process, are of primary importance. Surroundings which stimulate thinking and offer opportunities for social play and imaginative, creative expression both facilitate and expedite developmental growth stages set out by Piaget and even promote the contraction or elision of such stages. The child's egocentricity is countered at a very early age by obstacles and frustrations created by play materials or adults and the child is forced by the demands of his game and by the demands of the material world around him to see reality as opposed to the world of his imagination.

Isaacs classifies children's games into two types: escape into the world of imagination and escape into reality. When internal pressures, such as anxiety or pent-up aggressive feelings, become too strong, the child seeks refuge in real-life experiences, among real people in real-life situations, in an effort or as a means to reestablish his self-confidence. On the other hand, escape into the world of imagination or fantasy occurs when the child tries to evade reality in an effort to achieve wish-fulfillment. Providing suitable play materials and opportunities to play in a permissive, non-interfering atmosphere supplies the child with: (a) the best possible means to come to terms with reality on his own terms, and (b) the best possible treatment for minimizing fears and anxieties by the release of emotional energy through creative play activities.

In such a free and permissive atmosphere children reveal three main types of activity or play:

—Improvement of all types of physical skills, enjoyment of physical movement and the growth of control over such movement, for its own sake.

—A direct interest in physical phenomena, animals and plants, revealed in questions of the "Why is. . ." and "Why does. . ." variety.

—Numerous games of "let's pretend. . ." which differ in form according to the age, sex, play materials at hand and individual experiences of the children involved.

All three types of activity constitute the central point from which discovery, thought and thought processes develop. Isaacs, however, accords special significance to imaginative play over the first two because much of its energy derives from the first symbolical formations of the infant mind which is constantly revitalized and nourished by the suppressed desires and fantasies of that growth period.

Our experience confirmed that the children from high socioeconomic background did indeed engage in the three types of activity delineated by Isaacs; however, children from low socioeconomic background mainly engaged in the first type of activity. The second and third types were seldom noted. Apparently, the groups with whom Isaacs worked can be compared with our high socioeconomic groups of children.

Isaacs notes the ambivalence of the child-parent, love-hate relationship. Her hypothesis is that the hostility in children's play stems from unconscious fantasies: fantasies of danger, rejection and deprivation of love. Behavior such as biting, spitting, verbal threats, vomiting, scratching, provoking and throwing things is evidence of a relationship between aggressive feelings and infantile sexual fantasies. Isaacs felt that feelings of aggression and hostility tend to transmute themselves readily into dramatic play activities and that hostile, aggressive play constitutes a child testing reality to see how far he can go in expressing instinctual behavior, how much anger and avidity he can express without danger. In this way the child alleviates his anxieties and relieves inner tension.

Isaacs pointed out that a large number of children's games are centered around family life—solving problems within the family circle. This is the main theme chosen and directly played out by children up to the age of approximately four years. Later this theme appears albeit in disguise. Both boys and girls show a desire to have babies and to know about the relationship between the sexes in order to find out who can marry whom in wedding games. Isaacs interprets the selection of these themes as an effort to express the deeper-level fantasies of sexual relationships between the parents.

Isaacs' study demonstrates, how an environment with a great variety of "materials", where adults allow the children maximum opportunity of experience and experiment, but feel free to intervene when necessary, can influence the mental development of a group of highly intelligent children.

Our observation of children from high socioeconomic background revealed certain play behaviors described by Isaacs. For example, overt curiosity in the immediate surroundings: an avalanche of questions beginning, "Why is. . .?" "Why does. . .?"; numerous games of "Let's pretend. . ." which are entered into without tiring of it. On the other hand, many play behavior traits mentioned by Isaacs were not found in our groups: a multiplicity of aggressive play themes, aggressive play behavior (hitting, scratching, etc.) during the game itself or strong competitive feelings during the game. We surmise that the reason for these differences can be found in the fact that Isaacs' groups were composed of emotionally disturbed children. The fact that Isaacs found no groups of children who did not engage in play can probably be explained by the homogeneity of high IQ (average 131, range 114–166), and also, perhaps, by the small number of children aged from three to six years in her study (a total of 30 children, aged 2–10 years). While Isaacs attaches great significance to sociodramatic play for the child's healthy development, her theory does not provide explanation for the fact that large groups of children from low socioeconomic background do not develop imaginative play as do their peers from the high socioeconomic levels.

Piaget's theory of play is the most influential and comprehensive theory today; it was developed as an integral part of his dynamic theory of intelligence. In his description of the child's growing mental abilities Piaget details the early developmental progression of play behavior in general and symbolic play in particular. According to Piaget symbolic or dramatic play appears at the beginning of the second year. It marks a transition from pure empiricism to mental representation and transformation of sensory input (Piaget & Inhelder, 1971). All major elements of symbolic play are present at the age of three years (Piaget, 1962).

Although Piaget attaches considerable significance to symbolic play in the course of mental development, he looks at it mainly as having an assimilative function, the consolidation of past experience. He emphasizes the affective-expressive function of play, insofar as it enables the child not only to assimilate reality, but to interpret it in order to relive it and thus to dominate or compensate for it (Piaget 1962). The essential property of symbolic play is ". . .the deformation and subordination of reality to the desires of the self" (Piaget, 1971, p. 339). Through such play the child attempts to recreate experiences in an adapted form to suit his ego and his desires, and to repeat past experiences in order to enjoy the pleasure involved in activating augmented inner forces. Although this process of adaptation and reformation of experiences to suit the ego stands counter to the effort to adjust to reality, in fact such play combines the two aspects of regulation (balance) and catharsis. Children project and enact behavior patterns forbidden to them in real life through make-believe. During symbolic play a child may reconstruct frightening or painful situations, unbearable to him in reality. Piaget points to such instances as imitation or reproduction of a situation in order to conquer the facts and bend them to the child's will and not as an effort to adjust himself to the facts. "The ego can get its revenge on real life." Piaget clearly regards the pretend nature of play as a reflection of egocentricism. Therefore, it is not surprising that Piaget records a gradual decline of symbolic play when egocentric thought gives way to a more realistic orientation, expressed in the emergence of games with rules.

Despite the fact that Piaget's work stimulated much thought and research on pretend play, especially at early stages, and on its relationship to language development—another symbolic function—he does not provide answers to our dilemma: why are there large groups of children who do not demonstrate the developmental progression in symbolic play as described by Piaget? Why do we find five-six year old children with the linguistic skills of at least 3–4 year olds who still do not use these skills to elaborate symbolic play, not even at the level of much younger children?

An ontogenetic approach, like that of Piaget, often overlooks possible influences of the social milieu. (An article by Fein (1979) that compares the work of Piaget and Vygotsky demonstrates this point with regard to symbolic play.) Also, since Piaget's observations were conducted with middle class subjects, he was not confronted with the phenomenon of the lack of sociodramatic play in large numbers of children. This issue, as well as other elements of Piaget's play theory, will be discussed in further detail in the next chapter.

Summary

None of the play theories provide an explanation for the fact that certain groups of children do not engage in sociodramatic play activities. Despite the differences in historical time perspective and cultural settings in which the various theoreticians worked, all subscribe to two suppositions:
  —Play is a natural and universal phenomenon, and;
  —Children naturally advance through all levels, stages and
    types of play behavior.
None of the play theories link pretend play to learned elements.
These contentions might be due to the following.
  a. Empirically-based studies were based mainly on selective populations. Most of the theoreticians and researchers observed children from middle or high sociocultural levels. In Israeli nursery schools and kindergartens, as well, these children tend to engage in a great deal of sociodramatic play. Furthermore, Piaget's theory of play is based on his observation of his own and other middle-class city children. Valentine, too, uses observations of his own children as examples. Other researchers dealt with groups of disturbed children, rather than large, representational groups of "normal" children. Isaacs states, for example, that the majority of the children in her group were emotionally disturbed, with high IQ's and of high sociocultural backgrounds. Loewenfeld's observations were made in a closed institution for disturbed children in England.
  b. Early play theoreticians tried to formulate all-encompassing theories and tended to ignore details that did not fit into their formulations. Stanley-Hall, for example, based his theory on the law of biogenetics, and considered only those children's

games which reconstructed the various stages of human historical development. He apparently ignored the fact that most children overwhelmingly chose to play out themes dealing with
their immediate environment, and only rarely indulged in
games that might possibly be considered as reconstructions of
earlier or later primitive or civilized stages of human historical
development. Other researchers, like Groos, based their theories on parallels between human and animal play, emphasizing
mainly the function of play, and not it's cause. Similarly, Schiller
and Spencer tried to formulate *all encompassing* theories which
would explain the first stages of play behavior exhibited by the
infant and baby, children's games, young people's amusements
as well as the more indirect play behavior of adults! The problem
is that play constitutes an extremely complex group of human
behavioral patterns, including both conscious and subconscious
experiences, occurring in various manners, at various times and
at different stages of growth and development. It is hard to
imagine that a single theory could possibly contain satisfactory
explanations for all contingencies and sequences, even though
there is most likely a relationship between the various aspects
of what is called children's play at any age and the games,
activities and amusements of youth and adults. Indeed, play is
common to the entire human race, regardless of ethnic or cultural distinctions. It can also be found in the behavior of higher
animals.

Archeological research has unearthed children's play objects
and games. Surprisingly, the findings that a number of the
fundamental elements of play, or stages of play, or kinds of play
exhibited by a certain group of children with a certain cultural
background *are not exhibited* by children of a different culture or
sociocultural background, has not stimulated theoreticians to
question their generalizations.

For a variety of reasons, not one of the theories we have
mentioned accounts for the absence of sociodramatic play in
large groups of children. Therefore, it seems that we must coin
our own basic operational concepts.

Our main objective is to arrive at an explanation of observed
phenomena from which we may infer theses to be tested in
experimental studies. Our discussion deals with dramatic play

only, beginning with its first stage, (when pretend is prevalent, but the social context is not yet mandatory) and continuing with sociodramatic play, until its gradual decline which begins approximately at the age of seven.

2. Proposed Conceptual Framework for the Understanding of Sociodramatic Play Behavior

The key concept in the understanding of sociodramatic play is that of identification, the basis for all imitative behavior. Imitation is, in turn, the mainspring of dramatic and sociodramatic play. We regard identification as an integral part of healthy development for all children, including those from low socioeconomic background. However, the translation of identification and it's expression in the form of dramatic and sociodramatic play, includes learned elements, not present in other types of imitation. First, we will clarify the concepts of identification and imitation on the basis of existing literature; then, we will describe their translation into dramatic and sociodramatic play behavior.

Identification

Our thesis is that sociodramatic play in preschool children (aged two to seven years) expresses the child's need to model himself in thought, feeling, action and reaction after the adults in his immediate surroundings, mainly parents, and arises from an intense desire to be like these adults as exactly and in as many ways as possible. According to Murphy (1946), there is a wish to view oneself as one with another person and to act accordingly.

The term "identification" in the sense we refer to it, was coined by Freud and appeared for the first time in *The Interpretation of Dreams* in 1899. Freud stated that identification is not simply imitation, but assimilation. It expresses a resemblance and is derived from a common element which remains in the unconscious. Since then, this concept has enjoyed a variety of definitions at the hands of numerous theoreticians whose opinions, experience and knowledge has led them to diverge in many respects from the classical Freudian definition.

Freud's formulations have at least two distinguishing features which are not attributes of learning theory. First, the child is clearly motivated to become like the parent. Second, this motive functions in relation to a total pattern or Gestalt, not to isolated elements.

Parsons and Bales (1956) also regard a generalized motive, to become like another, as the core of identification. It is their thesis, however, that the developmental process involves a series of identifications gradually differentiating and modifying the role relationships of child-parent, child-society.

Mowrer (1950) distinguishes between two mechanisms in identification: "developmental" and "defensive." The first is based on the affection of the parents and the second is based on parental threat. Developmental identification derives predominantly from biological drives and is a simpler, milder experience, involving little conflict. Defensive identification stems from socially inflicted discomforts and is characterized by a violent crisis, in which anxiety and conflict are prominent.

Slater (1961) also distinguishes between two mechanisms: "personal" and "positional" identification. Personal identification is the identification of the ego with the actual person— adopting his personality, traits, values, and attitudes and is primarily motivated by the ego's love and admiration for the other ("alter"). The child who identifies in this way is saying, in effect, that he wants to be just like him.

Positional identification is the identification of the ego with the situation or role of the alter. There is no empathic understanding of the alter, but merely projecting the self, in fantasy, into the situation of alter and acting out the appropriate role. Positional identification is motivated by fear and envy, not by love. The child who identifies with a parent in this way is saying, in effect, that he wishes to be in his shoes. If he wishes hard enough and acts like him, he will attain his more advantageous status, he will be strong and powerful and beloved rather than weak and helpless. The uncompromising all-or-nothing quality of these desires expresses their unconscious fantastic basis.

Whereas Slater (1961) as well as Ausubel (1952) assume that only one of these mechanisms of identification is necessary for normal personality development, Mussen (1959) and Mowrer (1950), viewing identification from a social-learning standpoint, assume that both types are indispensable for normal personality development.

It is clear that the term identification is used in a wide variety of senses. These definitions, culled from classical psychoanalytical, social-learning and dynamics-oriented theory, are neither consistent nor unanimous in their terminology usage. At the same time we must take note that they all agree that identification is a fundamental concept, generally implying that a child gives his allegiance to his parent (adult) and attempts to duplicate the values, attitudes and behavior of the object of this allegiance.

We believe that this propensity, found to some extent in every infant and preschool child, is the preeminent cause of and major motivator for dramatic play in children of this age. We further hold that preschoolers' identification with the parent is not only with him as an individual model but also as (a) the representative of social norms and (b) as a sex role model.

Identification evolves from parent-child relationships and is rooted in basic emotions. However, in the course of social and cognitive development, the emotional basis becomes less central and identification more diffuse. The child observes other persons is attracted by some aspect of these figures' role behavior, identifies with some expression of their personalities, and tries to imitate and/or to act like them. The motive for imitation is still identification, but with less emotional impact and with more differentiation. It is usually related to some specific aspects of the alter's identity. This looser identification, more cognitive in nature, seems to be an expansion of the primary child-parent identification, which moves from close ties inside the family to larger social relationships. A clue that all role-playing has its roots in this primary identification is found in the fact that the role choices of children are mostly sex-typed and include mainly behavioral aspects admired by the child. In Slater's terminology we could say that the basic mechanism of identification is "personal," of positive emotional impact modified by the child's growing understanding of what is involved in different social roles. Positional identifications also develop, which are not necessarily heavily freighted with emotion (as in Slater's theory), and which extend to various role figures. The child is attracted by some feature in the position of a role-person. He may feel curious and/or envy about it, and he may wish to feel how it is to be in somebody else's place and to act like him.

It must be emphasized that it is only possible to identify oneself with one's image of another person. A child can never really know a parent. Freud stated that the child's superego is modeled after his "parental images," his perception of his parents, not after the parent as he is. The quality of the child's emotional relationship with his parents and his growing understanding of their behavior and the motives behind it, all influence this perception. Translation of the need for identification into imitative behavior will occur only in a very limited form without such understanding.

The same is true for all the child's "positional" identifications. He identifies with a truck driver as he perceives him—sometimes as a powerful and aggressive captain of a big vehicle, sometimes as a clever mechanic who knows all the tricks of a delicate machine, sometimes as a magician, etc. Because the child's limited information and ability to judge, his perceptions of a person may be unrealistic, and thus his role play will be distorted. We should not conclude from this, however, that the child is deliberately, or even unconsciously distorting reality to fit his needs and wishes. It is true that the perception of the identifying person is influenced to some extent by emotional forces, as well as by cognitive factors. Nevertheless, a normal child tends to make a conscious effort to conform to the perceived image while imitating its behavior.

Imitation

There are several important distinctions between identification and imitation. First, imitation is a means used by the child to fulfill his need—identification with his parents' image. In order to satisfy his need for identification, the child *imitates* this image. Second, whereas imitation is largely a conscious mechanism of behavior, identification is predominantly an unconscious process. Although there may be moments when its existence is recognized, the most important aspects of identification develop outside awareness.

Most importantly, the core of identification is the desire to become like another person; imitation is the means to this end.

Miller and Dollard (1941) have defined imitation as behavior in which one person learns to model his behavior on that of another and knows that his act is an acceptable reproduction of the model act. They also state, tentatively, that it is possible that a more detailed analysis would show that the mechanisms involved in copying are also involved in that aspect of character or superego formation which the Freudians have described as *identification*.

Miller and Dollard (1941) regard imitation as learned behavior. They state that parents, aware of the biological sex differences of their children, respond differently to each sex from early infancy. Their punishment and discouragement prevent a boy from learning a girl's role and keeps a girl from adopting masculine habits.

Our observations of sex-typed imitation in pretend play confirm their contention and indicate differentially applied reinforcement. Research on play reviewed by Fein (1981) also substantiates parental reinforcement sex typed in relation to imitation in the play framework.

Sears (1953) attaches less significance to parental reinforcement of imitation and internalization of parental values and behavior patterns. He considers that acquiring parental characteristics through the identification process occurs without specific training, either by direct guidance or by reward and punishment. Sears is, however, aware of a learned element within this process, probably established through partial reinforcement, in the form of a generalized principle acquired by the child "to be like father and mother", replacing any need for specific reinforcement in each instance (Sears 1967).

We feel that the need for identification motivates the child to imitate, but he will only imitate behavior which is positively reinforced; negative reinforcement will extinguish imitative behavior. This thesis has been borne out in experiments conducted by Miller and Dollard and explains sex-typed imitation. It provides us a partial explanation for the absence of imitative behavior in the form of dramatic play in children from low socioeconomic backgrounds.

Dramatic Play

Imitative behavior, especially that based on strong personal identification, is incorporated into a child's total behavior. He acquires behavior patterns, attitudes and ideals he observes through a partially conscious and partially unconscious imitation process. However, part of a child's imitative behavior is based on less intensive "positional" identification and is closely related to adventurous curiosity. The child, confined to a limited, passive and inferior role, identifies with active and more powerful adults; he imitates them consciously, tries to be like them at least for a limited period of time. This results in dramatic play episodes, in which he imitates (his images of) parents and other persons. These images exist in the child's memory and all dramatic role-play is based on these memory images. The more the child believes that his enactment of the role is true to his memory image, the more is his identification need fulfilled and the greater is his satisfaction.

Until he is approximately three years old, a child perceives most of his parents' behavior as a chain of single acts forming a continuum of action. In order to express identification he imitates and plays out each single act, as far as he has understood it and as exactly as he can remember it. A little girl puts on her mother's shoes and hat, takes her mother's purse in hand and says to herself, "I'm Mommy and I'm going shopping," or she might take a doll in her arms and say to herself, "I'm Mommy taking baby to the doctor." At this stage of dramatic play, social contact is less essential for the child, because his awareness and understanding of social relationships is still limited.

Sociodramatic Play

At about three to seven years of age the child further perceives that the thoughts, feelings and actions of his parents do not constitute merely a string of single acts, but are also their reactions to other people's thoughts, feelings and actions. At this point, he realizes the existence of *reciprocity* between people and reaches the *socio*dramatic stage of play. Now he requires social contacts with one or more children in his play activity. He needs to interact with other children in order to satisfy his need to identify with his parents. In order to identify he must imitate, as nearly as possible, *both the actions and the reactions* of his models.

The significance of a child's desire to imitate the images of his parents' world can be assessed by observing the influence of this desire on the choice and content of sociodramatic play episodes and on his play behavior. A great deal of playing time is spent on verbally creating and developing the content of the play episode, on the preparation of toys and other play materials, and on the constant comparisons and criticism voiced by the participating children. This activity reflects the children's continuous efforts to approximate what they believe to be "real life" in their play. The main conflicts or criticisms which occur generally are heated comparisons—an attack on or defense of the various "realities" as the different participants know and remember them, on the one hand, and the play behavior, actions and reactions of the participating children within the play context on the other.

Through imitation behavior the child is attempting to interweave himself into the interactions of the adult world. Thus he attempts to recreate the behavior patterns, actions and reactions of his parents and other adults and children he has observed directly. He does not try to distort the play reality to suit his ego or other psychological needs. On the contrary, *in sociodramatic play the child aims at reproducing, as exactly as possible, the world as he observes it, as he understands it, and insofar as he remembers it.*

.The child invests great energy in playing according to the rules of adult behavior, in producing a faithful imitation of the interpersonal and social rules of the adult world (". . .just like Daddy does. . ." "This is the way the doctor does it. . ."). When he feels he is succeeding—that is, when he feels that his role play is a faithful reproduction of adult reality—his satisfaction is so great, that he has the necessary strength to willingly post-pone gratification of immediate needs or desires that would be inconsistent with the role he is playing. In cases when such strong desires struggle for expression and the child cannot or will not postpone them, he tends to announce a change in role in order to justify his discrepant behavior both to himself and to the others in the group. Here once again is evidence of his efforts to adhere strictly to the rules of the adult world: A little girl is playing at being a baby. She very much wants to do the ironing. She announces, "Let's pretend that I have grown up and I'm now your big girl. A big girl is allowed to do the ironing."

Therefore, far from being a form of retreat from reality or a means of escape, sociodramatic play would appear to be a means of experiencing the adult world of "reality." They are, indeed, not running from the world but are *confronting* it with all the resources at their disposal.

Imitation through sociodramatic play helps the child crystal-lize his experiences and facilitates both an emotional and intel-lectual adjustment to the environment. It offers the child a way to experience the organizing of his behavior from "within a role" in an environment that supports him in the performance of that role. Being within a role in a supportive environment means that the child may organize his behavior in the following ways:

—Selectively choosing the stimulus to which he wishes to respond
—Spontaneously organizing a response which is clearly his own
—Expressing that response
—Seeing that response accepted by the others within the supportive environment
—Having his response turned into new cues by the others
—Using the new cues selectively to formulate a new response and thus continuing the play activities.

The play episode provides the child with a circumstance of interlocking events within which he can act out a role. From his position in the role he experiences himself as a creature who can make choices, formulate and carry out a plan of action, be spontaneously creative, compose something new which rebounds and stimulates further choosing, formulating, creating, etc., in a continuous cycle. He realizes what it is like to have a personal and significant effect on what happens in the world with him in it. He experiences his environment as a responsive and nurturing entity. He acts freely within the limits provided by the role, the play episode, and the players. As subsequent acts form a continuing flow of a "story line," he senses the factor of sequence and its development. He is caught by the drama and grows to meet the needs of the drama itself as it unfolds before him and within him.

3. The Place and the Function of Sociodramatic Play in the Context of Other Play Behavior

Piaget's work on cognitive development stimulated a great deal of research and theorizing on symbolic or dramatic play. The developmental sequence of early pretend activities as outlined by Piaget was substantiated in several studies: the developmental trend is from self-referenced to other-referenced pretend activity, from single-act to sequentially coordinated events, from solitary to collective symbolism; and a general move toward substitutive behavior (Fein and Apfel, 1979; Fenson, 1978; Lowe, 1975; McCune Nicolich, 1977).

However, there are several elements in Piaget's theory of play that cannot be reconciled with either our observations and findings or with other empirical works. Three main issues will be discussed:
— the place of symbolic play in the sequence of play development
— the adaptive function of Sociodramatic Play
— play as ontogenetic vs. learned behavior

A. Symbolic Play in the Sequence of Play Development

Piaget differentiated three major sequences of play: sensory-motor practice (functional play), symbolic play and games with rules. Piaget does not relate to constructive, goal-oriented play behavior as a distinct type or stage of play development. One might ask why an outstanding observer of child behavior like Piaget overlooked one of the dominant types of preschool behavior. It is possible that he did not attach significance to the difference between functional pleasure derived from sensory-motor practice as compared to the satisfaction derived from constructive play activity which results in accomplishing a goal or creating a product according to a predetermined plan.

We believe that constructive play activity is in fact the developmental extension and elaboration of random sensory-motor activities at an age level when the child has some representational capacities and is capable of acting according to a plan. Instead of throwing sand, he "builds a castle" or "bakes cakes." This activity occurs parallel to the first stages of symbolic play and often contains elements of pretend (neither the sand castle nor the cakes are real). The transition from manipulating material toward formation represents a distinct developmental path, a further elaboration of sensory-motor practice. However, in constructive play, as well as in most games with rules, the activity with the materials is the focus of attention. The child acts upon the the materials and enjoys doing something with them. Their physical characteristics are the main source of his satisfaction and, to a considerable extent, their properties dictate the child's activity. In sensory-motor artistic expression, like singing and movement, satisfaction is derived from goal-oriented activity of parts of the body.

In contrast to functional and constructive play, symbolic dramatic play concentrates on roles and themes and not on materials, even at the earliest stages during the second year. Therefore, dramatic play cannot be regarded as a natural transition from sensory-motor practice play toward a more mature way of relating to the material world. Symbolic dramatic play represents a unique behavior pattern expressing the child's growing understanding and interest in the social milieu—a development triggered by identification processes and made possible by the emergence of representational thought. In turn, this type of play facilitates further development of representational capacity. As dramatic play becomes more elaborate, the child continues enjoying functional activities that gradually become more complex and often involve goal-oriented creative construction.

Constructive play is sometimes included as part of sociodramatic play or as preparation for it—such as building a house with large blocks or having "Daddy" add a garage or a swimming pool. But even if these constructions absorb a great deal of attention and time, they rarely replace the original intention of acting out a theme.

Symbolic play serves different needs than functional or constructive play and activates a larger spectrum of dispositions, understandings and abilities. During pretend play, the child is interested in objects or toy replicas only insofar as they are instrumental for his enactment of a make-believe role. Of course, they are necessary because objects are as much a part of role behavior, as are other persons (or the doll that signifies "the other") a part of real-world roles and themes. At the early stages of pretend play, when gestural or verbal substitution has not yet developed, symbolic role behavior is more dependent on objects and replicas. Nevertheless, there is still a basic difference, even at this early stage, between the child's relationship to "things" in the framework of practice or constructive play and the use made of "things" in pretend play. In symbolic play the child is not interested in the material properties of play-objects (e.g. how it feels, what it does, what can be made from it), but rather in the symbolic valance for enactment of particular roles or themes (e.g. what does Mommy [people] usually do with it; how does it help me imitate Mommy's [people's] activities). The child is not interested in the signifier itself, but with what it signifies *within* the context of social roles and social interactions.

This does not mean that toy replicas and materials have no value for symbolic play. Even at higher stages of play development, they act as triggers, suggesting the acting out of certain themes and roles. For example, introducing a toy typewriter into a kindergarten might boost office-related roles or themes which had rarely, if at all, been part of the dramatic play repertoire before. However, especially at the higher levels, players soon neglect the toy replica and pretend to type on a box, a book or any object even remotely resembling a typewriter. They may even simply make typing gestures with their fingers, sometimes adding an explicit statement explaining their behavior more exactly: "I am typing a letter."

Thus, there is a fundamental distinction between the child's use of things, toys and materials in the framework of dramatic (symbolic) play and the use of toys and materials in the framework of functional and constructive play. In pretend play he is exploring and experiencing the social world, while in functional and constructive play he is exploring and experiencing the material surroundings. Therefore, we cannot agree with the assumption implicit in Piaget's play theory, in which the symbolic use of objects emerges as an ontogenetic extension, continuation and elaboration of the functional-practice play period. The developmental extension of practice play is most likely in the realm of constructive, creative, goal-oriented activity,[1] like block building, drawing, sand and clay work, construction play, etc., and in higher level sensory-motor oriented activities of parts of the body. Neither of these two forms of play—functional and constructive—are discontinued with the appearance of symbolic play or games with rules.

An important consideration in the discussion of the place of sociodramatic play in relation to other types of play is its relationship to games with rules. Piaget suggests that games with rules be regarded as successors of symbolic-dramatic play and an indication of a transition from egocentric thought and activity toward a reality orientation. However, certain games with rules are widespread quite early (before age four), before sociodramatic play reaches its peak (about age 5–6): like simple card games, lotto, dominos, or varieties of movement games—catching and jumping, hide and seek, etc. These games are not more "real" than pretend play (see Sutton-Smith's argument with Piaget, 1971).

The ability to adhere to rules is indeed a sign of reality orientation, in the sense that it implies the ability to make a cognitive assessment of what is required and to comply with demands by exercising self-control. Since Piaget views symbolic play as a

---

[1]These also contain imaginative, "as if" elements, but they do not include the transformation of the self or of others.

distortion of reality to fit egocentric needs, he regards games with rules as a higher level of play. We contend that games with rules represent *a different* but *not a higher* level of play behavior. A child is required to act according to agreed-upon rules which are imposed by thematic and role choice in sociodramatic play as well. In the framework of his role the child tries constantly to assess his behavior according to the "real life" behavior world in order to carry on the game. Moreover, he not only has to adapt his behavior to that of the role model, but also to coordinate it with the reactions and behavior of his playmates. Thus, the rules that govern sociodramatic play are a close simulation of real life rules as understood by the child, a fact that underlines the adaptive function of sociodramatic play.

It seems clear that a better description of games with rules is that of an extension of sensory-motor and constructive activity with the addition of externally defined rules and success criteria, whether competitive or not. The child focuses on the materials and what has to be done with them or on the activation of parts of his body in most games with rules, as in functional and constructive play. This focus provides the source of pleasure while playing rather than merely "winning" in competition, as can be observed by the fact that different children will show preferences for different types of games with rules, each of which might be competitive or not.

Although games with rules continue to be part of play behavior for many people into adulthood, even after sociodramatic play ceases, there is a long period where they coexist. For many children this period ranges from the age of three to the age of 10–11. Thus, it is not possible to accept the view of Piaget, that sociodramatic play gives way to games with rules, as a more mature form of play behavior. The two forms are distinct types of play, each of which fulfills different functions and satisfies different needs.

Cessation of Dramatic Play

The cessation of pretend play seems to be related to several changes which occur during school years.

—The child, whose previous role was mainly that of an observer of adult behavior, gradually becomes an influential actor himself. He is integrated into real life with its concomitant responsibilities, obligations and privileges.

—With a growing understanding of social relationships, especially family roles, there is less need to experience such behavior by enacting the roles. Children who continue with sociodramatic play at higher age levels usually play teachers, stars, tourists, discoverers or figures from television series rather than "House." That is to say, they tend to choose roles that are remote from their real-life experience, or are less well-understood. As at earlier age levels, playing a role serves the need to gain insight, to experience how it feels to be someone else. It provides the excitement of being like the role model of interest to the child.

—The acquisition of reading skills opens up new horizons enabling the child to identify with a variety of role models. In the lower grades children tend to seek out books about certain heroes and read about them for a long time, similar to enacting the same role for a certain period. Then, they tend to move on to another hero. Reading would seem to be an additional medium for experiencing how it feels to be somebody else.

—Cognitive growth plays also an important part in the cessation of pretend play, but not in the sense proposed by Piaget (e.g. moving away from egocentricity toward reality orientation). The older child has less need to enact a role in order to gain experience. He is better equipped to understand behavior patterns, motives and roles by observation, reflection and discussion. He uses mental representational tools to facilitate understanding and empathy at the cognitive as well as the emotional level. The need for actual acting in a role is thereby diminished.

—With all of the above factors taken into consideration, it is important to realize that the basic characteristic of dramatic and sociodramatic play—consciously pretending to be somebody else and behaving accordingly—never entirely ceases. It becomes more covert and more subtle, taking new forms. The adult internalizes several role figures which may change and shift throughout adult life, often without conscious awareness. A few of the children grow up to become professional actors while the majority become passionate consumers of movie, television, and literary drama.

Having examined the place of symbolic play within the context of other types of play, it seems clear that the concept of developmental stages does not necessarily imply one-way developmental routes. Representational thought opens up qualitatively different routes of behavior and development. Language, symbolic and constructive play all appear in some form during the second year. They coexist and become elaborated throughout early childhood. All types of play continue to be part of the behavioral repertoire of some persons, in some form, throughout life.

B. The Adaptive Function of Sociodramatic Play

Sociodramatic play is perhaps one of the most important expressions of a young child's growing awareness of social relationships as well as a powerful means for adapting to his environment. When a child is playing, he is intent on reproducing "reality" as he perceives it; by interacting with other players, he gains a more comprehensive understanding of real life roles and behavior.

This opinion does not accord with Piaget's view which emphasizes the "wishful" element of symbolic play—the distortion of reality to fit egocentric needs. At best, he assigns sociodramatic play an assimilative rather than an adaptive function. ". . .play manifests the peculiarity of a primacy of assimilation over accommodation which permits it to transform reality in its own manner without submitting that transformation to the criterion of objective facts." (Piaget, 1971, p. 338) Development, as he views it, proceeds through a continuous, complimentary process of assimilation and accommodation. Assimilation implies the incorporation of new experiences—skills, knowledge, objects and concepts—into previous formed schemata (mental structures that mediate between the child and the environment). Accommodation occurs when novel elements in the child's experience demand modification of the existing schemata. The child acquires knowledge and adapts to his environment through the reciprocal process of assimilation and accomodation.

Sutton-Smith (1971) criticized Piaget's view by emphasizing the unique intellectual function of symbolic play, especially with regard to divergent thinking processes and as a tool for expressing personal meaning. According to our view sociodramatic play is equally relevant for convergent thinking, problem solving and conceptual development. It seems to us that the adaptive nature of symbolic play is revealed mainly by the child's verbalizations during play, by what he *says* rather than by what he *does*. Unfortunately, no systematic research has been carried out on early pretend play which addresses specifically the verbal component, its nature, function, frequency, content and quality. The fact that, in general, the subordinate role of objects and materials in pretend play has been consistently overlooked, has also meant that the significance of verbalization in solitary, dramatic play has also been neglected.

Most recent observational and experimental studies on early stages of pretend play have concentrated on object use and object substitution, and relatively very little has been done on the nature and function of verbalization during pretend play. Features such as role announcement, imitative speech and make-believe verbalization (verbal announcement substituting for objects, activities or situations, often designated "metacommunications") also appear in solitary play, especially in doll play ("You must sleep here, dear!" "Mama's making your food now.") Vocal expression and language in role enactment functions in a variety of ways for very young children (from about age two).

A thorough observation of verbalization in early solitary symbolic play would probably disclose a prevalence of reality orientation already at these stages. The child's actions as well as his imitative speech tends to resemble those of his role-model insofar as his understanding permits (Mommy, driver, big brother). In order to attain as close a resemblance to real life as possible there is a constant interchange of observing, enacting and adjustment between the pretend situation and the real life model. An attentive observer can hardly overlook these elements.

However, the adaptive element of symbolic play is especially highlighted in analyses of verbalization in the framework of social play. Marshall and Doshi (1965) conducted an interesting study that pointed to the adaptive rather than the frustration-compensation element of play for upper class kindergarten children. The use of language, even aggressive language in role-play characterized well-adjusted children, rather than dependent and problem children who displayed aggression in non-play situations.

While playing with other children the child does not focus on his egocentric wishes beyond the general wish to experience being someone else, but on the world around him and on the behavior of the role figures in their life-sphere as perceived by him. Moreover, specific behavior in isolation does not interest him, but its relevance to the role and theme he chooses to enact. Each behavior unit is tested against and adapted to the general theme, the total situation and the reciprocal affirmation and reaction through interaction with the co-players. In this context the rule of the game is often explicitly verbalized as adherence to "real life" despite the overall make-believe situation.

The accommodative function of play finds expression with regard to the social and emotional domain as well as the cognitive developmental sphere. Adherence to the "real life" rule is regarded important to such an extent that the child willingly suppresses individual needs and wishes in order to continue the cooperation and enactment of the overall theme.

The effort to enact reality as it is perceived by each player has to be understood and accepted by the other players. Violation of the general rule to adhere to "real life" often causes temporary interruptions of the play while discrepancies between the internal representations of the role-behavior are discussed by the co-players. The one suspected of violating the rule has to convince his friends that his interpretation is based on reality according to his personal experience. Alternatively, the "violator" has to accept the limitations imposed by "reality" as perceived by the others and modify his behavior accordingly. This process introduces additional elements into the child's schemata. Thus, adherence to "real life" rules in the framework of sociodramatic play means the widening of knowledge and the modification of idiosyncratic concepts.

It could be stated that the *assimilative function* of sociodramatic play is due to the need to mobilize a wide variety of past experiences and to integrate them meaningfully while enacting a role within a general play theme. The *accommodative function* is brought to bear on the child's effort to comply with the rule of adherence to "real life" behavior, implicit in cooperative enactment of any theme. The child is willing to suppress egocentric fancies, accept the suggestions of his co-players, and be attentive to their interpretations in order to have the pleasure of participating and, thereby, he also will formulate more generalized concepts of roles, activities, situations and social interactions.

In this process language plays a central role and therefore the adaptive nature of dramatic and sociodramatic play can be detected mainly through a thorough analysis of the explicit verbal statements during play (Rubin and Pepler, 1982; Fink, 1976).

C. Play as Ontogenetic vs. Learned Behavior

Research findings of differences in sociodramatic play related to cultural and socioeconomic status raise many questions about environmental influences on symbolic play development. What do we know about this subject beyond the fact that there are differences in socioeconomic status? This question cannot be answered without reliable cross-cultural data on the early developmental progression of dramatic and socio-dramatic play.

Regretfully, while almost all of the basic research on symbolic play was at the early-formative levels, most of the studies on SES and cultural differences in play behavior were at higher age levels. Our work was with 3 to 6 year olds, and so was other work cited before. In the work of Piaget, who stressed the primacy of biological disposition and direct, non-mediate experience on early development, this issue was not addressed. His work was with middle class infants only. This does not mean, that Piaget was not aware of the possible impact of the social milieu. In one of his later articles, he expresses the hope that cross-cultural research might contribute to better understanding about the influences of culture and the social milieu on developmental progression (Piaget, 1966). Piaget cites research that demonstrates the same sequences in operational tasks in different cultures, in spite of large age delay, probably due to environmental conditions. But he expresses his belief, that, "in the area of figurative thinking, one could possibly find everywhere the same age for the appearance of the semiotic function (e.g. symbolic play, mental images, and the development of language), which develops in our culture between 1 and 2 years of age." (Piaget, 1966, p. 305).

Indeed there seems to be considerable consistency in the appearance of early imitative acts during the second year. This is our impression, on the ground of recent non-formal and limited observations with infants from various social strata.

Fein (1981) reports percentages of pretend acts at the age of 11 to 15 months with Guatemalan babies from impoverished villages to be similar to those of middle-class American babies (Fenson et al., 1976, Kagan et al., 1978). This study seems to indicate, that the disposition for imitative activity, the basic need for it, might be universal. In this case, we can assume that it is a typical expression of the infant's growing interest in his social surroundings, and his need to assimilate his experiences by means of imitation. Lacking additional cross-cultural data, it seems too early to generalize. But it is quite possible, that imitative acts at early ages will be found in all intact environments. If so, we still have to answer the question, why this imitative tendency does not develop in some cultures, into the kind of Sociodramatic Play that is observed in middle-class Western cultures? If so, at what stage of development and in which elements of symbolic play do environmental influences manifest themselves? These questions have only been addressed, as far as we are aware, by Soviet psychologists , who, typically, tend to emphasize the influence of the social milieu on development.

El-Konin (1966) presents experimental evidence from the work of Fradkina and others that seems to suggest the importance of adult suggestions and demonstrations at the earliest stages of symbolic play development. "Tanya (one year, 20 days old). . .always lulls to sleep, feeds only the animals, i.e., only those playthings with which these activities were shown to her. She still does not transfer them to other objects." (page 223) Similarly, "children gave a drink to a doll or animals from casks, pots, wine glasses, cups, pitchers, tureens, etc. because these playthings were used by adults in their joint games with the children." (page 223)

According to El-Konin the child gradually performs the same activities with different playthings than those used by the adult. Object substitution appears at the end of the second year. "Lida (two years, 23 days) sits on the carpet and holds a caster and a nail in her hands. The teacher gives her a doll and suggests that she feed it. Lida brings the nail to the doll's mouth and feeds it, using the nail as a spoon. . ." (El-Konin, 1966; p. 224) In view of the research evidence presented El-Konin concludes that it is debatable whether there is spontaneous development of symbolism in the child. According to him, at the very least, the possibility of play utilization and the renaming of objects needs to be suggested if not directly taught.

Another study about environmental influences on sociodramatic play was conducted by Marshall (1961). The study explores the relationship between behavior of 108 children (2½ to 6½ years) with peers and teachers in preschool and different aspects of home experience (upper class families). She found that ". . .if parents and other important adults talk with the child about more topics the child can use in play with other children, the child will talk about and play these topics more frequently with peers and will also have a better chance of social acceptance in the preschool group." (Marshall, 1961; p. 72)

The evidence presented by El-Konin and Marshall points to different elements of environmental influence. The first points to directly suggesting pretend activities and substitutional behavior; the second suggests the importance of providing knowledge and understanding of adult behavior, e.g., contribution to and clarification of content to be enacted by the child.

Lacking more comprehensive research evidence on the nature of environmental influences on sociodramatic play, we would like to suggest that both elements might influence the level of play—enriching experiences on themes that might be incorporated in play and also direct encouragement and demonstrations of imitative and substitutive behavior. The findings of our experiment described in Chapter V support both assumptions.

4. Some Elements of Parental Behavior and Their Possible Relevance for Sociodramatic Play Development

It is quite likely that the parental role may be decisive at all phases of developing dramatic and sociodramatic play. Some parental influence bears on the general emotional, social and intellectual development of the child, and therefore has only an indirect (but nonetheless decisive) effect on the quality of sociodramatic play. Some parental influence can be regarded as directly instrumental toward the development of sociodramatic play.

Indirect influences are assumed to be the following parental behaviors:

- Providing for normal emotional relationships, essential for healthy identification
- Providing conceptual, informational and verbal tools which contribute to understanding human behavior and social relationships
- Developing the power of abstraction, of imagination, and the ability to get beyond the concretely present toward grasping verbally described hypothetical existence
- Encouraging the child to develop positive social relationships based on tolerance and self-discipline, both with parents and peers

More direct influences might be the following activities:

- Providing conditions that facilitate sociodramatic play: toys, space, friends to play with, time, etc.
- Demonstrating and reinforcing imitative behavior in the framework of role play
- Suggesting and demonstrating verbal and non-verbal substitution

We assume that parental behavior enhancing the child's general development, is related also to the level of the child's sociodramatic play. However, without some direct encouragement and fostering of dramatic and sociodramatic play elements, the child will lack the essentials required for development in this specific area.

Parental behavior may affect child's play development in the following ways:

Emotional Relationships

It is Stoke's hypothesis (1950) that the process of identification is influenced by the degree of affection accorded to the child and the extent to which his needs are gratified by the person with whom identification is attempted. According to several theoreticians (Mowrer, 1950; Sears, 1953) children of both sexes tend to identify initially with their mothers. They are most likely to find it rewarding to participate in and imitate her activities, developing emotional attachments to her. Later, the father becomes the main source of reward for a male child. The father gradually associates more and more with his son and allows the boy to participate with him in an ever-growing circle of activities. Social pressures, too, demand that the boy adopt the proper sex role and so he shifts toward identification and imitation of his father.

Mowrer (1950) has pointed out that the extent to which the child is rewarded for appropriate sex-role behavior depends not only on the actions of the same-sex parent, but also on prevailing harmonious inter-parental relationships. It seems to us that, excluding pathological home conditions, families of both low and high sociocultural levels provide the potential for development of meaningful identifications. The mere presence of a loved parent, the availability of a suitable identification object is not in itself adequate for the identification process to develop fully.

The parents of children in Marshall's study (1961) who had low levels of sociodramatic play were more punitive than the parents of good players. This seems to indicate that sociodramatic play development is affected also by the emotional quality of the parent-child relationship.

Understanding Behavior

It is not necessary for a child to understand the larger, overall behavior pattern for him to be able to imitate parental behavior, but he must understand, to a certain extent, the activity or behavior trait that he wishes to imitate. Without such understanding he will only be able to imitate external, physical gestures—he will walk as he sees his father walk, move his hands or face in the fashion characteristic of his father, etc. As mentioned above, the child imitates the parental *image*, the father- or mother-image, limited only by his perceptual capability. It is impossible to derive the amount of understanding of parental behavior required in order to imitate this image from observation alone, but the child needs explanation, direct guidance and joint parent-child cooperation in certain activities.

The parent helps and encourages the child to understand his behavior better in many ways:

- By a conscious effort to explain the reasons behind any given action
- By answering questions raised by the child concerning adult behavior in a meaningful and comprehensive manner
- By directly teaching the child certain patterns of behavior which have particular importance to the parent
- By breaking down complex actions into simple actions which the child is capable of performing and in which both the parent and the child participate. The child learns to master and understand the parts first and, then, gradually learns to fit the parts together into a comprehensible whole.
- By consistently repeating certain behavior patterns with little or no change.

These behaviors enable a parent not only to help his child understand his own behavior, but also to provide information and explanation of phenomena observed by the child. A parent answering the ("what" "why" "how") questions of his children and offering explanation even without questions, sensitizes the child to a variety of behavior patterns. This parental mediation paves the way for the child to obtain a wider conception of behavior and relationships which will, in turn, enable him to enact differing roles in various ways and to accept different interpretations of roles.

Fostering Abstraction and Imagination

Not only do explanations bring presently observed phenomena closer to the child, but verbal means also mediate hypothetical situations and occurrences. Conversation between child and parent can focus on possibilities, wishes, future or past events: such as simple comments like "Some parents do give a lot of candy to their children, but I prefer not to because candy is not healthy." or "I wish our kitchen were twice as big" or "We have a president, but some countries have a king or queen instead." or "If we were rich, I would buy you that bicycle, but now we cannot afford it." (Mediation of Transcendence, in term of Klein, 1985.)

Reading stories or books, telling a child about past experiences are other methods by which a parent brings the child closer to non-concrete, not-experienced events. The child's imagination is awakened, and he begins to realize that reality offers countless possibilities and adventures. Both verbal and creative tools for make-believe are established.

Social Relationships

The extent to which a child is able to cooperate with peers in sociodramatic play depends partly on the points described above: his emotional relationship with parents, his understanding of broad categories of behavior, his ability to accept unfamiliar behavior as possible. In addition, the parents' own pattern of social relationships will influence the child by the very process of identification and imitation. The model of social intercourse between the parents themselves, between the parents and their children, and between parents and other adults in the immediate environment will probably be mirrored in the child's behavior. The child also needs training in social intercourse, impulse control, and in tolerance for other people's wishes. Enabling the child to meet other children and reinforcing positive behavior provides the best training (receiving praise for allowing others to play with toys, for not quarreling, for playing for a long time, for settling conflicts by discussion, etc.). This area of behavior is particularly relevant for the child's general social development and, therefore, is listed as one of the indirect influences on sociodramatic play behavior. However, as pointed out, social training is effectively achieved through the cooperative play situation itself; therefore, it may also be regarded as an influence directly relevant to sociodramatic play.

Applied to a greater or lesser extent, all the parental influence described above provides the child with the basic general requirements which make the appearance of sociodramatic play possible. These requirements can be regarded as the raw material from which the play tapestry is woven. But our observations lead us to believe that without direct training and reinforcement of the techniques of play such requirements alone do not necessarily result in sociodramatic play. Dramatic and sociodramatic play are not a natural extension of imitative behavior; rather, they are a specific form of it and demand special means of transition. Without training this transition will not take place or will appear in a most limited form. In the next section we shall relate to direct influences that concern dramatic play.

Providing Conditions for Play

Toys that are miniature replicas of real objects invite at least imitative activity. They serve as a signal that imitative play behavior is welcome as does the provision of time designated for play and encouragement of interplay with peers (comments such as, "Now go and play House with your doll" or "Go and call Dan to play doctor with your new kit")

At the initial stage of dramatic play development, it is important to provide these conditions and encouragement. The child still lacks the initiative for play and has not yet mastered the play techniques fully.

Demonstrating and Reinforcing Imitative Play Behavior

The provision of toys alone not only will not secure imitative activity, and certainly will not assure general role play. The child may continue manipulating toys for a long time, carrying them, etc. At best he may perform a certain observed activity or series of activities: rocking, dressing and undressing, nursing a doll without any story-line development and even without the pretense of being "Mommy." Some demonstration of the imitative possibilities inherent in toys is needed.

With all that, such toys are most suitable for evoking imitative action, but not verbalization and other general expressions of role behavior. Children can keep on for several years doing things like another person, but not talking like him or adopting his mannerisms, gesticulations etc. Toys may even limit a child to certain activities instead of encouraging him to adopt a role and enact it within all its rich and varied possibilities.

Parents may evoke real imitation by reacting to a child who is manipulating his toys as if they were a role player: "How is your baby today? Is she crying a lot? Did she eat her food? Did you do your shopping today?" By functioning as co-players themselves, parents demonstrate verbal imitation. The child gains a conscious realization of the play possibilities and he is provided with an outlet for the expression of identification and imitation motives.

Suggesting and Demonstrating Substantiative Behavior

Imitation alone does not constitute taking on make-believe roles. The child can imitate single actions of others *as a child*, without projecting himself into the role. The kind of demonstration described above is training in make-believe, pretending to be another person; play involves additional elements of make-believe. The toys at the child's disposal are limited. The technique of substituting similar objects, movements or verbal description for toys is probably taught and learned. Moreover, most of the experiences a child wants to express cannot be enacted by him even approximating reality. Again, he has to learn the technique of verbal substitution for sequences of actions, situations and events. This technique also enables him to abbreviate his actions: "Let's say that that's the room, those are the beds and there is the table. Let's pretend that Daddy has already left for work and Mommy is at home cooking" . . . "When he comes home later, they'll take the children to the zoo" etc. Using such a technique a rather exciting chain of events may be experienced, without really performing at all. Players can be substituted for verbally or their absence justified: "Let's pretend your Daddy went on a trip somewhere and won't be back for a long time."

Since speech is the central element in make-believe behavior, if a child does not learn how to use verbalization for make-believe purposes, the child will lack a major tool for sociodramatic play.

Conclusions

Identification is the source of imitation, dramatic and sociodramatic play, but it will not necessarily find expression in these phenomena. Imitation in it's complex forms is learned behavior as are dramatic and sociodramatic play. Some of the factors affecting the extent and quality of sociodramatic play are provided indirectly, as part of fostering the emotional, social and intellectual development of the child. But some of them, which we might call "play skills," or "play abilities," must be learned in direct connection with the play situations. We hold that parental fostering of areas of general development does not by itself naturally lead to dramatic and sociodramatic play; however, if the child does learn how to play, those indirect factors contribute greatly to the wealth of play. Learning how to play and engaging in sociodramatic play influences development in emotional, intellectual, creative and social areas.

The question now arises whether socio-economic differences in sociodramatic play might be attributed to differences in parental attitudes and behavior. After we initially identified the differences in sociodramatic play behavior, we carried out informal observation and interviews of 30 families from low

socioeconomic background and 30 families from high socioeconomic background. The aim of the interviews was to reveal
parental attitudes toward play in general and make-believe play
in particular. The observation focused on mother-child behavior
and interactions which might be directly or indirectly relevant
to play.

Since numerous systematic studies of the past two decades
have disclosed socioeconomic level differences on a variety of
parenting attitudes and practices known to affect the child's
general development, especially in terms of language and cognition, we will not concentrate on that area. The evidence is
clear that there is less adapted mediation of experience in low
socioeconomic level homes, a factor which very well may affect
play indirectly. However, since parental behavior directly relevant to sociodramatic play was not studied cross-culturally, we
will only briefly summarize the major points revealed by our
observation and interviews.

a. While there were toys suggestive of pretend play in low
socioeconomic level homes (dolls, household utensils, toy vehicles), they were less numerous and of lesser quality than in the
high socioeconomic level homes. More importantly, the attitude
of parents from the lower socioeconomic strata, when asked
why they buy such toys, was: "To make them happy" "for their
birthday" or "to keep them busy." They do not seem to attach
educational significance to the toys or to the type of play they
might evoke. In the high socioeconomic families there was more
awareness of the importance of dramatic and sociodramatic
play, albeit more for its emotional than its cognitive value. There
was also more interest on the part of the mothers in the content
of the play.

b. High socioeconomic level parents tend to join the play of
their children, constructive as well as sociodramatic. Children
from such families, especially when they have no other com-
pany, often assign their mothers to roles: "You will be the
grandma, let's pretend we came to you for a visit." "My baby
is sick, let's pretend you are the doctor." The mother, accepting
the role, reinforces the child's play, conveys approval and often
also demonstrates substitutive behavior within the context of
the play situation: "Let's pretend that grandma is sick, so she

cannot prepare us any snacks; here, take the pots and make her something to eat." "Oh, poor baby, she is very sick indeed. I think you will have to take her to the hospital. I will give her a shot in the meantime." The world of pretend was probably an enjoyed childhood experience for the parents themselves. Most mothers note that the child is happy even if their participation is minimal; it seems sufficient just knowing that mother is part of the play episode.

No low socioeconomic level mothers reported that they are involved in any way in their child's make-believe play. This form of play was probably not part of their own childhood experience and therefore it does not have a positive association for them. In fact, there were instances when mothers noted they were afraid of their child's "fantasy" especially if the child persists playing the same role for a long time: "She's always playing School with the pillows as her kids. Almost every day, it's the same thing. My friend says she might get crazy if she keeps it up!" Others just felt that there are more important things to do and that it is a waste of time.

c. High socioeconomic level parents show their approval of dramatic play by listening to the child's play-related problems, even when they are busy, and by attaching importance to their requests. They will offer solutions from the point of view of the child's play theme: "If you have no blanket, take this and let's pretend it is a blanket." "Here, this [pencil] will be the thermometer." In contrast, low socioeconomic level parents tend to regard interruptions of their important activities or conversations "with silly requests" as unworthy for serious consideration. They might be amused by the child's fantasy, if not rejecting it outright, but only rarely attach any importance to it.

d. The positive attitude of high socioeconomic level parents to sociodramatic play is also seen in their encouragement for inviting friends to play together. They will praise the children for cooperating over a longer period with their friends or siblings within the framework of sociodramatic play as well as other kinds of play. This reinforces persistence and cooperation—both essential elements of sociodramatic play. Low socioeconomic level parents are less happy to have other children coming to their houses—unless it is family-related. Often they justify this by a lack of space or other arguments: "They make too much noise" "They wreck the toys" "The children in the neighborhood are no good (this, even though their children might play outdoors with these very children)."

Socioeconomic differences in parental behavior and attitudes relevant to dramatic and sociodramatic play, similar to those enumerated above, were disclosed in a recent study in which extensive home observation and interviews were carried out for a different purpose (Shefatya, 1988).

It would seem that, since many low socioeconomic level children lack parental fostering of sociodramatic play, nurseries and kindergartens should provide the conditions and training necessary for the facilitation and acquisition of the basic tools of collective make-believe.

Chapter Five: Experiments Designed to Improve Sociodramatic Play and to Test Transfer to Other Cognitive and Socio-emotional Abilities

1. Adult Intervention in Make-Believe Play—
Theoretical Considerations

In the previous chapters we have emphasized the importance of sociodramatic play for child development in general and particularly for children from lower socioeconomic backgrounds. We have noted that lower socioeconomic homes do not tend to provide their children with whatever is necessary to develop such play behavior. Thus, it seems that some sort of adult intervention in the context of the kindergarten or nursery school is needed to help such children to benefit from sociodramatic play activities, which should also translate into a better chance to succeed later on in school.

However, we cannot overlook the fact that adult intervention in symbolic play, as well as in other creative activities, is almost taboo for many preschool educators. Therefore, before describing the various experiments aimed at promoting sociodramatic play with adult intervention, we will discuss literature dealing with cases in which dramatic play was used as a major tool, or working process, with children. The ideas contained in the literature helped clarify the implications of such adult intervention in children's play, decide strategies with regard to the role and behavior of the adult and suggested the organization of material conditions conducive to play.

We found dramatic play was instrumental in three different areas:

a. *Diagnosis:* employing dramatic play to uncover and explore the emotional, social and intellectual state of the child.

b. Psychotherapy: employing dramatic play as a therapeutic experience.

c. Education: using play to further intellectual and socio-emotional development.

Diagnosis through Dramatic Play

The assumption is that a child expresses in his dramatic play desires, thoughts, images and problems he is unable to express verbally. Therefore, the dramatic play situation is considered a possible method for discerning and developing understanding of children's emotional problems. Investigators using dramatic play as a diagnostic tool, accept wholly or partially a psychoanalytic interpretation of the dynamics of personality growth. They tend to concentrate on what they interpret as more or less unconscious symbolism of primary conflicts stemming from sexual drives and instincts and the constellation of relationships within the family circle.

Dramatic play in a diagnostic situation focuses on the individual child, supplied with toys and other materials intended as stimuli. The examiner observes the particular manipulation of the toys as well as the imaginative creations of the child which are related to his problems and which reveal the child's personal vision of the world, the people around him and the methods chosen to resolve his problems (withdrawal, aggression, etc.). In all the diagnostic approaches the basic assumption is that toys and other play materials stimulate the child to dramatic play. The major function of the adult is to encourage the child to use the toys and other materials and join in the child's game in order to understand the child and gain insights into his difficulties.

⨪ℱ   *Psychotherapy through Dramatic Play*

The majority of psychotherapists regard dramatic play as a means of influencing the child's growth and development. Professional literature on this subject abounds. The various opinions and approaches can be concentrated into three major schools of thought, although there are many nuances and individual variations:

    a. Theories of Melanie Klein (1955).

    b. Theories of Anna Freud (1946).

    c. The non-directive trend (Axline, 1955).

    a. *Theories of Melanie Klein.* Klein feels that play and play therapy are interchangeable with free association which is the basis of adult psychoanalysis. The interpretation of normal child play, rather than that of a disturbed child, is useful because it is interpretation that empowers the child to overcome tensions and pressures inherent to the normal growth process. Play left without interpretation tends to be harmful, or at the best not helpful. Each of the child's action in the play situation and each toy used is of deep symbolic significance.

The aim of play therapy is to make the child aware of the subconscious significance of the symbols during the course of his play activity. The therapist enters into "the child's world of the imagination" and participates; at the same time he directs the child's game with remarks, questions and interpretations and supplies him with toys or specific play materials which will stimulate him to reveal further symbols. Klein feels that psychotherapy is more successful with children than with adults because children are closer to their primary experiences and adults have not only gotten further away from their early childhood experiences but have had time to develop greater resistance.

Play therapy dredges up buried memories, interprets the meaning hidden in dreams and fantasies, identifies resistance and repression, and, when the child is capable, enables transference of these exigencies to the therapist. Describing the real significance of symbols revealed in the play activity effectively neutralizes them. Children do not view their adjustment difficulties critically, and the aim of the therapy is, therefore, to make the child aware of his problems at the earliest stages of the therapeutic process. The child's latent anxieties and guilt feelings are brought into the open at the very beginning. Then, with the help of the therapist's interpretations, the child begins to understand these feelings and with understanding the symptoms diminish until they disappear. Therapeutic rather than educational objectives are prominent and there is no necessity seen for imposing any limits on intervention during the therapy process.

b. *Theories of Anna Freud.* Not everything the child does in the play situation has equal symbolic significance. In fact, the greater part of the play behavior is simply the repetition of recent impressions and experiences with little emotional freight. Therefore, the therapist must take an active, educational role and redirect the impulses of the child, regulating his instinctual life through play intervention. The therapist's function is to strengthen both the ego and the superego through using the play situation, among other methods, and to use the insights gained through the play situation to give new form to or develop defense mechanisms of the ego. The therapist considers only a part of the child's play behavior for interpretation and play is only one of the many therapeutic means used.

c. *Non-Directive Play Therapy.* The child is provided with a permissive and open-ended atmosphere in which to play out whatever is bothering him. The assumption is that free play, without active participation of the therapist, using toys and objects contrived to stimulate the child's expressing his deeply hidden or repressed feelings, will enable a child to come to terms with his difficulties. According to Axline (1955) the therapist must not use his superego as exemplified by Anna Freud, nor interpret symbols as advocated by Melanie Klein. As far as it is safely possible, his role with the child should be a passive one. This type of nondirective play therapy, flavored with a certain educational influence is used widely in child guidance clinics in many countries around the world.

Intellectual and Socio-Emotional Development through Dramatic Play

Susan Isaacs (1933, 1935) uses dramatic play as a means to further children's intellectual and socio-emotional development. Her research reports that dramatic play enables the child to progress in the socialization process while, at the same time, it projects him into situations where he must think, explore and strive to achieve at a much higher intellectual level than that which would be expected at his chronological age. She gives numerous examples of how dramatic play works within an interactive social context in an imaginary world, that of "make-believe—let's pretend," and how it projects the children into higher intellectual activity and achievement.

Pestalozzi (1801, 1915) attaches special significance to dramatic play insofar as it acts as a means of developing the child's imaginative powers; developing "make-believe—let's pretend" is a means of advancing the child's educational learning progression.

A similar view is expressed by Froebel (1947) and later by Dewey (1902, 1934), and it is their influence that is the most marked in the kindergartens of Israel, America, and Europe up to the present day. Dewey contended that the child has to investigate his environment actively and learn from his experience. Although, for Dewey, adult intervention could be undertaken in order to enrich the possibilities of the child benefiting from the experience, popular attention has since focused on the child's experience, minimizing, overlooking and finally guarding against adult intervention. Dewey's ideas which are reflected in most western kindergartens have been embodied in giving the child an enriched environment (a variety of toys and work materials) and suitable play space. The adult's role is one of nonintervention, not even active guidance; the child is left to investigate his environment and learn from his own experience. This approach is the rule, even to an extreme degree, in terms of dramatic play of children within the kindergarten setting.

Environmental Factors to Encourage Dramatic Play

There is no significant difference between the various schools of thought regarding environmental factors used to encourage children to engage in dramatic play. Everyone assumed that toys and other play materials are excellent stimuli and sufficient for evoking dramatic play. Most theoreticians assumed that young children's interests and problems focused around family ties and immediate surroundings; therefore, they supplied the child with toy miniatures of people, objects, situations which would correspond to the immediate family environment (doll house, furniture, kitchen utensils, animals, vehicles, etc.).

Differences of opinion arise in terms of how the adult prepares and exploits the dramatic play behavior of the child in any of the above mentioned situations: diagnosis, therapy or intellectual and socio-emotional development. To summarize what has been covered in the first three chapters, it has been found that the majority of children from lower socioeconomic backgrounds do not engage in sociodramatic play; the play of those few who do try is inadequate, meaning it does not contain all or even most of the components deemed necessary to be considered sociodramatic play. Children attend kindergartens for a varying number of years and are provided with all the conditions necessary to stimulate and encourage such play (toys, play materials, space, time, freedom, nonintervention by the adults); yet, most of these children do not develop the ability to engage in sociodramatic play.[1]

The problem we are investigating involves finding methods by which it is possible to develop the ability of children from low socioeconomic backgrounds to engage in sociodramatic play. Then, we can investigate the use of sociodramatic play in furthering children's social and intellectual development in general terms. The theoretical assumptions about what constitutes "good environmental conditions" for dramatic play—everything connected with place, space, toys, play materials—remained the same for our purposes. In reality, this meant we did not need to adjust the conditions already existing in the kindergartens of our experimental groups: they were uniformly provided with large rooms, playgrounds, toys which were miniatures of real objects, people, materials and instruments found in the immediate family environment of the children as well as

---

[1]Kindergarten is compulsory and free at age five in Israel. At ages three and four children from lower socioeconomic level homes may attend nursery school for nominal fees. Children from higher socioeconomic levels attend nursery school for at least one year prior to kindergarten and most attend for two. Both nursery schools and kindergartens meet six days a week, four hours a day.

a variety of free-play materials (play-dough, clay, colored paper, blocks of different sizes, etc.).

The Adult in the Play Situation: Role and Behavior

Although theoretical assumptions and goals vary with the different schools of psychotherapy, they all agree on one point: adult intervention during dramatic play does not interrupt or disturb the play, but helps it to evolve and express the child's inner world more acutely. Such adult intervention consists of remarks and interpretation of almost all play acts according to Klein; in Anna Freud's view, it consists of educational redirection and relates to certain aspects of the child's behavior; for the non-directive school, such intervention is simply confirmation, repetition and clarification of the child's remarks and actions.

In contrast to the *affirmation of adult intervention* when using dramatic play for diagnostic or therapeutic purposes, there is an absolute value placed on the *nonintervention of the adult* when using play for furthering intellectual and socio-emotional development. Isaacs, for example, supplies materials and opportunities for sociodramatic play in as free an atmosphere as possible and with no adult intervention. Her children engage in numerous games of make-believe that take various forms depending on the age and sex of the children and on the materials available for them to use. It is important, however, to remember that the children whom Isaacs observed, were of high intelligence (average IQ 131) and from high socioeconomic background.

When we formulated our standards of adult behavior within the process of developing children's ability to engage in sociodramatic play activities, we accepted the general assumption of those using sociodramatic play for diagnostic and therapy purposes (i.e., active adult intervention) and rejected the assumptions of non-guidance or nonintervention characterizing those who use dramatic play for furthering intellectual and socio-emotional development. Furthermore, we also rejected the extreme tenets of this doctrine which held that adult intervention in children's dramatic play or artistic activities is highly undesirable.

We believe that the natural processes of child growth and a passive environment are not sufficient to give these children the necessary boost. The teacher, like the parent, is an essential part of the child's surroundings and must necessarily take an active part in the child's growth. Such children have something to say and, furthermore, the need and the ability to say it through dramatic play. Our data shows that these children will not make progress in dramatic play simply by being provided facilities and an encouraging atmosphere.

The first step is undoubtedly to leave the children alone and allow them to begin doing what they want. When they repeat themselves over and over again on the same sub-step of dramatic play or when they seem stuck and do not know what to do next or when they jump from one activity to another without carrying anything through to an elaborated end, then *intervention* by the teacher through suggestions, comments, questions, demonstrations and other relevant means can act as a stimulant. Children can be made aware of different possibilities and qualities inherent to dramatic play and can become conscious of themselves as resources of experiences and memories from which to draw. In this way the teacher encourages and enables the child to do what *the child wants to do* and does not leave the child to face the immense task of solving all the problems raised by his efforts at self-expression by himself. Adult intervention, properly exerted, can be a highly effective catalyst and open up sociodramatic play as a pleasant possibility within the children's play experience. We feel that adult intervention is necessary to develop sociodramatic play activities for children, both in terms of the diagnosis of the child's play behavior and in terms of its guided development.

There are similarities and differences between the therapist's diagnosis and treatment with play and the diagnosis and approach in our experiment.

We did not concentrate on the content of the child's play. We observed his play activities in order to see whether he engaged in dramatic or sociodramatic play and, if he did, whether his play displayed all the components of good sociodramatic play. Our intervention was not in order to interpret the play activities or bring out subconscious content or release repressed emotions, but in order to develop skills of sociodramatic play. We agree with the therapists that adult intervention will help the child express himself. Also we do not wish to influence the content of the play activity but rather aid the child in elaborating more fully.

2. The Israeli Experiment[2]

Once the decision was made to intervene in order to develop the ability to engage in sociodramatic play behavior, the question arises which methods would produce the best results? The children must be provided with learning experiences missing from the home environment which are regarded as basic for developing play behavior.

A. Experimental Procedures

Theoretical analyses and observations suggested two kinds of experiences that seemed to be lacking in homes of children from lower socioeconomic levels. (Chapter Four)

These two types of experiences include (a) general learning experiences mediated by the adult in a way that optimizes meaningful absorption of stimuli; and (b) specifically sociodramatic play related activities including encouraging make-believe and providing skills useful in imaginative play, especial the utilization of language for elaborating play themes.

We, therefore, applied two basic treatment approaches which we assumed would provide us with suggestions as to the relative importance of these two types of learning experiences in terms of developing sociodramatic play. We wanted to find answers to the practical problem of what is the best method of encouraging and furthering sociodramatic play for children and

---

[2]The Israeli experiment was described before (Smilansky, 1968). Since we did not find any large-scale experiment carried out by a random sample of regular kindergarten teachers, it was decided to describe the Israeli experiment as one possible effective model. The detailed presentation of procedures and processes might be of use to researchers and teachers as well.

to the theoretical question of what factors are most important in the development of sociodramatic play.

In Treatment Number 1, planned adult intervention concentrated on providing children with more thorough observation and better understanding of their daily experiences. This was done by means of guided visits, discussions, etc. We attempted to test the assumption that the inadequacy of the sociodramatic play might stem from the superficial and non-internalized quality of their impressions and experiences. IT was our observation that these children looked but did not *see*; they *did not understand* what they saw and experienced. Because they received no corollary explanations that would broaden and/or deepen their understanding, their impressions and experiences remain superficial and ineffective as stimuli for sociodramatic play. *Our hypothesis was that if we provided these children with meaningful impressions and experiences within their comprehension, they would begin to engage in sociodramatic play without adult intervention in the play episodes themselves.*

In Treatment Number 2, planned adult intervention concentrated on "teaching" the children how to utilize their previous experiences by converting them into raw material for sociodramatic play. In this group we tried to test our assumption that inadequacy in sociodramatic play for such children is more the result of a lack of guidance in play skills. In this case the assumption was that the children had sufficient meaningful experiences to serve as bases for play episodes, but they had not learned how to translate their experiences using verbal and non-verbal techniques into imitative and make-believe play behavior. *Our hypothesis was that if adults teach them how to play, they will begin to express their experiences in the form of sociodramatic play, just like the other children.*

Treatment Number 3 combined Approaches 1 and 2. Planned adult intervention was aimed at both providing raw material for play and teaching how to use it in the course of sociodramatic play. *The assumption here was that children from lower socioeconomic backgrounds lack both the understanding of behavior and phenomena and the experience in play skills. If this is so, the best results would be attained by the combination of the two approaches.*

Table 14 shows the difference in intervention with each of the different treatment groups. The teaching of sociodramatic play was carried out using the same techniques for both Groups B and C; the provision of meaningful impressions and experiences within the comprehension of the children was the same for both Groups A and C. An assumption implicit to all the different approaches is that the children have gone through basic processes of identification, the grounds for all imitative behavior. Also, it is assumed, that they all possess, at least to a minimum degree, the verbal, motor, intellectual and social skills required for play. Partial deprivation in these areas would not be a real obstacle to developing their play ability.

Table 14: Differences in Adult Intervention for Experimental Groups A, B, and C

Experimental Group	"Teaching" Sociodramatic Play	Provision of Meaningful Impressions and Experiences Within the Comprehension of Children
Group A	−	+
Group B	+	−
Group C	+	+

Treatment Number 1 can be considered "indirect" since it aims to affect children's play but it does not include direct intervention. The task is that of a conventional teacher. Treatment Number 2 applies direct intervention of the adult in the children's play where he directs it both from the outside and as a co-player from the inside.

Description of the Play Themes

In order to minimize interference from uncontrolled variables, the same play themes were developed in all three treatment groups during the experimental period. The play themes chosen were:
    a. The Clinic (doctors, nurses, patients, medicines, etc.)
    b. The Grocery Store (shopkeeper, shop assistant, shoppers, groceries, etc.)

The following criteria guided us in our choice of play themes:
  a. the themes allow for both sexes to participate
  b. the themes should be those that generally appear in children's play, indicating their overall appeal to children
  c. roles and behavior involved in the themes should be part of the life-experience of the children, at least to some extent.

a. The Clinic. The Sick Fund, Kupat Holim, is the most widespread medical service in the country with clinics in every residential area. All the parents of children in the experimental groups were members of Kupat Holim. Both children and adults are served by these clinics both for illness and for preventive medicine: inoculations, vaccinations, injections, etc. The clinics also provide guidance and medical attention for nursing mothers, and doctors and nurses make house visits. Since there is no separate fee for clinic visits, everything being covered by the membership fees, the families tend to pay frequent visits to the clinics, mostly with their children.

b. The Grocery Store. Although there are large supermarkets in Israel, containing a large variety of groceries and other goods, the majority of shops in the areas where the children in our experimental groups lived were small and specialized. This is particularly true for grocery stores; small shops are plentiful in these areas and the parents frequently send their children to the little store down the street or around the corner to buy a few things.

The requirement for familiarity with the themes was particularly important for approach Group C. This group learned techniques with which they could utilize their past experiences as source material for dramatic play. Therefore, we had to be certain that the themes were based on real experiences of all the children. The criteria of familiarity is also important for approach Group A. We realized that in the short experimental period we could give the children a better understanding of phenomena and behavior they often experienced as observers and participators; we could not provide them with a deep understanding of new experiences within the framework of the experiment. In other words the methods were designed to awaken the children's awareness of familiar phenomena that had been passed over before, and to explain and clarify all the implications of such phenomena for them.

Assessment of Play Level

The purpose and method of pre- and post-experimental evaluation of the children's play level was the same for all groups. This assessment was performed by the experimental aides and not by the kindergarten teachers, although they engaged in the process as part of their training for the experiment. A systematic assessment was necessary for evaluation of the experimental results.

Observation was carried out in each kindergarten during the period reserved for "free play" or "dramatic play." Each child was observed on three separate days; his play behavior was observed and recorded in minute detail including his physical movements, behavior and a complete record of every word he said. This material was then used to decide which of the six evaluating factors defined as essential for sociodramatic play were missing in the child's play behavior. The six evaluating factors are as follows;

   a. *Imitative Role-Play.* The child undertakes a make-believe role and expresses it in imitative action and/or verbalization.
   b. *Make-Believe with regard to Objects.* Toys, non-structured materials, movements or verbal declarations are substituted for real objects.
   c. *Make-Believe with regard to Actions and Situations.* Verbal descriptions are substituted for actions and situations.
   d. *Persistence.* The child continues playing in a specific episode for at lest ten minutes.
   e. *Interaction.* There are at least two players interacting in the context of a play episode.
   f. *Verbal Communication.* There is some verbal interaction relating to the play episode.

Missing factor judgments were made by two experimental aides working separately; one was the observer and the other made his assessment purely on the basis of the written record of the child's behavior at play. Each experimental aide was asked to record his judgment on each factor, using one of the four following responses:

a. +—sign that this factor was used by the child in his dramatic play during one of the observation periods.

b. ?—sign that the child used this factor in his dramatic play, but only in part or only for a very short time.

c. 0—sign that the child did not use this factor at all in his dramatic play behavior during the three observation periods

d. NP—sign that the child did not engage in dramatic play at all during the three observation periods.

The teachers of both experimental and control groups were told that observations were being made on the children's play behavior. They were also informed about the standing of each child within their groups. There were no detailed reports given to teachers of the control groups on the behavior of certain children or on the play behavior of the class as a whole.

Work Methods in the Experimental Groups

Group A

We tried to supply the children in the kindergartens and nursery schools designated as Group A with as wide and rich a variety of meaningful impressions and comprehensible experiences as possible during their visits to clinics and grocery stores and during the discussions which followed those visits.

The Clinic. The teacher and experimental aides took the children to visit a clinic in which they made every effort to give a thorough and detailed explanation of everything they saw: the clinic equipment, the various waiting and treatment rooms, the different staff members and what they did, the teamwork, the interrelationship of the various staff members. They also discussed the reasons that people came to the clinic, what people are supposed to do in order to get help, what they might expect to happen when they come to the clinic, etc. Doctors and nurses spoke to the children, showed them around, explained and answered questions. Other clinic workers gave demonstrations and further explanations. In addition, the teacher and experimental aide elucidated or gave additional information when necessary. After the visit there were small group and larger group discussions in the classroom. Books and poems were read on the subject and pictures were shown. The subject was raised and discussed for an entire week, for one and a half hours a day. Additional toys relating to the theme were brought into the preschools: toy replicas of medical instruments, nurses' uniforms, doctors' bags, stethoscopes, etc. During the visit to the clinic, the doctors and nurses had given the children different sorts of instruments for the children to take back and play with in the kindergarten.

In addition to meaningful impressions and comprehensible experiences, the group was provided with a free environment: toys, space and no intervention on the part of the adults involved. The teacher merely announced: "Now it is play time. Everyone is free to play what he wants and enjoy himself. Perhaps someone would like to play clinic?" Treatment procedures in group A were designed to answer the question, whether it was sufficient to have meaningful impressions and comprehensible experiences available to change or develop the ability of these children to engage in sociodramatic play.

The Grocery Store. Three weeks after beginning the theme of The Clinic, Group A started the second theme, The Grocery Store. The visits to the grocery store, discussions, etc. were carried out similarly to those to the clinic. There were new toys related to the theme and a suggestion that they might want to play the new theme.

Group B

The children from the kindergartens and nurseries included in Group B were "taught" how to engage in and sustain sociodramatic play. The adults (preschool teacher and experimental aide) helped the children to exploit their experiences and convert their impressions into sociodramatic play material. The impressions and experiences included those connected to the two themes described above. However, there were no *new* or *additional* impressions or comprehensible experiences provided for the children as were done for the children of Group A. Thus, we were hoping to learn whether adult guidance and encouragement in play skills would be sufficient to change or develop the children's ability to engage in sociodramatic play activity.

Identical sets and numbers of toys, play objects and materials relating to the theme, The Clinic, were delivered to the kindergarten and nursery school classes of Group B on the same day as they were delivered to Group A. The adults took the opportunity while unpacking and setting up the toys to suggest their use (as in Group A) and also began their intervention in the play behavior itself.

As in Group A adult intervention concentrated on The Clinic theme for a three week period. At the end of that period, new toys and play materials relating to the theme of The Grocery Store were brought in and arranged. The toys relating to The Clinic were left in the classroom, as with Group A, and The Grocery Store toys were grouped in another corner of the room. The children were free to play The Clinic, but adult intervention was based on the theme of The Grocery Store during the subsequent three week period.

Adult intervention in the children's play took two basic forms: a) participation in the play itself, and b) intervention from outside the play activity.

a. Adult Intervention from Outside the Play Situation. The teacher observed the children at play and knew where each child stood in terms of the six evaluating factors. Her aim was to evoke missing factors in each child's play behavior without herself entering into the play situation. If, for example, the diagnosis of a certain child indicated that none of the six evaluating factors were missing, the teacher would not intervene in his play at all. If, however, a child is found playing by herself with a doll and had been evaluated as not participating in interactive behavior, the teacher might say, "How is your baby today?" The child could answer, "She is ill" or if she does not respond, the teacher could suggest that her baby might be ill and "Let's take your baby to the clinic. I did the same thing with mine when she was ill." The teacher would then bring the child to the corner where other children were playing Clinic and say, "Here is Mrs. Mizrahi with her baby. She thinks her baby is sick, could you please help her, nurse?" At this point the teacher would stop her intervention and observe whether the little girl began interaction with the other children and whether the others included her in their play world. If the child began to play with and within the group, she needed no more help from the teacher. If, however, the child did not respond by interacting with the other children, even though they spoke to her and tried to involve her in the game, the teacher would try again by saying, "Mrs. Mizrahi, the nurse asked you what is the matter with your baby. Show the nurse where it hurts your baby. Tell her all about it." etc.

Intervention from outside the play situation takes several forms: questions ("How is your baby today?"), suggestions ("Let's take your baby to the clinic."), clarification of behavior ("I did the same when my baby was ill."), establishing contact between players ("Can you please help her, nurse?"), and straightforward direction ("Show the nurse where it hurts your baby. Tell her all about it."). It is important to note that all the different kinds of interventions are from the point of view of the make-believe theme. The teacher addresses the role person, not the child. Thus, the distinction between outside intervention and participation in the play is minimized. By intervening from the outside the teacher does not take on a role in the play, but his intervention comes as part of the child's play world. It is both a confirmation of the validity of the play world and a demonstration of how it works.

b. Teacher Participates in the Play Situation. Active participation in a play episode implies that the teacher joins the child's play by taking on and enacting a role relevant to the theme of the episode over a period of time. The teacher's participation functions as a demonstration: it is a model of how to participate in sociodramatic play activity.

Furthermore, by being inside the play the teacher is in a position to direct the children almost in the same way as if she were on the outside. By being an actor she can activate a whole group of children, emphasizing the missing play components for each child in her contact with the child. Thus, if she knows that Miriam, who is playing a mother, does not use make-believe with regard to objects, the teacher can say to her, from within her role as a nurse, "Here is the medicine, Mrs. Ohajon" and pretend to give her something. She can elaborate further: "Give two spoonfuls to your baby twice a day. Now call a taxi to take you home since your baby is very ill and should not go out in this cold. Here is the telephone" (she points to a nearby box). If the missing element in Dan's play is the ability to use make-believe as a substitute for actions and situations, the teacher-nurse can address Dan, the doctor, who very much wants to do the nurse's job: administer injections. "Let's pretend that I am now on vacation and you can't wait to give these shots and so the doctor is going to have to give them. I am going now and when you need me again, you will call me on the phone and I will come." Here the pretended situation is used for problemsolving.

The act of being a co-player can activate the other children to develop the missing elements of their play or it can demonstrate the possibilities inherent in the play activity itself. Such demonstration evokes more than passive recognition, it forces the child to react to the demonstrated play element. The make-believe situation demonstrated by the teacher becomes a cue for the child's subsequent activity.

Teachers of Groups B and C used both kinds of intervention, depending on the situation. There were no definitive directions given, recognizing the fact that only the teacher was in the position to decide what would be most appropriate for the particular play situation and for the specific child's play level.

An analysis of observation notes did not reveal any single area which could be used to improve dramatic play behavior. There were six components, (as described in previous chapters) any one of which could be lacking. There were children who used make-believe and "let's pretend" in their play but did not do it in groups ("interaction with more than one other child"): a girl might put on high-heeled shoes, a "lady's" dress and say to herself: "Let's pretend that I'm Mommy and I'm going shopping" referring, verbally or with gestures, neither to another child nor to an adult. Other children might interact with a group of children but neither take on a role ("I'm Daddy) nor use make-believe with regard to toys or play objects ("Pretend that this is a plate"). There was no attempt to direct the teachers to develop any one missing component rather than another; they were to evaluate specific situations with regard to the particular child and plan their intervention according to which component was missing in that play episode.

We recommended developing interplay between children even if the solitary dramatic play was still undeveloped. Verbal make-believe seems to develop best in interactive situations, and therefore we felt it was better methodology to work towards sociodramatic play. We did not feel it was necessary to stick rigidly to the natural developmental sequence. Our rule of thumb was to accelerate the "technical" ability or skills of the child in sociodramatic play while minimally influencing the content.

As soon as the child is observed demonstrating participation in all six components of sociodramatic play, the teachers ceased their intervention. The assumption was that once all six components were present in the child's activity, the level or intensity of using each component, both separately and together, would develop *through the play activity itself.* If, for example, a child who played alone reached the stage of playing with another child, the teacher would not continue intervening in order to get that child to play in a group of four or five other children. Even with only a single partner the child has achieved *sociodramatic* play. Future participation in sociodramatic play episodes will develop this activity further and eventually he will play with larger and larger groups. This principle was followed with regard to the development of all six components.

In order to facilitate the teacher's control of the learning process, we proposed the record sheet reproduced below to be used by the observer (or the teacher) as a supplement to the pre-experimental diagnosis. The record sheet was seen as an aid to teachers in focusing and choosing how to implement the intervention.

The record sheet includes two dimensions: the play level of the child at the time of intervention and the effectiveness of the intervention according to the child's response. The numbers included in the sample record sheet indicate that when the

Sample Record Sheet: Progress in Play Behavior

The level of the child's play at time of intervention	Reactions to intervention					
	1	2	3	4	5	4
	No reaction or negative reaction	Passive participation, interested observing, smile, confirmation by word or nod	Active participation doing as the teacher says or repeating his words	Adds to adult's suggestions, also his own words or ideas	Interprets adult's suggestion independently, reacts originally	Initiates new plots, adult not needed
No dramatic play	1					
Dramatic play			2			
Sociodramatic play				3		
Play elements						
(1)						
(2)						
(3)						
(4)						
(5)						
(6)						

teacher began intervening, the child was not playing and reacted passively (number 1); the second intervention (number 2) evoked active participation with the child contributing something; the third intervention found the child engaging in sociodramatic play and brought play element (2) into the child's play behavior although he did not show initiative in using it.

The sheet helps to point up the three possible states the child will be in with regard to play behavior and enables the teacher to focus his intervention appropriately. Thus, if the teacher finds the child at the first level, not playing at all, she will need to try to initiate him into dramatic or sociodramatic play, whichever seems more appropriate to the child and the situation. In any case she must suggest the theme ("Would you like to play Hospital?"), the role ("Let's pretend you are the doctor.") and the role-appropriate activities ("You examine the sick baby and tell her mother what medicine to give her."). In order to avoid imposing content on the child, the teacher will try to get clues from the child about what he would prefer doing. She may present the child a variety of toys and ask him which he would prefer: the doll, the wheel or some scales. The child's choice may indicate which role and theme he would prefer. If he chooses a wheel, it is probable that he would like to imitate a driver and the teacher can develop the theme along these lines.

If the child is already engaging in dramatic play (the second level), there is no need to intervene in terms of role or theme; however, it will be more important to get the child involved within a group—either by joining him to a suitable preexisting group or by involving another child who has not yet begun dramatic play.

Intervention for a child on the third level is aimed only at redressing any missing components. For example, if a child tends to interrupt his play episodes frequently, after only a few minutes, the teacher could suggest new variations of his theme in order to encourage elaboration of a theme and continuation with the play episode. The original theme and role is preserved. If the child is rigidly attached to "real" objects, he can suggest, "Let's pretend this is a . . ." until the child begins to substitute independently.

All intervention is predicated on sensitivity to the child's responses. Note that the range of the six response levels goes from no reaction to independent imitation of the teacher's intervention. The child does not to merely imitate or mechanically follow the teacher's suggestions. When the teacher says, "Go to the doctor and tell her that your baby is sick," it is not sufficient for the child to walk over to the "doctor" or even to hand the doll to the "doctor" and say, "My baby is sick." The idea is that the child will take the hint and act on his own: "Doctor, my baby is sick; please examine her, she has a fever." Or even better, the child could begin to plan the entire story: "Okay, Dear, just be quiet until we get to the doctor, don't cry!" and begin an entire chain of self-initiated interactions.

If the teacher sees that a child responds habitually at low levels, she will need to change her strategy. If she has been directing play from the outside, she may have to try to take on a role and interact with the child from within a play episode. The primary function of the sheet was as a teaching aid rather than for evaluation purposes.

Group C

Children in kindergartens and nursery schools included in Group C were supplied with as wide and rich a variety of meaningful impressions and comprehensible experiences as possible around the same two themes (culled from visits, field trips, discussions, etc. exactly like that which was done with Group A). In addition, the children were "taught" by the adults how to exploit and convert their impressions and experiences into sociodramatic play material (exactly as was done in Group B). It should be noted, however, that the adults and children in Group C were exploiting impressions and experiences *shared at that time*, which both the children and the adults knew were familiar; in Group B adult intervention was based on stimulating the use of *past impressions and experiences* which varied from child to child and which was, in fact, an unknown entity to the adults.

During the three-week period allotted to each theme, identical sets and numbers of toys and other play materials were made available to the children of Group C, just as with Groups A and B.

Although Group C was on the surface Group A experiences plus Group B experiences, the new whole was far greater than the sum of its parts. In Group B the adults never quite knew or could be sure of what the children had seen in their environment, how far they had understood what was explained and what impressions they carried away with them. The adults had to feel their way, gingerly, and uncertainly. However, there was a firm basis of *shared* impressions and experiences between the adults and children in Group C which could be used to encourage development of any given element in their sociodramatic play.

For example, if a child from Group C were to begin playing "Grocery Store" by himself, the teacher or experimental aide could ask, "Did the grocer in the store we went to yesterday work all by himself? Who was helping him? Why did he need a helper? What sort of things did the assistant do for him?" In this way the adult could help the child recall impressions of an experience they shared. She might continue by asking, "Where is your helper today, Mr. Grocer? Did he forget to come to work? Why don't you get another assistant?" Then, after the child invites another child to join him in his game, she could continue, "Have you told your assistant what you need him to do?" (recalling the discussion of duties of the assistant at the time of the trip to the corner grocery store). She could turn to the "assistant" and say, "Do you work here all day? Do you get any pay for all your hard work? Did you ask Mr. Grocer about your salary and when you have to come?" (reflecting the discussion of the grocer's assistant about his hours, pay, how he moved from one job to another in order to make better pay, etc.). Thus, the adult working with children in Group C can lead the child who generally plays alone toward playing with other children and toward theme planning and elaboration as a group effort, i.e., sociodramatic play activity. She draws on experiences that she has in common with the children to develop roles (like the Grocer) to be used in a sociodramatic play episode which reflects a real-life situation she experienced together with the children.

Thus her role is both meaningful and comprehensible to the children.

This is not true for a situation where a child from Group B plays by himself. The adult has no way of knowing whether the child has ever been inside a grocery store with an assistant or to what extent he understood the duties and function of either the grocer or his assistant. Wishing to stimulate group participation the teacher can ask "Who else works in the grocery store where you get things besides the grocer?" If the child answers that he doesn't know, the teacher has no common experience on which basis she can lead him to agree to inviting other children to join him in the game. The personal experiences and impressions of the child are an unknown quantity to the adult; therefore, her scope for broadening, deepening and manipulating them is limited. Similarly, when an adult takes on a role in a sociodramatic play episode in Group B, she always wonders if her interpretation is familiar to the children from within their real-life context and suspects that they might not fully comprehend her actions.

Duration of the Experiment

Each group in the experiment engaged in sociodramatic play for a total of one and a half hours per day, five days a week for six weeks (three weeks per theme). The one and a half hour period included time to clean up and put things away. Each group spent a total of 45 hours in sociodramatic play activity.

Group A. Field trips and visits were made during the first week of each three-week theme-period. These visits and discussion time is not included in the 45 hours, which were dedicated solely to play activity. New toys and play materials were made available and "free play conditions" obtained for one and a half hours per day five days per week throughout the entire three-week theme period. There was no difference in the arrangements for the two themes.

Group B. The adults involved "taught" the children how to engage in sociodramatic play with regard to the two themes, spending each three-week period on one of the themes. The adults worked with the children during a play period of one and a half hours a day five days a week, basing their work on the children's *past* impressions and experiences.

Group C. As with Group A, field trips and visits took place in the first week of each three-week theme period and at the same time the children spend one and a half hours a day in sociodramatic play with adult guidance, as in Group B. This continued five days a week throughout each three-week theme period.

The Sample and Matching Procedures

There were five groups of children involved in the study: three experimental groups and two control groups. The three experimental groups, A, B and C, included children we termed "low socioeconomic status non-European" which meant their families consisted of three to seven children, their parents were born either in Middle-Eastern or North African countries and had no more than an elementary school education; their fathers were semiskilled or skilled laborers. The first control group, Group D, included low socioeconomic status non-Eurpean children, who matched those in the experimental groups. The second control group, Group E, included children we termed "low socioeconomic status European" and "high socioeconomic status European." The term "low socioeconomic status European" meant they came from families consisting of two to five children, their parents were born in Europe and had no more than an elementary school education, and their fathers were semiskilled or skilled laborers. Group F, including "high socioeconomic status European" meant they came from families consisting of two to four children, their parents were born in Europe and had a high-school or higher education, and their fathers were professionals.

The three experimental groups, A, B and C, were composed of 12 experimental classes totalling 420 children. Each of the groups consisted of four classes—two kindergarten class with children aged 5–6.6 years and two nursery school classes with children aged 3–5.6 years. Control Group D was composed of ten classes totalling 362 children including five kindergarten classes (children aged 5–6.6 years) and five nursery school classes (children aged 3–5.6 years).

Control Group E-F consisted of 12 classes totalling 427 children including six classes with mainly low socioeconomic status European children and six classes with mainly high socioeconomic status European children. The E control group ("low socioeconomic status European" children) included three kindergarten classes (5–6.6 year-olds) and three nursery school classes (3–5.6 year-olds). The F control group ("high socioeconomic status European" children) included three kindergarten classes (5–6.6 year-olds) and three nursery school classes (3–5.6 year-olds). See Table 15 below.

Table 15: Composition of Experimental and Control Groups by Age Level

Age	Experimental Groups			Control Groups			Total No. of Classes
	A	B	C	D	E	F	
3 to 5.6 (Nursery)	2	2	2	5	3	3	17
5 – 6.6 (Kindergarten)	2	2	2	5	3	3	17
Total Number of Classes	4	4	4	10	6	6	34

Note: The average number of children per class was 35, ranging from a minimum of 29 to a maximum of 40.

The matching of the children of Control Group D to those in the experimental groups was according to the following characteristics:

1. the nature of the family
2. the nature of the child
3. the school environment
1. *Family Characteristics* included:
   parents' country of origin
   number of children in the family
   parents' education
   father's occupation
2. *Attributes of the child* included:
   age
   sex

IQ as measured by the Stanford-Binet test

play level (according to the six criteria)

3. *School Environment* included:

number of children in class

teacher's education and experience

quality and quantity of equipment

There was no noticeable difference between each of the three experimental groups when compared with one another or when compared with Control Group D in all three characteristic categories. All children in the class participated in the experimental activities even those whose data was excluded from the study because of the necessity for matching.

There was no significant difference between Groups A, B, C, D and E in terms of parents' education, father's occupation, age, sex and school standards. Group E-F, as a whole, including (those of high socioeconomic European status) differed from the other groups in all family characteristics, mean IQ and play attainment. Only age, sex and school standards remained similar (see Table 16).

Because our primary interest was in the influence of sociocultural background on the child's ability to engage in sociodramatic play activity, we did not include children coming from problem homes or families within the groups. It was our opinion that the introduction of such children into the experimental groups would have clouded the issue with extraneous, for this study, issues such as pathological family patterns vs. sociocultural influences. For the purpose of this study a "problem" home was defined as one in which a child was an orphan or whose parents were divorced or one or both parents were in a mental hospital.

B. Teacher Training Procedures

Experimental Aides and teachers were given guidance by means of thorough explanation and discussion in general meetings and through classroom demonstrations until it was clear that the teachers understood fully how to work within an experimental framework. Each teacher had an experimental aide to

Table 16. Matching Control and Experimental Groups

| Name of Group | FAMILY | | | | | CHILDREN | | | | | Number of Pre-School Classes |
	Education of Father and Mother	Occupation of Father	No. of Children in Family	Parents' Country of Origin	Child's Age	Mean IQ Stanford-Binet	Boys	Girls	N	
Experimental A	Elementary or less	Semi- or unskilled	3-7	Asia/N. Africa	3-6.6	90.6	49	51	140	4
Experimental B	Elementary or less	Semi- or unskilled	3-7	Asia/N. Africa	3-6.6	91.0	48	52	140	4
Experimental C	Elementary or less	Semi- or unskilled	3-7	Asia/N. Africa	3-6.6	89.9	50	50	140	4
Control D	Elementary or less	Semi- or unskilled	3-7	Asia/N. Africa	3-6.6	91.5	47	53	362	10
Control E	Elementary or less	Semi- or unskilled	2-5	Europe	3-6.6	102.2				6
Control F	High School University	Professional	2-4	Europe	3-6.6	130.6	51	49	427	6

All the children were born in Israel. Their parents immigrated to Israel 8-12 years earlier.

work with during the time dedicated to dealing with sociodramatic play.

First Group Meeting: Teachers and Investigators

After observation periods in all the experimental and control groups, a meeting was held between the teachers and the investigators, consisting of a short lecture, the presentation of prepared material, discussions, questions, etc. Problems connected with sociodramatic play were discussed in detail.

—an outline of differences found in sociodramatic play behavior of children from middle to high socioeconomic background as compared to that of children from low socioeconomic background

—a detailed definition of sociodramatic play including the six evaluating factors (play elements) commonly found in sociodramatic play of children from middle to high socioeconomic backgrounds

—a discussion of the possibilities inherent to this form of play behavior in terms of developing those abilities necessary for the child's successful integration into school life

—a demonstration of how to carry out observations in the preschool situation in order to diagnose which factors were lacking in each child's dramatic play behavior.

Second Meeting

Individual guidance was provided for the teachers and experimental aides in terms of observation, recording and diagnosis of missing factors in the sociodramatic play behavior of individual children. They observed and recorded behavior of a number of children under the direct tutelage of the researchers, making use of techniques which they had learned earlier, and gave interpretations in light of the explanations and discussions of the first meeting. Each teacher and experimental aide carried out at least three instances of guided observation, diagnosis and interpretation; some teachers received additional individual guidance in the techniques until the researchers felt all the teachers and experimental aides were fully conversant with this side of the experimental material.

Third Group Meeting

When all the adults involved had learned how to observe and record the children's play level a third meeting was held to explain the approaches to be practiced in their particular classes. Each group attended this third meeting separately.

—*Group A*. Adults working with Group A were told the rationale behind the approach and the work method was described in detail. They were asked to do their best, through field trips, discussions, reading, illustrations, etc., to elaborate the chosen themes and make them understandable to the children. They were told that the children should be expected to begin playing and to improve their play level as a result of these learning experiences, the stimulus of the new toys and the suggestion to use them in dramatic play.

—*Group B*. Adults working with Group B heard an explanation of the assumptions behind the approach they were about to employ and a description of the work methods. Four main problems associated with the conscious development of children's sociodramatic play were raised and discussed:

1. Planned adult intervention, based on knowledge of missing elements in a child's sociodramatic play, must take into account both the child's personality and the specific play situation of the moment and the necessity of trying to help the child to develop the play skills he lacks
2. The adult is *not* to intervene or try to develop further those factors that have been observed existing in the child's sociodramatic play behavior.
3. Adult intervention is to be planned to encourage the use of one specific element at a time and is to continue for a specific period of time, taking advantage of various opportunities as they develop. When the adult is satisfied that the factor which has been at focus has been integrated into

the child's sociodramatic play behavior, he may then go on to encourage the development of an additional play element. For example, if diagnostic observation shows that a particular child is lacking three factors in his sociodramatic play behavior: make-believe with regard to an object, persistence, and verbal communication, the teacher should choose one of the factors and focus her intervention around it, taking into account the play situation, the child's personality and the activity itself. If she thinks the play situation makes "make-believe with regard to an object" particularly suitable, she will consistently encourage this element with the child over a period of several days or until she observes the child "making-believe" with regard to objects on his own. Then, she will concentrate on one of the other factors missing from that child's sociodramatic play behavior.

4. Planned adult intervention is to concentrate on teaching *how* to play and to interfere as little as possible in the content of the play activity. The point is to help the child be able to play using any and all content he might come across.

—*Group C*. Both approaches were explained and discussed in terms of purposes and methods. In addition, the advantages of integrating the two approaches were emphasized.

Fourth Meeting

The preschool teachers and experimental aides of Groups B and C were given individual guidance in furthering the development of missing play elements attending their classes. The researchers gave each teacher a table, similar to Table 17 below, containing a detailed diagnosis of the sociodramatic play behavior of each child in her class.

From tables like the example the teacher can see that Dan does not utilize play elements b, c and f at all (make-believe with regard to objects, make-believe with regard to actions and situations and verbal communication) in his sociodramatic play. He uses element e (interaction with one or more children) only partially and needs planned help and encouragement with this

Table 17. Attainments in Sociodramatic Play (sample sheet)

Name of preschool　　　　　　Name of Preschool Teacher
Address　　　　　　　　　　　Date

Factors Existing and Missing from Sociodramatic Play — Play Elements

Names of Children in Classroom	a			b			c			d			e			f		
	+	?	0	+	?	0	+	?	0	+	?	0	+	?	0	+	?	0
Dan	x					x			x	x				x				x
Shoshana		x				x			x			x		x				x
Hanna	x			x			x			x				x	x			

factor. He has fully integrated elements a and d (imitative role behavior and persistence) and needs no intervention at all. Shoshana, on the other hand, does not engage in sociodramatic play behavior at all and needs planned intervention to encourage her to begin playing. A teacher can tell at a glance how every child rates with regard to a single factor—whether most of the children seem to be using one particular play element or whether the majority lack any specific element. If there is a situation where most of the class lacks a particular element, the teacher can plan her intervention in the form of a class project.

Only half the preschool class was present during the first three observation and recording demonstrations in order to make the activity easier to handle. From the fourth meeting on the entire class was present and the teacher and experimental aide began planned interventions according to the diagnostic sheet. After a few days, if the teacher is satisfied that a child has integrated one of the play elements into his play, she will cross out the old diagnosis and fill in a new one, noting the changes. Thus, the diagnostic sheet becomes a constant source of information for regulating and directing their planned interventions as well as an up-to-date record of the changes taking place with each child. The Teacher's Remarks column was utilized to note children's reactions to the interventions. This proved a useful tool for guiding the teacher's intervention strategies. As soon as a child received a + (plus sign) for all six play elements, the adults no longer intervened in his play activity. The assumption was that if a child used all six play elements, even if in a limited fashion, in his play activity, there was no more need for intervention and the child would develop his ability further through involvement with other children and through imitation. We felt that imitation had not been useful to these children before intervention by the adults because the children had not reached a high enough stage of sociodramatic play development to be able to benefit from their own personal observation and to learn through imitation of other children. When we carried out individual guidance sessions with the teachers, we worked on the possibilities and methods of developing the six essential play elements appropriate to the rate of progress of the teacher's children.

The teachers and experimental aides of Group A also received individual guidance in terms of theme elaboration and the use of various materials and verbal explanations that fit the needs of each child. During the first week dedicated to elaborating the theme, a variety of teaching experiences, aimed at small groups as well as individuals, was suggested by the researcher and innovated by the preschool teachers and experimental aides themselves.

Although additional staff meetings in group form were not held until the close of the experiment, the teachers were free to consult with the researchers at any point throughout the experimental period.

It is instructive to note the reactions of the teachers to the ideas and demands of the experiment as expressed in group meetings and during the individual guidance sessions with the researcher.

The teachers in Group A identified easily with their role, which differed from the usual preschool teaching practices only in its intensity and ultimate goal. In contrast, a high percentage of the teachers in Groups B and C had great difficulty accepting, theoretically at least, the idea of active intervention as presented in the third meeting, although they were quite familiar with their children's play deficiencies. Most of the teachers had children of their own. In the discussion they admitted guidance and active intervention in their own children's play and were able to demonstrate various strategies they employed. They presented examples pointing to all six imitative and make-believe play elements in their own children's play. Yet, the majority resisted the idea of intervention in preschool, saying "this is different." Two main points were raised:

1. Intervention in free play might have negative effects on the mental health of their pupils. When we noted that they did intervene in their own children's play, they replied that they had closer emotional ties to their own children and better knowledge of their emotional and experiential state.

2. Intervention was too sudden and went against the slow, "natural" process that children must undergo. With their own children, intervention was gradual, from birth on.

Both objections reflected their training as preschool teachers. The experiment's demand for intervention conflicted with the theories and work practices they had been taught. It is interesting to note that they admitted this training had had little effect on their own child-rearing practices while influencing their professional work quite heavily.

After thoroughly discussing the theoretical points, everyone agreed to try the method. Demonstration and individual guidance soon resolved most doubts and the teachers carried out the fostering with enthusiasm and resourcefulness. The relatively quick progress and the children's obvious pleasure in their play activities were sources of satisfaction and reinforcement for the teachers' efforts.

It was also to note the difference in reactions between the preschool teachers and their experimental aides. The aides had participated in the planning of the details of the experiment, the preparations and the preceding observations. None were professional preschool teachers, but some were school teachers and most of them had children of their own. Their experience as mothers and school teachers probably made it easier to accept the idea of adult intervention; training of school teachers emphasizes the active role of the adult in the class and the need for intensive intervention into the children's development. They were not afraid of hurting the children by teaching them play skills they lacked.

C. Hypotheses

The previous sections have described the treatment variables in detail, not only as were foreseen but as were observed during the process of the experiment itself. Below we will present our hypotheses, clarify the dependent and independent variables, and describe our methods of evaluation.

Hypothesis 1

Each of the three experimental groups will improve its play behavior; that is, more children will engage in dramatic and sociodramatic play episodes. Improvement will be evaluated in terms of each group's performance at the end of the experimental period, as compared to the following:
1. Performance prior to the experiment
2. Performance of the control group consisting of children from lower socioeconomic status groups
3. Performance of the control group consisting of children from the higher socioeconomic status group

Hypothesis 2

The results of the three treatment groups will not be the same. Different degrees of play behavior improvement will be evaluated by comparing the attainment of each experimental group with the attainment of the other two.

Hypothesis 3

There will be a positive relationship between sociodramatic play attainment and IQ. The group of children with higher attainment in sociodramatic play will have a higher mean IQ.

Hypothesis 4

There will be no correlation between sex and achievement of sociodramatic play.

Hypothesis 5

There will be a positive relationship between age and attainment of sociodramatic play. Older children will have more success at attaining sociodramatic play.

Variables Involved in the Hypotheses and Their Evaluation

Since the experiment was designed to investigate the effect of different approaches to improving sociodramatic play among children from low socioeconomic backgrounds, the first two hypotheses were central.

Occurrence and Quality of Play

All children were placed into one of four categories according to the level of their play behavior before and after the experimental period:
1. Not playing (no kind of dramatic play behavior)
2. Dramatic play behavior only
3. Poor sociodramatic play behavior
4. Good sociodramatic play behavior

Evaluation of the quality of the play behavior was based on the presence or absence of the following six essential play elements:
1. *Imitative role-play.* The child undertakes a make-believe role and expresses it in imitative action and/or verbalization
2. *Make-believe with regard to objects.* The child substitutes toys, non-structured materials, movements or verbal declarations for real objects.
3. *Make-believe with regard to actions and situations.* The child substitutes verbal descriptions for actions and situations.
4. *Persistence.* The child engages in a play episode for a period of at least 10 minutes duration.

5. *Interaction*. There are at least two players interacting in the context of the play episode.
6. *Verbal Communication*. There is verbal interaction of some sort with regard to the play episode.

Any role-play was accepted as dramatic play whether it was displayed by verbal declaration or make-believe ("I am a bus driver") or by imitation (running around the playground with a wheel and shouting "Beep-beep!"). "Poor sociodramatic play" consisted of the elements of role play and interaction with a partner plus one other component. "Good sociodramatic play" included the elements of role play and interaction with other role players plus two or more other components.

The classifications were based on systematic observation of each child over three free play periods unless the child was seen displaying "good sociodramatic play" on the first or second day. Therefore, the classification reflects his maximal performance from the three observation sessions for the period of time usually given over to free play.

Aside from assessing the level of each child's play, the observer also described what the child was doing and saying. When sociodramatic play occurred, he recorded whatever verbal interchanges took place for a maximum of ten minutes and stopped only if he was sure that all the co-players were displaying "good sociodramatic play." These records served two purposes: they controlled the judgment of the observer by a nonpresent researcher and provided speech samples for the verbal analysis (see Chapter 3).

Three play levels were considered for evaluation of Hypotheses 1 and 2: No Play, Dramatic Play and Sociodramatic Play (both "poor" and "good" together). The other hypotheses employed three different categories: No Play, Poor Sociodramatic Play, and Good Sociodramatic Play.

IQ, Sex, Age

We investigated the relationship between level of engagement in sociodramatic play activity and the independent variables of IQ, sex and age. For the purposes of making these evaluations all children were classified into the following three categories:

1. Not engaging in sociodramatic play.
2. Engaging in poor sociodramatic play.
3. Engaging in good sociodramatic play.

These categories were based on the same observations that served to evaluate Hypotheses 1 and 2.

IQ was established before the experiment by administering the Stanford-Binet test for children. The hypothesis about IQ was raised on speculative grounds. We expected that children with higher IQ scores might profit more readily from the learning experiences provided in the various approaches. Our previous observations did not point to any correlation between IQ and play behavior (see Chapter 3, Section 8), but at that point we were dealing with play behavior without special training and with a very small number of children from lower socioeconomic levels.

We expected no sex-related differences in terms of level of play behavior, since the teaching was directed to all children individually and the themes were role-appropriate for both boys and girls.

Our expectation of age differences was based on the assumption that older children might profit more from the relatively short learning period, especially since the variable was studied in terms of interaction with other children within the sociodramatic play context. We dealt with only two age groups: younger (3–5 years) and older (5.1–6.6 years).

D. Findings and Interpretations

Hypotheses 1 and 2: The Effect of the Three Experimental Treatments

The three experimental groups (A, B, and C) were matched with the lower socioeconomic level children of control group D according to play level (in addition to other variables discussed previously). About 69% of all four groups did not engage in any sort of dramatic play, about 20% engaged only in dramatic play and about 10% engaged in sociodramatic play (Table 18). Three percent of the children of European origin (control Group E) did not engage in any sort of dramatic play and 78% engaged in sociodramatic play.

At the conclusion of the experiment, the following results were recorded:

1. There was no significant improvement in Group A's play level (no direct instruction in play skills). The slight improvement that occurred is similar to that in Control Group D.
2. Highly significant[1] improvement occurred in Groups B and C in comparison to Control Group D and to their performance prior to the experiment.
3. The improvement of Group C is significantly higher than the improvement of Group B.
4. Control Group E has still significantly higher achievement than Group C in terms of play level.

We can conclude by saying that Hypothesis 1 was only partially confirmed (Group A did not improve) and Hypothesis 2 was wholly supported by the findings.

Table 18: Children's Play Level Before Experiment, By Group

| | | | | Play Level | | | | | |
| | | No Play | | Dramatic Play | | Socio-dramatic Play | | Total | |
Groups		N	%	N	%	N	%	N	%
Experimental	A	96	68	29	21	15	11	140	100
Experimental	B	98	70	27	19	15	11	140	100
Experimental	C	98	70	29	21	13	9	140	100
Low SES Control D		250	69	72	20	40	11	362	100
High SES Control E		13	3	81	19	333	78	427	100

[1]The X2 test for independence was carried out separately for each experimental group with Control Group D, for the experimental groups between themselves and for Group C with E. In all cases, except Groups A and D, the hypothesis of no association between group and play level was rejected at the 0.01 level of significance.

Table 19: Children's Play Level After Experiment, by Group

Groups		No Play N	No Play %	Dramatic Play N	Dramatic Play %	Socio-dramatic Play N	Socio-dramatic Play %	Total N	Total %
Experimental	A	88	63	35	25	17	12	140	100
Experimental	B	48	34	45	32	47	34	140	100
Experimental	C	16	11	57	41	67	48	140	100
Low SES Control D		76	63	28	23	17	14	121*	100

*A random sample, of about a third of the total number in Group D, was reevaluated after the experimental period. Group E was not reevaluated.

Hypotheses 3, 4 and 5

Our examination of the relationship between various independent variables and play level included only the results of Groups B and C at the end of the experiment. Since there was no significant improvement for Group A, it was excluded. We wished to test whether IQ, age and sex affected the children's ability to profit from the different approaches designed to improve their sociodramatic play level.

IQ and Play. There was no significant difference between the average IQ of "good," "poor" and "no" players. Thus, Hypothesis 3 was not confirmed.

Sex and Play. There is a significant difference in play level between boys and girls (the hypothesis of independence between sex and play level is rejected by the X^2 test at 0.01 level of significance). Girls showed remarkably better achievement and so Hypothesis 4 was not supported by the findings.

Age and Play. There is a significant difference in play level of older rather than younger age groups (the hypotheses of no

Table 20: Mean IQ and Play Level

	Good Sociodramatic Play	Poor Sociodramatic Play	No Sociodramatic Play
Mean IQ	89.9	91.1	90.2

Table 21: Sex and Play Level

| | Play Level | | | | | | |
| | Good Sociodramatic Play | | Poor Sociodramatic Play | | No Sociodramatic Play | | Total |
Sex	N	%	N	%	N	%	N
Male	14	10	28	20	95	70	137
Female	37	26	36	25	70	49	143
Total	51		64		165		280

Table 22: Age and Play Level

| | Play Level | | | |
| | Good Sociodramatic Play | Poor Sociodramatic Play | No Sociodramatic Play | Total |
Sex	%	%	%	
4–5	6	13	81	100%
5.1–6.6	31	31	38	100%

relationship between age and play level was rejected at the 0.01 level of significance on the X^2 test of independence). Children from the older age group showed much higher achievement and Hypothesis 5 was supported by the findings.

Interpretation of Findings on Treatment Effects— Hypotheses 1 and 2

Group A

Although the expectations were that there would be improvement in all three experimental groups, Group A showed little noticeable improvement despite the treatment applied. We arrived at four possible interpretations of this finding, further clarified by interpretation of the results of the other two experimental groups.

1. A total of 45 hours spread over a six-week time period is insufficient to both expose the children to impressions and experiences and render them meaningful and comprehensible enough for the children to utilize them in their dramatic play. It may be necessary to supply meaningful impressions and experiences, both around the same themes and around other

themes, for a longer period of time in order to inspire dramatic play. Such an interpretation assumes that the main prerequisite for dramatic play of preschool children is meaningful impressions and comprehensible experiences; it also assumes the preschool environment can replace the home environment in terms of supplying such impressions and experiences. Supporters of this interpretation would aver that the cultural deprivation of these children has continued for a number of years and such a relatively short experimental period could not possibly be effective.

2. Another possibility could posit that it is impossible to introduce supplementary impressions and experiences into a preschool context. Children from environments similar to Control Group E receive such impressions and undergo such experiences within family circle relationships (parentchild, brother-sister, uncle-nephew, etc.). Such relationships are far warmer and more intimate than those existing between children or adults and children in a preschool context. In addition, the family group is comprised of people of varying ages, whereas the preschool group is relatively homogeneously the child's peer group. Furthermore, events occurring within the family may have a deeper, more lasting impact on the child. Sibling rivalry and jealousy could impel a child to greater activity, intensifying his impressions and experiences. A number of questions arise with regard to these interpretations: how do "only" children among Control Group E make up for the lack of sibling rivalry and jealousy? why don't similar experiences within the context of the family from lower socioeconomic levels produce similar results? must all the factors operate together, or are they equally important singly? Indeed, interaction within the family circle for children of lower socioeconomic backgrounds is virtually the same as that of those from higher socioeconomic backgrounds, except in terms of actively explaining and mediating events occurring within the child's immediate surroundings and in creating supplementary situations which would stimulate further the child's impressions and experiences. It was for this reason that the experimental situation provided impressions and experiences which were to *supplement* those encountered

within the family circle and its immediate environment. Supporters of this interpretation would agree with the previous interpretation that meaningful impressions and comprehensible experiences constitute the main prerequisite for preschool sociodramatic play, but would continue to say that experiences and impressions from a preschool context could not be expected to *replace* those originating in the family. It would seem that in order for the impressions and experiences to be effective for stimulating sociodramatic play, they must occur within a home and family atmosphere.

3. A third interpretation would simply say that the fundamental hypothesis on which the experiment for Group A was based was invalid. The immediate environment of these children may indeed provide them with sufficient meaningful and comprehensible impressions and experiences, but such impressions and experiences are not in themselves a prerequisite for sociodramatic play. Since the experimental environment did nothing to further their play skills, the children in Group A did not change or improve their play behavior patterns. Supporters of this interpretation would state that fostering play by means of supplementary impressions and experiences is a waste of time; that the immediate environment of such children provides them with sufficient meaningful and comprehensible experiences to provide grist for their dramatic play; and their inability to engage in sociodramatic play is caused by some other factor.

4. The fourth possibility might admit the requirement for meaningful impressions and comprehensible experiences and accept the possibility of a preschool context supplementing those provided by the children's family and day-to-day environment; however, this factor is insufficient *by itself* to guarantee the development of sociodramatic play activity. Thus, some other factor(s) must be provided in addition to meaningful impressions and comprehensible experiences. This interpretation seems to be borne out by the findings: we did not succeed in involving the children with increased sociodramatic play through providing these impressions and experiences *alone*. Supporters of this interpretation would hold that provision of supplementary meaningful impressions and comprehensible experiences to children from lower socioeconomic backgrounds

is necessary, but needs the development of an apparently essential complementary factor.

Group B

The results for Group B are according with the expectations. It can be stated with confidence that Treatment Number 2 resulted in significant progress for this group. Planned intervention on the part of teachers and experimental aides into various aspects of sociodramatic play behavior by means of comments, suggestions, demonstrations, participation, etc. proved to be fruitful stimuli to make the children aware of different qualities and possibilities inherent to the sociodramatic play situation, of their own ability to draw on the repertoire of experiences residing in their memories as a rich resource of material to use in play episodes, and to make them aware of the potential of verbally elaborating play and problemsolving activities. The teachers and experimental aides actually were encouraging and helping each child to do what *he wanted* to do instead of simply abandoning him to face the immense task of solving all the problems involved in self-expression alone and unaided.

A comparison of the results of Group A with those of Group B supports the assumption that the deficiency of sociodramatic play behavior in children from low socioeconomic families stems mainly from a lack of guidance in converting their experiences into play material rather than from a lack of experiences per se. The children in Group B learned how to play and were not provided with new experiences or better insight into old ones.

Group C

The treatment for Group C combines those from Groups A and B: the provision of knowledge and experience which could be used as play material and instruction in play skills and demonstrated significantly greater improvement than did the approach for Group B. A most interesting factor in the differential results of the three groups is the non-additive effect of treatments 1 and 2 as revealed in Group C. The question arises:

what interactive factors are at work in the combination of the two techniques? There are two possible answers.

1. One answer would say that Approach 2, teaching how to play, is the most important factor in the combination. The role of Approach 1 was only methodological, facilitating a better application of Approach 2. It was much easier for the adult to suggest, encourage, demonstrate, etc. all the possibilities of play activity on the common ground of experiences and impressions provided by Approach 1. Also the common ground of experiences resulted in better interaction: there was a stock of shared experiences, vocabulary, knowledge and concepts.

2. Another interpretation would suggest that both Approach 1 and 2 are decisive in improving children's play. Children from low socioeconomic backgrounds lack both experiences necessary for play and the skills and techniques by which to express those experiences. However, play skills and techniques must come first. Without them old and new experiences will not find any outlet in sociodramatic play. As soon as the play skills instruction bears fruit in creating a play outlet, the children will immediately utilize their newer, more thoroughly understood experiences and engage in play activity on a much higher level than they could on the basis of their previous, vague understanding of behavior recalled from the past.

The two possible interpretations are not mutually exclusive. It would seem more likely that Approach 1 both facilitates Approach 2 methodologically and provides raw material for the children to play with. In practical terms what seems important is the fact that the combination was efficient in increasing the number of children engaging in dramatic and sociodramatic play.

The Relationship Between IQ and Sociodramatic Play Achievement: Hypothesis 3

Contrary to expectations, there was no relationship found between IQ and sociodramatic play achievement. The fact that less intelligent children profited from the learning experiences provided by the experiment the same as the more intelligent children can be interpreted in several ways.

a. It is possible that successful participation in sociodramatic play is not related to intelligence. Intelligence is not the main variable affecting sociodramatic behavior of children. However, an attempt to develop sociodramatic play among a small group of retarded (IQ = 50–75) children which proved fruitless may point to the necessity for a minimal level of intelligence in order to be able to carry out such play activities. It is possible that once that level has been reached, any child can develop sociodramatic play successfully.

b. The findings may reflect the method of evaluation, which dealt only with the *minimal* inclusion of play elements. We did not measure the extent of the elaboration of form and content of play; we did not discriminate between a child who played for 15 minutes and used make-believe once or twice and interacted with a single partner and one who played in lively interaction with a whole group of other children for a much longer time, creating verbally and actively successions of imaginative make-believe events and situations.

c. A third possibility could be related to the structure of the experiment itself, especially the time factor. Since the children were "taught" sociodramatic play individually by means of planned adult intervention, and this intervention was based on a diagnosis of missing or lacking factors within each child's play behavior, and since there were only 45 hours spread over a six week time period for the adults to work in, it is possible that the adults tended to spend more time with those children lacking several or all of the play elements and that perhaps these children were those with the lowest IQ's. In such a case, the children with higher IQ's may have been benefiting from comparatively little individual "teaching" and guidance. This possibility could only be confirmed by carrying out a further study wherein sociodramatic play achievement would be measured after the time spent "teaching" and giving guidance would have been divided equally between the more and less intelligent children.

The Relationship Between Sex and Play Level: Hypothesis 4

Contrary to our expectation, the girls' play achievement was significantly better than the boys'—even though both groups made progress. There are several possible explanations for this:

a. It is possible that boys have more difficulty understanding the behavior involved in male roles. Boys see, know and join in the daily activities of their fathers to a greatly lesser degree than do girls see, know and join in with the daily activities of their mothers. As a result a boy's ability to imitate his father is less well developed and this weak imitative ability is reflected in sociodramatic play behavior. Despite efforts of the preschool teacher and experimental aide to "teach" both boys and girls how to imitate their parental models, presumably in equal measure, this process apparently remained unchanged.

Moreover, the mother's home role is far more uniform than the father's occupational role. The girl has a rather specific, concrete role model, whereas the father's occupation is remote and vague and often blurs the outline of the boy's role model. Preschool girls often play "House" where they are "Mommy." This play-theme is not as limited as it might seem; it expands to include numerous roles: Mommies and neighbors cook, care for children, walk in the park, clean the house, wash and iron, get dressed, go shopping, etc. Not only have the girls seen their mothers do these things innumerable times, but the mothers encourage, demand and even teach their daughters to take over these tasks gradually. This process is far more in evidence in the homes of children from lower socioeconomic levels than in the homes of children from higher levels. Women's roles and tasks are much more clearly defined and strictly adhered to in a lower socioeconomic milieu. Mother always performs her specific tasks; nobody else ever does them for her (a maid or the husband might very well help out in a middle or high socioeconomic level household). The daughter of the house is expected to help her mother and from an early age is taught to do so; her ability to perform such tasks is taken for granted.

Boys from low socioeconomic level homes know their father in his major role: "Daddy has gone to work" and they have no contact or relationship with the types of work their fathers may be performing. Boys from such backgrounds probably understand the general division of labor in society; they see the work-world controlled and manipulated by men while at home the private world is managed and worked in by women. Therefore, boys identify themselves with the men as "workers" and not as "Daddies" because they do not see their fathers playing a parenting role. In isolated instances when boys see fathers taking care of children or helping around the house, the surrounding environment does not accept such behavior as "normal"; therefore, the boy cannot see such behavior as "real" male behavior with which he can identify. The small boy is not introduced into the work world of men by his father either through visiting his father's workplace or through discussions with his father about his work, his fellow workers, ambitions, etc.

A preschool boy, from the lower socioeconomic levels, therefore finds himself in a sociodramatic play situation in which he may want to imitate and tries to imitate his father's role; however, he does not have the minimal degree of knowledge and understanding of how a father behaves, necessary to be able to undertake such an imitation.

b. Another possible explanation for the difficulty that boys seem to have in achieving the same standard of sociodramatic play as girls could be that boys are having greater difficulties with the identification process itself at this stage in their lives. Boys are in a transition period during which they are shifting from identification with the mother to identification with masculine images.

Mowrer (1950), Parsons and Bales (1956), Lynn (1947), and others stress the early closeness of the girl to the same-sex parent (the mother), which gives her an initial advantage in progressing towards appropriate identification. The boy must shift his initial identification from his mother to a masculine role model, whereas the girl need make no such shift. Identifications learned early in life tend to be resistant to modification which would suggest that shifting from identifying with the mother to a masculine identity must be a difficult psychological process for boys.

c. A third possible explanation is that a boy is under considerably more pressure from a very early age to adopt the masculine role despite the fact that there are fewer men than women models available for identification in the immediate surroundings. Cultural mores demand that the boy child model himself after a somewhat conventional, stereotyped, abstract masculine role where the abstract quality comes about because it is out of his reach, out of his experiential sphere. Hence boys have difficulty turning to the home situation for sociodramatic themes and that proved an obstacle to the teaching of sociodramatic play in our experiment.

The soundness of this explanation was supported by observations made in the homes of children from lower socioeconomic background. Mothers and other women in the home derided and even punished any signs of feminine behavior in the young boy child from the very earliest age. The females in the home demanded and praised what was considered "male" behavior without ever clearly defining, either verbally or through example, what exactly was expected of the child. The following remarks, directed to the young boy child were frequently heard: "What do you think you are, a girl?" "Aren't you ashamed of yourself, behaving like a girl?" "Be a man, like you're supposed to be."

The male child from a low socioeconomic background lives in a world controlled by men in which he, too, occupies a superior position, enjoying a privileged status. He is rewarded for adopting a masculine role and punished for deviation. It could be assumed that this will eventually reinforce the process of moving to a wholly masculine identity. At preschool age, however, the young male suffers from a deficiency of available male role models as well as from the cultural pressures which present him an abstract (to him) male identification model to which he is to conform. We feel that this social and cultural pressure on very young boys, allowing for little or no deviation from the vaguely defined male model, inhibits the child's scope and inclination for imitation and results in a weak imitative ability reflected in poor or little sociodramatic play.

At this point it is interesting to note the social pressure that preschool children exert on the various boys and girls to conform to his or her sex role as defined by their parents was strongest and most conspicuous with regard to the boys. Although the children could accept a girl dressed in boys' trousers playing at doing "man's work" (apparently because society does not adopt a punitive attitude towards a woman undertaking male activities), they could not accept a boy dressed up as a girl or doing "woman's work."

d. In addition to what has been said, the teachers and experimental aides were all women. This is important in two ways: First, teachers and aides may have operated in the eyes of the students as "mother surrogates" who would be expected to punish the boys for engaging in women's activities. Hence, the boys could not be quite sure the teachers meant what they seemed to be saying and would resist the teaching. Second, it was much easier and more natural for the women to guide and demonstrate mother tasks for the girls than father tasks for the boys in the group. We found no preschool teacher or experimental aide guiding and demonstrating a gathering of a group of men at a local coffee house or Turkish-bath to a group of boys and this was almost certainly a weekly experience in the lives of most of the boys' fathers. The boys knew about it, but had not experienced it themselves; the experimental aides and preschool teachers were totally unfamiliar with its existence.

e. A further explanation for the predominance of girls in terms of level of sociodramatic play could be the actual play conditions of the kindergarten and nursery classroom itself. They may be more suitable to sociodramatic play episodes instigated by girls rather than those required by boys. Toys and play corners are more suitably planned to fit episodes girls might plan in imitation of the mother role than to fit episodes fitting the male role. There are doll buggies, dolls, women's clothing and shoes, kitchen utensils and equipment, all of which center of women's activities around the home. There are few men's clothing, cigarette cases and lighters, pipes, briefcases, tool kits, etc. The only play corners suitable for male role enactment are the Store corner and the Hospital corner. The Store corner can only accommodate a single shopkeeper at a time and the Hospital corner usually ends up with a flood of female doctors, nurses, mothers with their sick children, etc. overwhelming a one or two male doctors who might attempt to join them. We failed to provide special male-role objects in the experiment.

Relationship Between Age and Play Level: Hypothesis 5

Most children from high socioeconomic backgrounds evince "good" sociodramatic play at age four, which means that their play includes all the basic play elements, albeit to a lesser degree than older children. Therefore, the expectations of the study were that the younger children would achieve less than older children and the findings supported these expectations. We propose several explanations:

a. Younger children from lower socioeconomic groups tend not to have the opportunity to play with older children, as do children from the higher (European) groups. Our observations of Control Group E noted that the younger children participated in sociodramatic play *together with* the older children; whereas the younger children from Groups B and C did not have an opportunity to play with the older children in their groups. The younger children did not seem to have the courage to dare participate in the sociodramatic play episodes of the older children and would usually be passive participants, standing and watching the older children play. The older children, furthermore, tended not to accept the younger children as active participants, and used them rather for running errands and taking orders. Planned adult intervention modified this passive participation only to some extent.

b. It could be that the younger children lack basic prerequisites for engaging in sociodramatic play whereas the older children, who have been in preschool for a longer period of time, may have acquired these prerequisites. In addition to lacking specific play skills, younger children tend to lack social, intellectual and verbal skills which are necessary. Therefore the experimental approaches, A which tried to provide knowledge and understanding, B which tried to teach the play skills and C which attempted to provide both knowledge and understanding and the play skills, were insufficient to close the gap. The older children already possessed a greater stock of raw material for utilization as sociodramatic play activity than did the younger children.

c. A third explanation would be that the methodology of planned adult intervention was not tailored to fit the needs of the younger children. Perhaps it should have been administered more gradually, at a slower pace and with a great deal more time allotted to individual, younger children in the lower socioeconomic groups than to the older children. Perhaps the younger children should remain in a separate group until they reach a certain level of achievement after which they could be guided and encouraged to participate in the sociodramatic play of the older children. We would assume that under such circumstances the children would move in the same direction as those children in Control Group E (including both E and F children), where a large number of the younger children participate in the sociodramatic play of the older children and the difference between the two groups is a matter of quantity rather than quality.

It should be noted here that all of these possibilities may be working together rather than as separate options.

E. Findings and Remarks, not Directly Relevant to the Hypotheses

There were also findings which were significant and which did not relate directly to the hypotheses proposed.

The Children's Reaction to the Experimental Treatments

Throughout the duration of the experiment the researchers conducted observations in order to pick up hints concerning the improvement progress and provide feedback to the teachers. Although there was no reaction expressed in specific play activity in Group A as a consequence of the visits and other experiences, there was an increase in interest in the themes themselves. During the trips and afterwards children asked questions and discussed what they observed. They started playing with the new materials and toys as well; however, the children playing with the new things were the same as those who were playing before and they played at the same level they had been playing at before.

Improvement in play for Groups B and C was noted in the first week of the experiment, mainly in terms of the number of children engaging in dramatic play. As time went on, the improvement continued. The engagement in play seemed to be satisfying to the children as well, for there were fewer signs and outbursts of aggression.

It is both interesting and important to note that when adults began "playing" with the children, the amazed reaction of the children lasted for only the first few days. Most of the children soon joined the adults willingly and played happily along with them. On the sixth or seventh day, when the adults began to withdraw gradually from the play activity, the children did not demand their further participation, nor did they invite the adults back into their games. The fact that the adults had actively participated in the games of certain children (whose sociodramatic play lacked one or more of the essential elements) and had not participated at all in the games of other children (whose sociodramatic play had included all six of the essential elements) did not cause any special jealousy among the children, although we had expected it might. We felt that the children had accepted adult participation as a temporary measure and once they had mastered the art of playing among themselves, they felt no particular need to be dependent on the adults any further.

Another fear which we had had was that we might create a stereotype in the minds of the children; we might be encouraging them to *play like* the adults teaching them and to *speak like* the adults playing with them instead of developing their own styles and patterns. However, such mechanical imitation hardly ever showed up; the children started to play in their own way, not imitating the adults, but participating with them. They moved to play corners where the adults had not ever intervened and where they had no adult example to follow. Yet the change in the direction of better play remained apparent.

An example illustrating how the children responded within their own behavior patterns comes from a preschool in a village just outside of Jerusalem. A little girl asked her friend, "Where's your Mommy?" The friend answered, "My Mommy is going to have a baby and she's waiting for the car to come and fetch her." The adult intervened and suggested, "Let's pretend that there in the distance is the car and inside it is the doctor coming to help your mother." "No," corrected the child, "let's pretend that it's the ambulance and there's a nurse who takes my Mommy quickly, quickly to the hospital so she won't have the baby in the ambulance on the way." Here is a clear example of children not accepting the adult suggestion, when it does not agree with the reality familiar to the child. There were no hospital facilities in that village and the custom was to call an ambulance to take expectant mothers to the hospital in nearby Jerusalem; in addition there had been instances when the babies were born in the ambulance on the way to the hospital.

Degree of Improvement in Each Essential Play Element

Hypothesis 1 stated an expectation that a larger number of children would include the basic elements characteristic of "good" sociodramatic play in their own play behavior; however, there was no prediction as to which of the six elements would be included. The observations provided us detailed data in order to make such an analysis.

In both Groups B and C improvement occurred in all of the factors; that is, each of the factors was displayed by more children after the intervention than before. In Group B there was marked improvement in only four factors; in Group C it occurred in all six. The degree of improvement in each factor was in the same order for both groups. The list of elements below is rendered in order of achievement, with the factor which showed the greatest improvement being first.

  a. Imitative Role-Play
  e. Interaction
  c. Make-Believe with regard to actions and situations
  d. Persistence
  f. Verbal communication
  b. Make-Believe with regard to objects

Improvement in Factors (a), (e) and (c). The games involved large numbers of children; roles were plentiful and assignment procedure was good. External patterns of the games were imaginatively contrived; the majority of the participants identified fully with their roles. Flexible planning was noted particularly among the girls; role exchange (i.e., the shopkeeper became the shopper, etc.) was effected with ease by certain participants. It was interesting to note the amount of cooperation existing between the different play corners. There were groups playing in the Store corner, the House corner, the Clinic (Hospital)

corner, the Blocks corner, and the Bus-Driver's corner simultaneously. Children participating in these various games also
participated in the games of the others from *within* their roles;
for example, a mother with her baby and grandmother (the
"mother's" mother) would go first to the clinic to see the doctor
and then take the bus to go shopping.

Improvement in Factor (d). There was great improvement in
terms of sustaining the game. Most of the games which were
the subjects of detailed observation during the experimental
period, were broken up due to external circumstances (the
teacher announcing that play-time was over) just when it
seemed they were reaching their climax. Some grocery store
games continued for 40 minutes and Hospital games continued
for 45 minutes. The ability to carry on a game for such lengths
of time had been very rare in the play behavior patterns of
children from lower socioeconomic backgrounds prior to the
experiment.

Improvement in Factor (f). Although the improvement in verbal
elaboration of content was slight for those in Group B, it was
conspicuous enough to constitute an improvement. After the
six week experimental period, the children engaged in lively
verbal interchanges (itself an innovation), although the discussion quality was far from adequate to satisfy the demands of a
play situation. Such discussion had still not become a means
through which a child could express his personal impressions
and experiences during role-play.

Improvement in using verbalization for imitation, make-
believe and planning was much more marked in Group C. This
was especially so in the Hospital and Grocery Store corners.
Language related to these two themes constituted one of the
main ingredients for the games and verbal expression was
widely used as a means of role identification, vis. example
below.

Doctor   "Mother, you must leave your baby here in the clinic;
          she is very ill and you must bring food for her every
          day so that the nurses can feed her."

Mother   "But, it is a long way away and I cannot manage to
          come every day. What shall I do with my other chil-
          dren at home?"

Nurse	"What do you want us to do? You made the baby ill; you left her out in the rain without any clothes on."
Mother	"Give me a note and I'll take the baby to the hospital. They'll feed her there and I won't have to bring food every day."
Doctor	"I can't give you such a note."
Woman	"Don't be mean, give her a note. What's the matter, does it cost you something?"
Nurse	"Come here, let me give your baby a shot in the meantime."

Improvement in Factor (b). The improvement to set aside reality with regard to an object (let's pretend this is food, this is a plate, etc.) was very slight in Group B. Despite the planned adult intervention endeavoring to develop this factor (as with the other factors), the children still tended to look for real things or at least toy replicas of the real things they needed for their play episode. They had difficulties accepting the suggestions aimed at diverting them to using make-believe with regard to object. They did, however, show considerable, significant improvement in make-believe in terms of roles and situations ("make believe I'm a doctor and I'm examining your baby [a doll]").

Experimental Group C's results regarding this factor showed marked improvement. It was particularly evident in play behavior related to the clinic and the grocery store themes, around which the children had received supplementary meaningful impressions and comprehensible experiences. Apparently the adult intervention served to illuminate the matter for the children, enabling them to see, both physically and in their mind's eye, the many different objects with regard to their functions and the various people as they related to their jobs, the public and their co-workers. When the children became involved in these theme later on during their sociodramatic play and searched for a toy replica of one of the objects they saw on their visits, a greater number of children were prepared to accept, with relative ease (compared to those in Group B) the adult suggestion to make-believe the object. There are two main reasons for this difference.

a. Adult intervention resulted in Group C children understanding the function and various uses of the objects more clearly and explicitly, and therefore, they were able to use their understanding in an imaginative way ("Do you want a pound of sugar? Make-believe I'm weighing it out for you on the scale.")

b. Since adults working with Group C knew exactly which activities, functions and objects were viewed by the children and were receiving corollary explanations and elucidation, they were surer and bolder in their encouragement and suggestions about which objects to make-believe. The contrary was true for Group B where the adults never really knew which objects impressed the children the most and which functions had been understood during the unguided and unsupervised visits to the grocery store and clinic which were a part of their normal activities in their immediate environment.

We shall not attempt to explain the specific ranking of the elements in their achievement order; that may come as a result of the approaches and their application; or it may be determined by the psychological make-up of the children involved (looking for concrete goods; unused to verbal expression of thoughts and feelings, etc.). It is important to note that the method for Group C resulted in improvement in *all six factors* to a greater or lesser degree, even if it did not reach the level of the control group representing children from high socioeconomic levels.

3. Extent of Improvement vis a vis Short Duration of Experiment

Teaching sociodramatic play in the experimental circumstances was attempted during 45 hours spread out over a six-week period. The question must be asked why such a short experience could have had such all-encompassing effects on the play and language achievement of these children.

It is possible to consider such teaching as a sort of catalyst, tripping a sequence of activities which had been ready to go. These children were ready to perform and conform to such behavior patterns. Perhaps the sense of satisfaction afforded children from lower socioeconomic levels by sociodramatic play is the sense of well-being derived from the harmonious adjustment of a psychological structuring (the sociodramatic play behavior) to the demands and necessities of the psychological structuring of the growing, human creature. These children have an appetite for sociodramatic play just as they have an appetite for the food necessary for balanced and wholesome physical development. Even though the previous diet was deficient in the vitamins needed to stimulate the imitation of adults with whom the children identify and to express this imitation through sociodramatic play, they were able, nonetheless, to sense the nutritive value of the new diet offered them, once given the chance to taste it. Prolonged deprivation might cause such a sense to wither, but it would seem to be very much alive in these preschool children, despite their coming from lower socioeconomic homes, as described above. The children, therefore, responded to even a very short period of guidance and demonstration in the techniques and skills of sociodramatic play behavior.

The suddenness of the change and improvement in the ability of these children to engage in sociodramatic play seems to suggest that the requisite processes and essential elements existed within these children already; they simply lacked play skills which would enable them to express themselves through sociodramatic play activities. Although the children were ready to learn these skills and needed them, they had *not* learned them on their own. *Perhaps such skills cannot be learned without adult intervention.* After a certain degree of conscious development in the necessary skills, other factors required for sociodramatic play were triggered, so that the children "suddenly" became aware of and were in control of resources and abilities hitherto unexercised.

This outlook seems feasible with regard to the language achievement factor as well (see the last chapter). We did not teach the children to speak in longer sentences or to speak within the context of the play theme or to indulge in fewer repetitions or to introduce new words, etc. By helping them to engage in sociodramatic play, we *created a situation* that required the children draw on their store of scattered facts, words, concepts and experiences, that they select those (facts, words, concepts, experiences) relevant to the play situation and use them in such a way as to become a meaningful part of the play situation, both for themselves (playing particular roles) and for the others (co-creators of a common play theme). Sociodramatic play, encouraged by planned adult intervention, enables the child to utilize past and present experiences, knowledge and abilities, formerly unexploited for want of the necessary situation and techniques, in a meaningful way.

It must be noted that Group C, which attained the best results, did not reach the level of Control Group E. This is not surprising considering the fact that the six-week experimental period was applied to provide for what has been missing for several years. It is even more understandable taking into account the complex nature of sociodramatic play which utilizes many of the intellectual, social and emotional resources of the child.

The Reaction of the Preschool Teachers to Their Diagnostic and Didactic Tasks

The training of the teachers and some of their reactions were described before. We noted that most had some difficulty accepting the principle of active intervention in children's free-play activity. We were not sure if we could consider using regular preschool teachers to carry out the task of active intervention, and so therefore we will elaborate the teachers' reactions before, during and after the experiment. The questions in our minds were whether they would be able to adapt to the demands of the experiment, which were quite different from that to which they were accustomed and sometimes even contrary to the principles they had learned. We tried to use two means to evaluate the change in the teachers' attitude to and their ability to apply intervention.

a. A rating scale checked by the researcher observer. The rating scale was based on the observation of the teacher's ability to further the development of sociodramatic play in her class. This was applied two weeks after the start of the experiment, again at the end of the fourth week and finally at the end of the experimental period. Observations were made of the teachers of *all* the experimental groups in all the preschool classes included. A considerable improvement was measured between the first and final ratings of Groups B and C.

b. Written reports (free-form) of all the preschool teachers as well as structured reports (special questionnaires and rating scales prepared for this purpose) were presented at the end of the experimental period.

Below are five of the most frequent reactions found in the free-form and structured reports of the teachers when they were asked to assess their own ability and development in furthering sociodramatic play of their children after the experimental period.

a. The teachers felt themselves capable of observing and diagnosing each child's sociodramatic play level and achievement.

b. The teachers felt they had initiated different ways and means of intervention, specifically suited to help particular children to develop essential elements which were lacking in their sociodramatic play.

c. The teachers felt that the majority of the children in their classes had improved their ability to engage in sociodramatic play. The fact that some children achieved more than others was explained by the short time-span of the experiment itself. They were convinced that had they taken more time, they would have raised the level of sociodramatic play of all the children to include all six elements.

d. At the end of the experimental period the preschool teachers felt that planned adult intervention and teacher, based on an individual diagnosis of the child's sociodramatic play level was possible and useful, not only with respect to sociodramatic play but also to other activities which might be classified as artistic.

e. The teachers felt that their learning how to observe the individual child at play had taught them not only about that particular child's attainments in play behavior but also how to observe a child's behavior in relation to a larger frame of reference. It enabled them to see the child against the background of the group with greater clarity and in far greater detail.

Both the individual diagnosis and the intervention methods were applied reluctantly and doubtfully. The positive reactions at the end of the period are a result of the reinforcing effect of the intervention's success. The teachers could see the changes that had occurred in the children's play after a relatively short period of time. This, in turn, caused more creative and more intensive intervention.

Individual and group training of the teachers was designed to help them accept intellectually the demands of the experiment. Some of the different points of resistance encountered are described below.

a. The most common opposition was raised against the idea of intervening in the child's creative or artistic activities: drawing, painting, dramatic play, clay modeling, etc. All the teachers viewed any intervention in these activities as highly undesirable and possibly harmful to the natural development of the child's personality. Teachers were content to provide the children with the "right conditions": toys, space, time, and freedom from adult interference or instruction. They were convinced that these "conditions" promised a "natural" unfolding and development of the child's creative and artistic powers.

b. Another difficulty which was found among many of the teachers was a lack of knowledge and practice in evaluation of a particular achievement of an individual child or a group of children with regard to or on the basis of a specific criterion or structured frame of reference. The teachers tended to include all the children with regard to a certain behavioral trait or achievement, in a generalization based on their impressions gained from just a few of the children. For example, in one of the group discussions, the majority of teachers were able to characterize sociodramatic play on the basis of their experience with their own children, but not on the basis of their experience with their preschool pupils. When we moved on to the question of how far this sort of play exists in preschools where the majority of children are from lower socioeconomic backgrounds, many of the teachers said that the majority of the students engaged in this kind of play in their preschools. When we asked for examples, they cited them all from a very small number of children.

We suggested that the teachers visit preschools selected for Control Group E, including both low and high socioeconomic status children of European background, during a free-play period and make an exact written report on the activities in certain play areas. They could then check to see which factors, as we had previously defined them, existed in the children's sociodramatic play and which did not.

c. Some of the teachers resisted the idea of written observations. They agreed that observation was important, but the majority felt that *writing* reports and analyses and conclusions was just a waste of time. They felt they could observe and compare notes without writing anything down; thus, they could learn more and it would take less of their time away from the children.

d. During the period of actual intervention, some teachers showed a marked tendency to want to work with the group as a whole rather than with the individual children comprising the group. After being guided in the diagnostic methodology and having themselves carried out individual diagnoses, they were handed the diagnostic sheets of individual children within their classes. Some of the reactions were: "Good. We've carried out the observations and written detailed reports; we analyzed the results and each of us now has a diagnostic sheet showing the exact picture of the sociodramatic play level of each child in her class. Now we can put away these diagnostic sheets in the drawer and think of a way to develop the sociodramatic play of *all* the children in the preschool." Even after the teachers had worked with the individual children and diagnosed their individual abilities to engage in sociodramatic play, they would have preferred to rectify the individual inadequacies through *group* work and methods.

e. After a relatively short period of individual and group guidance, the teachers saw no more need for using the diagnostic sheet as a regulator and director of the development of the individual child. At this stage the reaction was that if they were to teach a child (or children), that child (or children) would automatically grow and progress and there is no need to check up or examine the results. When we asked them how we could be sure that it was our method which was developing the children's ability (and with which children was it more successful), the reaction was that they "felt" the activity was having a positive effect on *all* the children except for one or two who showed no signs of improvement and who probably never would. Such teachers were expressing the feeling that if a teacher teaches, the majority of children will learn and that there is no need to follow the teaching up with verifying observation or other means of checking results.

f.   Some teachers were unwilling to use the results of recurring tests as a basis for looking for new methods for those children not affected by previously tried approaches. The reaction seemed to be as though children who showed no improvement were either retarded or rejecting the teacher. Such teachers' feelings were approximately, "Either the methods are good, in which case they will be good for *all* the children, or the methods are no good, in which case we must not use them at all."

All of the above difficulties can be traced to the novelty of the demands that the experiment made on the teachers. Active intervention in artistic activities, individual diagnosis according to fixed criteria, written observational records, individual-oriented teaching, systematic evaluation of teaching results and experimentation with methods to reach *all* children constituted new approaches in the training and experience of preschool teachers. This does not mean that until now they worked only with groups, or that their work was guided merely by subjective impressions, but that most of them did not apply the above approaches consciously and systematically.

Despite these difficulties, most of the teachers adjusted easily and all of them became deeply involved in the research and experimental work far more quickly than was expected. They were eager to achieve objective and explicit knowledge of both the quantitative and qualitative deprivation of the children from the lower socioeconomic levels and of the most suitable methods for developing and fostering these children. The teachers quickly became skilled in observation methods and in writing detailed reports of the particular achievement of a specific child; they became skilled in intervening strictly according to the diagnostic sheet; they became curious and returned again and again to the same child or group of children to check objectively for any change. Despite the clearly defined and explicit context of the experiment in the preschools and despite the presence and participation of the experimental aide, who supervised, counseled and strictly forbade any deviations from the experimental framework, the majority of preschool teachers were extremely creative in adapting to the demands of the method to the behavior of individual children in a specific play situation. Although the best proof of a teacher's efficiency is the results of the experiment: the marked improvement in sociodramatic play of the children, nevertheless, it may be true that because of initial resistance the results do not represent the optimal possibilities of these methods.

Relationship between Socio-emotional Adjustment and Play Level

We conducted a pilot study to investigate the possibility of a relationship between socio-emotional adjustment and play level. Our expectation was that socio-emotional adjustment would have no effect. We assumed that in a group of normal children (some special cases were excluded from the experimental samples in all groups) all would have the need to play and to identify through imitation; regarding those taking advantage of intervention, we would find no relationship to level of adjustment.

Before the experiment, we asked the teachers to rate all the children using the "Rating Scale of Adjustment" (Smilansky & Shefatya, 1976) designed for use with preschool and school children. The Scale is comprised of 19 categories representing various aspects of behavior. Each category contains a number of sentences that the preschool teacher marks in order of relevance to the child; she later chooses one sentence as being most relevant to and most characteristic of the behavior of that child when compared to the rest of the children in her class. Grades in each category range from 1 to 5 with 5 denoting the highest degree of emotional adjustment and 1 the least. The numerical values used to grade the sentences are, of course, unknown to the teachers. This scale can yield both a general picture of the child's state of emotional adjustment and a picture of the state of his adjustment with regard to specific aspects of his intellectual, emotional and social behavior. For the purposes of this study, we used the grade denoting the child's general state of emotional development, because all rating were relative within each particular preschool class. The following grades were used to divide each class into five groups:

1. Children whose state of emotional adjustment fell within the average range within their class.
2. Children whose state of emotional adjustment was one grade higher than the average achieved in their class.
3. Children whose state of emotional adjustment was two grades higher than the average achieved in their class.
4. Children whose state of emotional adjustment was one grade lower than the average achieved in their class.
5. Children whose state of emotional adjustment was two grades lower than the average achieved in their class.

In the pilot study, only three levels were used: below average, average and above average (levels 2 and 3 and levels 4 and 5 were combined). Evaluation of play level was based on the same categories that served to test the relationship between play and other independent variables (IQ, sex, age): "good," "poor," and "no" sociodramatic play.

The findings agreed with our expectations. There was no relationship between play level and level of adjustment. Planned adult intervention had a positive effect on the development of sociodramatic play of children with adjustment difficulties. This fact invites further investigation—not only on the effect of adjustment on play level, but also on the possibility that sociodramatic play positively affects the level of adjustment.

The Effect of The Experiment on Verbalization during Play

In the first section of this book we compared the verbalizing during sociodramatic play activity of children from high socioeconomic background to that of children from low socioeconomic background. We found differences in several verbal criteria. In the theoretical discussion we argued that verbalization is central to the play of children from higher socioeconomic groups, serving as a tool for imitation, make-believe, planning and discussion. Therefore, we decided to examine the experimental results and look for improvement in verbalization as a by-product of improved play levels. "Improvement" is used in terms of a change in the direction of the children from the higher socioeconomic group. The linguistic superiority of children from higher socioeconomic backgrounds, which has been demonstrated in numerous studies, as well as their superiority in terms of play level, seems to justify such a procedure.

Five verbal criteria were applied:

1. Fluency—the average number of words uttered in 15 minutes
2. Length of utterance—the average number of words in an utterance
3. Length of sentence—the average number of words in a sentence
4. Contextual speech—the average number of words uttered in 15 minutes if all speech not relevant to play is excluded
5. Vocabulary range—average number of words uttered in 15 minutes with repetitions excluded

Speech samples analyzed include the verbalizations of all children who played in any sociodramatic play (including "poor" play). The material utilized for judging the play level served for the present analysis as well.

Results are presented in Table 23.

We present our results with some reservations because the data do not allow for testing significance of differences. Even so it seems worthwhile to us to present these first findings, which show promise of interesting possibilities.

a. All experimental groups remained markedly inferior to Control Group E, the children of higher socioeconomic levels.

b. Improvement in Group A was only in terms of one criterion: Fluency. There was no improvement in play level itself; it was possible that the approach applied to this group (knowledge and experiences relevant to play themes) facilitated the quantity of verbalization during play by those children who had engaged in dramatic play before the experiment even though it did not evoke sociodramatic play by additional other children.

c. There was improvement in all verbalization categories except length of utterance for Groups B and C who had shown significant improvement in play level. The improvement in fluency seems to be too slight to be accepted without a significance test.

Table 23: Verbalization Patterns During Play Before and After Intervention, by Groups

Groups	Average Number Words during 15 Min.		Average Number Words in Utterance		Average Number Words in a Sentence		Average Number Contextual Words during 15 Min.		Aver. No. Words NOT Repeated during 15 Min.	
	Before	After	Before	After	Before	After	Before	After	Before	After
A	142	177	4.0	4.1	2.6	2.8	80	81	28	30
B	137	155	3.8	3.9	2.7	3.3	78	107	26	43
C	139	156	3.9	4.0	2.5	3.5	79	124	28	46
D	146	146	4.1	4.0	2.9	2.9	80	80	30	30
E	243	—	5.4	—	4.4	—	221	—	102	—

d. The most conspicuous improvement appears in the quantity of play-related verbalization (contextual words), mainly for Group C. Also the growth in vocabulary range (words without repetition) seems to be more than pure chance for both groups.

e. Groups B and C speak in longer sentences by the conclusion of the experiment. Once again, this result must be viewed with reservations.

We can conclude the summary of results by raising a few hypotheses which need testing:

It seems likely that improvement in sociodramatic play results in an improvement of verbalization during play. It seems that this is reflected not so much in the quantity of speech as in its quality. That means that there is more play-related conversation, a utilization of a broader range of vocabulary and longer sentences. It is possible that some other aspects of verbal behavior (like the use of parts of speech) which has not been investigated in this pilot study are also affected.

Improvement of verbalization patterns during play as a result of improvement of the play level itself supports our contention that the sociodramatic play situation forces the child to draw on his resources and utilize them. We did not *teach* the child to speak more or use longer sentences during the experimental period, but it would seem that by playing on a higher level, by imitating and using verbal make-believe, by cooperating with other children and processing their use of vocabulary, the children made more use of their existing vocabularies, articulated their sentences better and concentrated more on the play theme than they had before.

3. American and English Experiments Designed to Investigate the Effects of Adult Intervention on Sociodramatic Play and on Cognitive and Socio-emotional Abilities

Since the experiment conducted in Israel, there have been other experimental studies conducted utilizing adult intervention for improving dramatic and/or sociodramatic play. The majority of these studies investigated the transfer of the effects of training in play to a large variety of related skills. Despite basic differences between the various studies in terms of the conceptualization of symbolic play and in the experimental design and process, almost all the studies report positive findings. There are no reports of negative findings.

Following is a brief description of those studies known to us, in chronological order. Other studies cited in various sources have been omitted either due to difficulties in obtaining primary source material or because of limitations in the experimental design. It should be emphasized that the studies which we have decided not to include also reported positive or at worst neutral findings.

a. Marshall & Hahn, 1967[1]

This study is the earliest work known to us that attempted to improve dramatic play experimentally. Interestingly enough, it was conducted in two university nurseries with high SES children. There were 12 matched triads of preschoolers (33-66 months), randomly assigned to one of the following conditions: doll play, fantasy training, use of toy training (with eye-hand coordination and science concept toys), and no training. Tutoring was arranged by means of active participation of a trainer and controlled for the amount of warmth and verbal interaction. The duration of the experiment was four sessions of fifteen minutes each. Results were that the group which underwent doll-play training increased the frequency of dramatic play with peers significantly; there was no increase with the other two groups. The doll-play trained children used significantly more language than the other children (friendly, neutral, aggressive verbalizing as part of acting out the dramatic role).

The study was designed to explain findings from a previous work (Marshall, 1961) which found correlations between parents' reported verbal behavior with the child (e.g., discussing topics at home which might be utilized by the child in his dramatic play) and the amount of the child's sociodramatic play

---

[1]This study was conducted independently of our first study, as evidenced by the year of publication.

as observed in nursery school. It is suggested, based on the findings, that the exposure to ideas during doll-play training fostered the use of ideas in playing with peers rather than adult warmth or attention provided during individual sessions, which also characterized the toy-training group. The following elements of the training was seen as important: verbal suggestions geared towards the child's ideas, acting out of ideas which furnished a model for the child to imitate, reinforcement of the child's contributions.

b. Freyberg (1973)

A study in the United States using children from lower socioeconomic level families as subjects, was designed to evaluate the effect of training in imaginative play on three play variables: imaginativeness of play, positive affect and concentration. It also investigated the relationship between fantasy predisposition and the improvement of play as a consequence of training.

Subjects were 80 five-year old children from New York, defined as "ghetto-school" kindergartners, whose parents had eight years of schooling or less; 8% of the families were on welfare and of the rest the head of the family was an unskilled laborer. 27% of the families had no father. Children were assigned to the experimental and control groups randomly; each group contained equal numbers of boys and girls as well as equal numbers of high and low fantasy-play children. There was no difference between the groups in terms of verbal IQ and M.A. Play behavior was assessed on the basis of written records by two observers which consisted of six five-minute pre-training protocols and twelve post-training segments. The protocols were rated on five point scales for imaginativeness, affect and concentration.

The imaginativeness scale was developed by the investigator, where the lowest level (1) implies no pretend elements and stimulus-bound play and the highest level (5) implies highly original play with many pretend elements, high activity organization and role playing and resistance to interruption by others.[2]

---

[2]Instructions and description of the scales are in Singer, 1973, pages 265-267.

The other two scales were taken from Pulasky (1973). Fantasy predisposition was evaluated by Singer's Imaginative Play Interview and the Barron Movement Threshold Inkblot Test.

Imaginative training sessions were conducted in groups of four in a room equipped with a variety of mostly unstructured materials during eight 20-minute sessions. The investigator introduced a theme and began to act it out, using the play equipment imaginatively. Children were encouraged to adopt a role, to choose play equipment and act out a character in the story. Four themes were utilized: two of them were very close to everyday experiences, the other two more remote. Children in the control situation had the same number of sessions devoted to adult-given construction activities. The emphasis was on providing a balanced experience of warmth and interest and training in a game of mastery.

Results were significant improvement of the experimental group in all three play measures with no change in the control group. Greater imaginativeness of the experimental group continued consistently during the two month post-training observation period. As expected, the high fantasy predisposition group improved more than did the low fantasy group in terms of imaginativeness and concentration. The investigator explains the considerable improvement in play as a result of the short-term training as indicating the children had the potential for more varied and complex play than they were displaying. They lacked specific techniques to actualize their potential, probably because of a lack of adult models. This interpretation was supported in findings from structured interviews conducted by Freyberg with parents of six high and six low fantasy children (1973, pages 148-150). The investigator describes the implications of the findings for preschool curriculum and points out topics for further research with more exact assessment tools, long term effects and the relationship of play to other dimensions of personality development.

c. Feitelson & Ross (1973)

A laboratory study conducted at the Center for Cognitive Studies at Harvard University aimed at clarifying the role of modelling in the emergence and level of thematic play as well as investigating the link between this type of play and performance on creativity measures. Thematic play, a broader category than dramatic play, is defined by the authors as play in which a theme is the mainspring of activity. The theme can change as play progresses, but some kind of content is always indicated. Thematic play can be carried out in solitude or in interaction with others.

Subjects were 24 white 5-6 year old children from working-class families, enrolled in public school kindergartens in the Boston area. Testing and tutoring sessions were individual; they took place in a mobile laboratory specially equipped with structured and non-structured play materials. Play behavior was recorded simultaneously on video tape and by an observer over 40 minutes (divided into quarter-minute units) and rated on an 11 point scale. The rating was subsequently collapsed into four categories of which only one, labelled combinatory play, can be regarded as equivalent to dramatic play. Creativity was assessed by three subtests from the Cincinnati Autonomy Test Battery and the Picture Completion subtest of Thinking Creatively with Pictures Test by Torrance.

Children were assigned to four groups randomly:

Play-tutoring   aimed to raise the level and amount of combinatory play and to decrease dependence on ready-made toys. Fancifulness and inventiveness were encouraged.

Toys only   children have access to the same equipment and a friendly adult, but although they were encouraged to play, they were not provided guidance.

Music-tutoring   children learn to play the tonette

Classroom only   no intervention at all.

All the children in the first three groups received ten individual tutoring sessions.

Pre-post test comparisons point to a significant rise in combinatory play for the play-tutored group only. Moreover, there was also a significant difference for the play-tutored group on one of the creativity measures (Torrance originality score) and nearly significant gains on two of the CATB subtests.

The findings support the researchers' hypothesis that some modelling is essential for developing symbolic (or thematic) play. Also an increase in this type of play is linked to performance on conventional tests measuring innovative and original behavior. They recommend further studies linking thematic play to other skills and attitudinal constructs.

d. Rosen (1974)

An intervention study was conducted to assess the effect of training in the basic techniques of sociodramatic play on different measures of social skills.

The subjects were 58 black children from low socioeconomic backgrounds from four kindergarten classes in a small, southwestern city in the United States. Two experimental classes received sociodramatic play tutoring during free-play period for a total of 40 hours. Training methods were similar to that in the Smilansky study and they included suggestions as well as active adult participation. The control group received about the same amount of time from the experimenter who led the group in various activities, showing interest and support but without any specific training.

Children were pre- and post-tested for sociodramatic play using a six-point scale (an adaptation of the Smilansky criteria) which ranged from functional play (manipulation of objects) to complex sociodramatic play (involving interaction with co-players and utilization of verbal descriptions as substitutes for objects, actions and situations). Children were also pre- and post-tested on group problem-solving tasks, on psychological distance and perceptual role taking. On the post tests another measure of role-taking skills was added: prediction of others' preferences and needs.

The experimental group gained significantly higher change scores than the control group except on psychological distance, where the difference was not significant, though still in favor of the play-trained groups. It is interesting that effectiveness in group problem-solving behavior was improved only for cooperative tasks, as expected, and not for competition tasks.

Rosen suggests the possibility that the training facilitated the evolving of a sense of competence and efficiency in problem-solving.

e. Saltz, Dixon & Johnson (1977)

A three-phase experimental study aimed to evaluate the effect of two training conditions on cognitive functioning and impulse control: employing fantasy material vs. more realistic materials (everyday experiences) and training for play enactment vs. no enactment.

It was a two by two design with four groups:

Thematic Fantasy Play (both fantasy and enactment); stories were read to the children, discussed and then roles chosen or assigned with the adult taking a key role; four to six sessions were spent on each story.

Fantasy Discussion (fantasy without enactment); children heard and discussed the stories, were asked to retell them following the pictures but did not act them out.

Sociodramatic Play (play enactment without fantasy); two main sources for play themes were common experiences such as visits to the doctor and the grocery store as well as supervised field trips of the preschool to a gas station, a fire station, the zoo, etc. Children were encouraged to describe and reenact these situations.

Control Condition (neither fantasy nor play enactment); children were given the same opportunity as the others to meet in small groups, to interact with the staff and be reinforced by them while being engaged in typical preschool activities (cutting and pasting, categorizing, etc.).

Subjects were 150 preschool, 3-4 year-old children, from lower socioeconomic level families and from various ethnic groups (black, Mexican, Detroit white and Appalachian white) in approximately equal proportions.

Training was provided for 15 minutes, three days a week through a six-month period. Children were pretested and matched for verbal IQ before beginning the program, and post-tested on a variety of tasks, measuring cognitive development and impulse control shortly after termination of the program.

Findings show that the two conditions involving play enactment (thematic fantasy play and sociodramatic play) were consistently superior to the other two conditions on most of the cognitive tasks and the impulse control task. Also, the thematic-fantasy trained group tended to be superior to the sociodramatic play condition. With regard to this second finding, it should be emphasized that in the sociodramatic play group there was no adult participation, but only discussion of experiences and encouragement to enact them. This condition resembles Group A of our experiment and not Group B. Despite this fact this group attained considerable gains as compared with the no-play control group, especially on verbal intelligence (PPVT), story interpretation, fantasy judgment test and impulse control measures.

Also post-training observations of play disclosed a much higher proportion of children from the sociodramatic play condition who engaged spontaneously in sociodramatic play with everyday experiences than the other groups (93% as compared with 57% in the other three groups). There are relatively high percentages in all the groups because of a minimal criteria—presence of symbolic enactment in any one of 20 observations.

It is interesting to note that on some measures the largest differences appeared for the above medium IQ children in both fantasy enactment groups. This finding supports our contention that cooperative enactment of symbolic roles requires a minimal level of mental ability. Maybe a more graded, individualized training program over a longer period of time could overcome this limitation.

f. Smith & Syddall (1978)

A small scale, but carefully designed study in England, controlling for the amount and quality of adult-child interaction in the experimental and control groups, which the researchers felt had not been dealt with properly in most studies.

Subjects were 14 3-4 year-old children from skilled working class and lower middle class families divided into two matched groups. Each child was pretested for level of spontaneous play (fantasy vs. no fantasy) and social participation as well as on various measures of competence.

Following assessment the children participated in a five-week summer program which included free-play activities with little adult involvement and 15 40-minute tutoring sessions by experienced preschool teachers, described (page 320):

"In play tutoring sessions the tutor aimed to initiate and maintain fantasy play in the children. This was generally done by providing a theme and suitable materials, and encouraging the children to join in. Typical themes were 'going to the seaside', 'the farm', 'the circus', 'Christmas', 'doctors', 'lion-hunting'.

In skills tutoring sessions, the tutor aimed to encourage activities with some definite end product in mind. For example, clay modelling, shape printing, painting, collage work, construction and number games, making cakes and jellies, and games involving concepts of colour, shape, size and position were used.

The tutors were asked to attempt roughly equal levels of interaction in the two conditions. They were otherwise unaware of either the theoretical rationale of the study or the assessment procedure."

An analysis of tutor-child contact, based on carefully structured observations, revealed no difference in amount of verbal contact, but a significant difference on object contact for the skill-trained group. There were some differences in contact quality, in which the play-tutored group enjoyed more suggestion and the skill-tutored group more explanation and approbation.

There were significant gains for both groups on most measures. However, while the skill-tutored group, with more intensive adult-child contact, demonstrates no advantage over the play-tutored group in any of the assessment measures (language comprehension, basic concepts, draw-a-person, dog and bone creativity test), the play-tutored group had significantly higher gains on all play-related tasks (fantasy, activity, group activity in free-play and a role-taking task).

It is interesting that the authors are reluctant to describe the merits of play-tutoring and emphasize only the differential improvement in this group in variables directly related to play-tutoring. These reservations appear also in a report by Smith (1983) summarizing the implications of this study as well as those of a larger scale replica of that study (Smith, Dalgleish and Herzmark, 1981) in which the findings pointed in the same direction. As far as we are aware this is the only study which included a follow-up testing session one term after intervention. Although achievement measures were somewhat different, there was improvement of both play-trained and skill-trained children on observational measures, such as complexity of play, attention span during activities and also on a variety of tests— language, cognitive ability and social cognition.

While the skill-trained group did not improve more than the play-trained group on any of the measures, the play-trained group gained more on several: frequency of fantasy play, more cooperative play, more gross motor activities in play and on the WPPSI geometric design subscale (one school only). These effects persisted by and large a term later as well. It should be pointed out that many of the tests where equal improvement is reported seem to be more related to skill-training than to play-training (Caldwell Cooperative Preschool Inventory in the first study and some of the WPPSI subscales and Flavell cube and card test in the second study). Thus, equal attainment on these measures and more attainment on the sociability and play measures deserve more merit than admitted by Smith.

g. Burns & Brainerd (1979)

The study was designed to reaffirm previous studies on improvement in perspective training as a result of short-term play training and to attempt an interpretation of these improvements in terms of the distinction between performance vs. competence effects.

Fifty one preschoolers from a three-day care center (socioeconomic status not specified) were randomly assigned to three conditions: the first experimental group received ten adult guided constructive play sessions of 20 minutes each with the goal of constructing some specified object, working in small groups; the second experimental group received ten sociodramatic play sessions (similar to Smilansky methodology); the control group received no special treatment.

The two experimental groups improved significantly more than the control group on a composite score of five perspective-taking tasks. Post-hoc tests by specific tasks were significant for three tests (perceptual, cognitive and affective) and nonsignificant, but in same direction for one other cognitive and one other affective task.

The group that received sociodramatic play training gained a significantly higher total perspective-taking score than the constructive-play trained group, but the difference was not significant according to subtests.

Since the gains of the play-trained subjects were found to be non-related to their pre-test scores, the authors conclude that the improvement in perspective-training cannot be regarded as performance effect. Accordingly, the gains disclose a real competence effect of training methods.

e. Dansky (1980)

A study attempting to examine the influence of sociodramatic play on two spheres of cognitive functioning:
- a. "the ability to comprehend, recall and produce meaningful, sequentially organized verbal information, and
- b. the dimension of imaginativeness or creativity." (page 42)

Subjects were 36 preschool five-year olds from lower socioeconomic background families in a day-care center in Toledo, Ohio (75% black and 25% white). Children were randomly assigned to one of three treatment conditions:

Sociodramatic play training
> children were introduced to a room with a variety of structured and non-structured equipment, and encouraged to take on roles related to a general theme suggested by the trainer (family picnic, visit to the doctor, grocery store).

Intervention was similar to that described in the Smilansky study (suggestions, adult participation).

Exploration training

children were encouraged to interact among themselves and with the trainer, but on a reality basis. Emphasis was on exploring and discussing the properties of present stimuli, utilizing description and guessing games, as guided by the questions: "What is it?" and "What can it do?" (hiding objects, group discussion on properties, etc.). The trainer actively participated in all games.

Free-play condition

in the same environment children were invited to play as they wished. The trainer answered questions but did not intervene.

Training was in groups of four, three times a week for a three-week period (a total of nine half-hour sessions for each group). Play level was evaluated through observation and rating of free-play sessions prior to intervention and a week after its termination.

The presence or absence of several behavior categories was rated during observations (6 X 40 15 sec. intervals) by two observers: role-play, object transformation, verbal communication within the context of role-play, non-verbal interaction during role-play and make-believe (a superordinate category including all of the preceding); pre-play (manipulative and other activities not related to dramatic or constructive play); and constructive play. Also the observers rated the imaginativeness of the entire play segment according to a five-point scale developed by Freyberg (1975, page 265) immediately following each five-minute observation period.

Post-treatment testing included seven tests that asses fifteen different cognitive functioning tasks; these were combined for some analyses into three composite scores: measures of imaginativeness, measures of verbal comprehension, production and organization and measures of exploration and identification of stimulus properties.

The play-trained group was superior to the other two groups in level of play as well as in the tests included in the first two composites. There was no difference in these between the two other groups.

The exploration trained group was superior to the sociodramatic play trained group in one measure only: the description of subjects (CATB curiosity box recall). It scored significantly higher on ITPA verbal expression tests as well when compared to the no-training group, but was not superior to the play-trained group.

The author states that relatively short-term training through modelling and encouragement increases the quality and the imaginativeness of children's play. Moreover, it has a significant impact on children's subsequent performance on cognitive tasks for which children received no direct training, especially relational thinking and sequential memory.

i. Udwin (1983)

This intervention study was conducted in South Africa with institutionalized children. The purpose of this study was to test the effect of sociodramatic play training on a group which was different from those previously studied: mainly emotionally deprived children who have been removed from their families because of inadequate or abusive parenting. The author found that this group of children was deficient in imaginative play as well as in social skills and positive affect when compared to home-reared children attending the same nursery school (Udwin, 1979).

Thirty four children aged 36-74 months were divided randomly into an experimental and control group with no significant difference according to sex, IQ or age. All children were assessed before and after training with a variety of measures:

a. imaginative play with criteria outlined by Singer (1973, page 266), including the rating of positive affect, concentration, aggression, interaction and cooperation with peers as disclosed during play (two ten-minute periods of free-play activities).

b. measures of imaginative predisposition (based on Guilford's Unusual/Usual Uses Test and a CAT subtest).

c. intelligence tests—WPPSI verbal scale and the Goodenough Draw-A-Man Test.

There were no significant differences between the two groups on any of the pretest measures. Training was provided in small groups for ten 30-minute sessions for both groups. However, the control group engaged in construction type activities unrelated to make-believe. The emphasis here was to provide the children with a balanced experience of warmth and interest and equal verbal input by the adult facilitator.

The sociodramatic play training aimed to provide a disinhibitory or eliciting function of modelling, rather than generate direct imitation of the tutor. Exercises and games utilized in the program were based on those described by Singer & Singer (1978), and the training was designed in three phases—first mainly sensory-awareness exercises and play with puppets, then enactment of stories read to the children and at last enactment of roles and themes originated by the children themselves.

The results revealed a significant increase in the imaginative play of the experimental group, as well as in positive emotionality, social interaction and cooperation with peers, reduction in aggression (which persisted also a considerable period after termination of the experiemnt and in different situations). It turned out that this institutionalized group reached the levels of imaginative play manifested by a group of middle-class children living with their parents.

The control group did not show corresponding changes in play.

The study also indicates that imaginative play training procedures are effective in enhancing subjects' verbal fluency and the production of imaginative material as measured by a conventional test of creativity and by a story-telling task.

The author also emphasizes the possibility of a beneficial effect of imaginative play training for the emotional and social adjustment of institutionalized children.

The data presented indicate, that following our first experimental program (Smilansky, 1968) numerous researchers have intervened in children's play activity in many subsequent studies in order to improve the quality and quantity of dramatic and sociodramatic play activity. The majority of these studies investigated the transfer effect of the play activity on a large variety of areas relevant to school behavior and achievement.

In Table 24 below all the studies are grouped together to give the reader a visual picture from which to make generalizations.

A glance at the first column of Table 24 indicates that these experiments cover a 16-year period (1967-1983). The second column indicates the range of age and socioeconomic level of the children included: between two years nine months and six years of age, from the middle and lower socioeconomic status, and from various racial and ethnic groups.

The third column needs closer examination since it describes what was done with the children. All the studies included adult intervention in the make-believe play activities of the children with the aim of improving dramatic and sociodramatic forms of play. What the adults did varied from one study to another: some discussed possible topics which could be incorporated into dramatic or sociodramatic play activity. Others concentrated on play skills and did not intervene in the content. They encouraged the children to use non-structured material, suggested partners and interaction within the framework of the theme episode, helped elaborate the theme, encouraged role adoption, etc. Still others not only introduced themes but began to act them out, encouraged the children to use the play equipment with imagination, and suggested acting out characters, etc. Others dealt with dependence of children on ready-made toys; while others looked outside the classroom for experiences which could serve as topics of dramatic and sociodramatic activities such as visits to a doctor's office, a grocery store, the fire station, etc. Make-believe itself became the topic as children in some of the studies were encouraged to engage in directed, adult-initiated fantasy or to create pretended episodes and then explain what was "pretending." Other studies described varied techniques used by the adults in order to encourage the children to take on roles, relate to certain general themes, and even made specific suggestions as to what to do in order to carry out the role more completely.

With all the variation in the process of the study and the setup of the experimental approach, the active intervention of the adult in the affairs of the child is a characteristic shared by all

Photocopy

Table 24: The Effect of Adult Intervention in Make-Believe Play on Areas Relevant to School Behavior and Achievement

Investigators	Subjects	Intervention	Gains in Play	Changes in School-Related Areas
Marshall & Hahn (1967)	2.9–5.6, Middle SES	Active participation of adults in children's play; discussion topics that might be utilized by the child in his dramatic and sociodramatic play.	+	More language used; More play with peers
Smilansky (1968)	4–6, Low SES	Active participation in child's play skills (not in content): encouraging children to use non-structured materials, encouraging children to invite others to play as partners, helping to elaborate a theme; encourage adoption of a role	+	Language criteria—quantity, quality of vocabulary; richness of vocabulary
Freyberg (1973)	5 years, low SES	Simulation of plot with pipe-cleaners; encouragement by adults: introduced the theme and began to act it out; encouraged the children to make use of the equipment imaginatively; encouraged to act out a character	+	Positive affect; concentration on imaginativeness in play activity
Feitelson & Ross (1973)	5–6, Low SES	Encouragement of fancifulness and inventiveness; decrease dependence on ready-made toys	+	Curiosity, innovative and original behavior; creativity assessment tools

Table 24: (Continued)

Investigators	Subjects	Intervention	Gains in Play	Changes in School-Related Areas
Rosen (1974)	5–6, Low SES, Black	Suggestions and active participation of adults, similar to Smilansky Study	+	Group problem-solving tasks; perspective taking; prediction of others' preferences and wants
Saltz, Dixon & Johnson (1977)	3–4.5, Low SES; mixed ethnic	Enactment of fairytales; encouragement of sociodramatic play; visits to the doctor, grocery store, fire station, etc. Encourage children to describe and reenact these experiences	+	Cognitive tasks, impulse contro; empathy, verbal intelligence, story interpretation
Smith & Syoldal (1978)	3–4 Low to Middle SES	Encouragement and suggestions by adults; imitate and maintain fantasy play in children; encourage children to join in play with others	+	More group activity; equal gains on intellectual and socio-emotional competence assessment tools as compared with skill tutored group; language comprehension; basic concepts; creativity tests; group activity; attention span; cognitive ability and socio-cognition
Golomb & Cornelius (1977)	4–4.6, Middle SES	Creating pretend episodes, prompting child to explain pretense	not tested	Conservation tasks
Burns & Brainerd (1979)	4–5	Active participation of adult	not tested	Perspective taking

Table 24: (Continued)

Investigators	Subjects	Intervention	Gains in Play	Changes in School-Related Areas
Dansky (1980)	5, Low SES, Black and White	Active participation of adult encouraging children to take on roles related to the general theme; intervention similar to that in Smilansky Study; suggesting the child do certain things related to his role	+	Assessment of imaginativeness, language—verbal comprehension, production and organization, cognitive tasks, thinking and sequential activity
Golomb & Bonen (1981)	5 – 6, Low SES	Intervention similar to Golomb & Cornelius	not tested	Conservation tasks
Udwin (1983)	3 – 6, normal & institution-alized	Variety of techniques used by adults to encourage	+	Assessment of creativity, verbal fluency (e.g., Goodenough Draw A Man Test); increase in imaginative play, positive emotionality; social interaction and cooperation with peers; reduction in aggression; emotional and social adjustment

the studies. The fourth column "Gains in Play" indicates that all groups show significant gains in their dramatic and sociodramatic play activity as the result of adult intervention.

The last column deals with the question of transfer effects of the adult intervention in children's play to related cognitive, social and emotional skills necessary for success in school. The results point to dramatic and sociodramatic play as a strong medium for the development of such cognitive and socio-emotional skills. We can summarize these results (note the last column in Table 24) as follows:

Gains in Cognitive-Creative Areas

Better verbalization
Richer vocabulary
Higher language comprehension
Higher language level
Better problem-solving strategies
More curiosity
Better ability to take on perspective of others
Higher intellectual competence
Performance of more conservation tasks
More innovation
More imaginativeness
Greater attention span
Greater concentration ability

Gains in Socio-Emotional Areas

Playing more with peers
More group activity
Better peer cooperation
Reduced aggression
Better ability to take on perspective of others
More empathy
Better impulse control
Better prediction of others' preferences and desires
Better emotional and social adjustment

Summary

Our experiment in furthering sociodramatic play of children from low socioeconomic levels was described in detail; in addition a series of other studies experimenting with imaginative play training were described briefly. Our purpose was not to provide a review of the field, nor do we pretend to have given a balanced review of the research studies present. The aim of this chapter was to present solid research evidence about the effectiveness of training in make-believe play and the ability to generalize from our findings. Moreover, the majority of the studies presented in this chapter went one important step further, they tested the transfer effect of training in imaginative play. The significance of these studies is twofold: they underscore the educational value of the training for the development of play ability; they also lend empirical support to the theoretical contention about the significance of sociodramatic play behavior for the child's development in a variety of spheres relevant to school behavior and achievement.

Chapter Six: An Integrative Overview and Implications for Further Research, Early Childhood Education and Teacher Training

In the preceding chapters an attempt was made to clarify and emphasize the significance of sociodramatic play for child development and early childhood education. We
—described and analyzed the complex and manifold nature of this type of play behavior.
—discussed the rationale regarding sociodramatic play as one of the most important milestones of early childhood.
—presented research studies which point to basic differences among groups of children in terms of their dramatic and sociodramatic play behavior, including the theoretical points of view which attempt to explain these differences.
—detailed experimental studies which demonstrated the feasibility and effectiveness of adult intervention in promoting make-believe play of children aged 3–7 years.
—reviewed empirical data testifying to the usefulness of sociodramatic play as a tool for promoting child development in a variety of cognitive and socio-emotional fields.
—formulated a reliable and valid rating scale for evaluating dramatic and sociodramatic play behavior and described procedures for its use.

In this chapter the major issues previously discussed will be summarized in an integrative manner and their implications for future research, early childhood education and teacher training will be discussed.

223

1. Summary of Major Issues, Based on Empirical Evidence

—Sociodramatic play is an important behavior pattern. It utilizes a wide spectrum of the young child's ability, skills, knowledge, interests and affective resources, and in turn provides an opportunity for enriching these further by means of interaction with peers. Sociodramatic play is a micro-world of active experiencing of social roles and relationships.

—Despite the probably universal tendency of 3–7 year-old children to imitate the activities of significant others, it cannot be taken for granted that this tendency will develop into genuine dramatic and sociodramatic play activity. There are children who engage in play at a highly elaborated level for long periods of time, indoors and on the playground, while there are others who never play or, if they do play, remain at a very concrete level that comprises merely sensory-motor manipulation of toys. Some differences might be due to individual preferences, but empirical evidence points to cultural factors (see details in Chapter Three). Certain cultural groups seem to encourage this form of play from a very early age; in other groups, however, this type of play behavior is not the norm. Regardless which group variables are related to sociodramatic play and which are not, it is clear that sociodramatic play behavior is highly influenced by environmental factors. Evidence supporting this contention comes from various ethnic and socioeconomic groups.

—Sociodramatic play can be taught in preschool with relatively little investment of time and effort. Since the capacity for symbolic representation develops at an early age, the prerequisites for developing sociodramatic play are there by the time most children enter a formal educational framework. The task of the teacher in teaching how to play is essentially facilitative: suggesting the legitimacy of this form of play, providing some basic techniques of communicating make-believe, demonstrating the various possibilities, etc. Experimental studies with very different methods yielded amazingly quick and large-scale changes in dramatic and sociodramatic play behavior in a variety of settings and with various populations.

—Improving dramatic and sociodramatic play improves cognitive and socio-emotional skills. This fact is supported by rich experimental data with a variety of intervention methods, evaluation tools and populations (see details in Chapter Two). These studies indicate the relevance of play for school adjustment. Aside from correlational evidence, there are experimental studies now available suggesting the direction of the correlations. Sociodramatic play not only utilizes cognitive and social skills, but this type of play is also a means for improving and enriching cognitive, socio-emotional and academic skills. (see details in Chapter Five).

Before discussing the implications of the above statements, it is necessary to respond to doubtful or critical comments about our work and that of others which various researchers in the field have raised.

a. Some researchers challenge our contention about socioeconomic differences in sociodramatic play because the issue of socioeconomic status was confused with ethnic background. We don't deny the facts, we only disagree with their significance. We don't claim that any one specific factor is responsible for the group differences found in Israel and in the United States. The point is that there are environmental influences, probably cultural factors, that work through the familial environment of the child. Whenever a teacher encounters a child or group of children who don't engage in sociodramatic play on a level which enables growth, she should be aware of her duty to provide what the family either did not or could not provide effectively.

b. Another criticism deals with the circumstances in which socioeconomic differences were evaluated. The argument is that the setting, the toys or the play topics were unfamiliar or threatening to children from lower socioeconomic levels. In our work this was by no means the case. All children were observed in a free play situation in the same kindergarten where they spent five hours every day for at least the five-month period prior to that in which the structured observations took place. Most of these children were in similar settings more than a year. The argument could hold for some of the other studies where observation took place in laboratory conditions. However, in most of the work reported from the United States (see Chapter Five), evaluations of children's dramatic and sociodramatic play took place in a free and familiar setting.

c. Some criticism was raised about the effectiveness of intervention, especially about the claim for improvement in cognitive and social skills, on the grounds that the control groups were often "no treatment" groups. This was neither the case for our experiment nor for the studies cited in detail in Chapter Five. It should be added that the claim of "no treatment" control groups is not justified for other studies as well since all experiments were conducted in settings that were designed to provide enriching activities throughout the day. In no case were experimental children compared to groups with no educational activity.

It should be emphasized that the effect of cultural factors on sociodramatic play is well-founded only with regard to children aged 3–6 or seven. Also the feasibility and effectiveness of intervention as a means of promoting sociodramatic play is established only for these age levels as well. Little is known about younger children (age 1–3) on these issues.

2. Implications for Future Research

Keeping present knowledge about sociodramatic play in mind, it would seem important to point out areas of theoretical and practical importance that have not received adequate attention in past research. Since research into socioeconomic differences as well as intervention studies have concentrated on children ranging in age from 3–6 years, there is little known about earlier ages. It is important to know if socioeconomic status is related to dramatic and sociodramatic play even at the earlier age levels and for which play criteria. This could suggest intervention at even earlier stages, adapted according to the needs and individual characteristics of the young child. Follow-ups of early intervention studies might indicate long-term effects of early intervention, not only in terms of play behavior but also in terms of other behavior patterns.

Studies of early formative stages of dramatic play have concentrated mainly on object use and imitative actions. There is no systematic research on verbalization during solitary or social make-believe for ages one–three. Observation of middle-class children reveal a great deal of verbal imitation and declaration of pretense even for very young children.

Studies of verbal output during sociodramatic play are rare for the age range of 3–6 years as well. Any investigation of the characteristics of verbalization during play activities should concentrate on a variety of areas including content, linguistic properties, and function of language in terms of developing and sustaining the play. Studies concentrating on these issues might contribute important information on the developmental function and significance of dramatic and sociodramatic play. In addition a study of the verbal output as well as observation of other behavioral characteristics expressed in the course of sociodramatic episodes, compared with behavior in other play and non-play contexts, might clarify the role of sociodramatic play for socio-emotional adjustment. Important dimensions for study would be pretended positive and negative emotions, complying with limitations imposed by the role, impulse control, problem-solving behavior, leadership style, etc. On all these issues there is only sparse descriptive data.

Another important direction for further research concerns the relationship between the level of sociodramatic play ability and a variety of other variables—concurrent characteristics of the child, future school adjustment, parental correlates. All of these should be investigated with proper control for socioeconomic status. Several topics are of special interest:

—What characterizes "good players" as opposed to "poor" or "no" players? Studies cited earlier indicate better social adjustment. In terms of future correlates, the only study known to us points to higher school adjustment for good players. Replication for these findings is necessary, as well as establishment of additional criteria for measuring adjustment and achievement. Longitudinal studies would provide most valuable information. Little is known about parental correlates of play (aside from socioeconomic status). Studies should assess parents' attitudes toward make-believe play and forms of positive or negative reinforcement for pretend play in the form of toys, equipment,

actual participation, etc. Also general child-rearing attitudes should be considered as a correlate.

—Another interesting area for study would be the influence
of the media on sociodramatic play roles and behavior,
especially from a developmental perspective. At what age
do elements from the media begin to appear in the children's play? What characterizes children who adopt roles
based on television programs in terms of play level, intelligence and socio-emotional adjustment? Is the attraction to
roles and topics from the media long-lasting or does it fade
fairly rapidly.

—It seems important to learn more about the developmental
sequence and dominance of different forms of play. In
previous chapters we argued that dramatic and sociodramatic play, as a unique type of play behavior, does not
represent a stage between functional play and games with
rules. Symbolic play has its own developmental course that
runs parallel with the development of other types of play.
This content can be substantiated by careful observational
studies that should be conducted in natural settings with
abundant materials for distinguishing between constructive and symbolic play and games with rules. Observing
children's preferences at different age levels, their performance level, time spent on each type of play, and the
content and quality of verbalization during play might provide extremely valuable data about trends in play development.

3. Implications for Preschool Education

The question that should be raised at this point is how to
explain the fact that the knowledge accumulated on the importance of dramatic and sociodramatic play was not translated
into preschool educational practice? Studies point to a general
neglect of symbolic play at the preschool level and a growing
tendency toward formalized and structured learning activities
disguised as "play" which often disregards basic developmental
needs and inclinations of young children (Elkind, 1988).

Although all preschool and kindergarten settings include some equipment designated as "doll play" (often of impressive quality and quantity), activities around the "doll corner" or "house" corner are not regarded as an integral element of the curriculum, are not encouraged by the teachers and serve mainly as an option for children who have finished with some other task that is believed to be "really" important. Dramatic and sociodramatic play are perceived as convenient for children's relaxation after meaningful activities (see Appendix B).

This attitude is communicated in various ways to the children who, in spite of it, are attracted by these play corners, especially if they are of middle class background. There seem to be forces stronger than the teachers' attitudes at work!

Our present knowledge about the significance of dramatic and sociodramatic play for cognitive growth and academic success, demands a radical change in attitudes as well as in daily preschool and kindergarten practice, at least for the age-range of 3–7 years.

The following suggestions or points should be stressed:

—"Sociodramatic play" "free play" "doll play" "make-believe play" should be included as a central element in the daily schedule of the preschool and kindergarten curriculum. All children in the classroom should be invited from time to time (at least twice a week) to participate in pretend play, indoors and outdoors, with clearly declared expectations that they will cooperate with others and engage in enacting a theme for a certain period of time. Children who hesitate, manipulate materials, wander about, etc. should be helped by the teacher through suggestions and other types of gentle intervention. It is the teacher's task to see to it that each child engage in some role-play, developing ever growing levels of elaboration during the school year.

In order to be able to help the child develop his dramatic play ability, it is essential that teachers should use some evaluation tool and procedures to diagnose the child's present state and plan and follow through further progress.

—It is important that intervention should be skill-centered and not content-centered. The teacher has to help the child to develop skills that will enable him to express the content that interests him in his play and not to impose on him roles and themes from outside sources. The child's choice of toys, his declarations of role ("make believe I am the doctor") or a direct question might indicate his preferred content areas and the theme to be encouraged and enriched by the teacher.

Experience indicates that there is no risk of distorting or suppressing children's make-believe play if adult intervention is aimed toward sociodramatic play skills and adapted to the child's present state of play development. Rather, adult suggestions and intervention have a facilitative effect that results in dramatically rapid progress.

—Equipment and toys, while not of great importance in and of themselves for children engaging in sociodramatic play, do have a facilitative effect on sociodramatic play especially for poor players. A new toy can inspire roles neglected before or may trigger poor players to begin playing a shared role. Intervention with non-players might start by providing a new toy that would arouse associations with a theme in which the child had previously shown an interest.

Therefore, equipment for make-believe play should be diverse but in small quantities. Large quantities of toys tend to encourage children to manipulate them. It is important that a new toy or new non-structured material should be introduced, if possible once a week. However, the teacher should be aware of the fact that good sociodramatic play is based on substitutive behavior which demands a gradual move away from real objects toward make-believe using non-structured materials, body gestures and words.

—The discussion of intervention in sociodramatic play has focused mainly on socioeconomic differences in play behavior. It should be emphasized here that we observed sociodramatic play of children from middle and high socio-economic backgrounds as well. Most of these children, but not all, engaged in quite a highly elaborated level (Marshall and Hahn, 1967; Smilansky, 1968). Whatever the reasons for poor play, it is the teacher's duty to help each child to acquire the skills necessary in play behavior which will enable him to elaborate themes the child wishes to experience through pretend role-playing.

—Stressing the inclusion of sociodramatic play as an integral part of the preschool curriculum does not mean neglecting other important areas. In preschools and kindergartens with a developmental orientation there is a time and place for diverse activities—creative as well as more formal, however, with a proper balance adjusted to the needs, interests and abilities of young children. We do believe that the adult has a central role of intervention not only in cognitive, academically oriented areas (Smilansky and Shefatya, 1979), but also in all creativeexpressive activities of the child, such as drawing, working with clay, play, etc. (Mooney and Smilansky, 1973; Smilansky, Hagan and Lewis, 1988). But it is important that intervention and adult guidance in all areas (cognitive, academic, creative, expressive, etc.) should be matched to the child's needs at each stage of his development, should utilize the child's spontaneous inclinations and preferences and lead him gradually to higher levels of performance in each area.

The natural tendency of young children for imitation and pretense, even if manifested on the most concrete level, offers a unique opportunity for enrichment and growth while building on processes from within.

4. Implications for Teacher Training

The fact that sociodramatic play does not receive proper attention in the preschool and kindergarten educational system is at the very least surprising considering the massive body of theoretical as well as empirical literature on the subject. One possible explanation for this situation is the fact that most research during the past 20 years which demonstrates the value of sociodramatic play for promoting abilities in a variety of areas was conducted in the form of small-scale experimentation, mostly by sophisticated researchers and senior educators. Research findings are slow to reach the field. The experiment conducted in Israel and described in this book is the only one to our knowledge which was carried out by regular preschool teachers after a short training period and in which a large-scale intervention strategy was implemented. However, this experiment did not cause schools in Israel to include sociodramatic play as a central ingredient of the official preschool curriculum, despite the fact that many teachers who had participated in the study reported they were continuing the program several years after the study had been carried out.

It seems that the realization of the pedagogical opportunities offered through the promotion of sociodramatic play depends on changing attitudes at the teacher-training level. Advocates of structured curricula tend to overlook the learning potential of sociodramatic play and regard it as just "play for the sake of relaxation"; those who uphold classical developmental schools of thought and believe that provision of proper settings and encouragement is sufficient for the child's growth, regard intervention as neither necessary nor desirable. Since pretend play as well as drawing, working with clay and other modes of creative expression are regarded as important mainly for their emotional valance, most teachers regard adult intervention in these activities as disruptive.

Our 1987 survey on the attitudes and practice with regard to sociodramatic play of teachers in the United States and Israel indicates the ambivalence felt towards play (see Appendix B for details).

The major findings of this survey are as follows:

1. All teachers in both countries reported that there is an equipped "house" corner in each preschool class.
2. The vast majority of the teachers in both countries did not expect all children to play in these "house" corners.
3. 90% of the teachers did not regard sociodramatic play to contribute to the children's future learning and school readiness; the remaining 10% perceived the value of sociodramatic play in terms of socio-emotional adjustment.
4. About half of the teachers rejected the idea of any kind of encouragement or intervention in children's play.
5. None of the teachers knew how to evaluate sociodramatic play except for anecdotal descriptions
6. None of the teachers reported having studied assessing and facilitating sociodramatic play. Only a few Israeli

teachers had some experience in such areas during their practice teaching period.

These findings reflect the fact that play in general and socio-dramatic play in particular seems to receive only negligible attention in a teacher's initial as well as inservice training (Bowman, in press; Globman in press). Very few colleges and universities offer courses on make-believe play.

Teacher education on Sociodramatic Play should include familiarity with the empirical studies of the last two decades, acquaintance with different observation and evaluation methods; and practice in intervention methods[1]. To be efficient, teacher training programs should stress several differentiations in regard to Sociodramatic Play , which regretfully are not always made explicit in the relevant literature, a fact that often obscures the issues discussed. We will point out here the differentiations we regard as most important:

1. A clear distinction should be made at the theoretical level between the early stages of solitary pretend, when symbolic play elements are the manifestation of the child's growing representational ability, and between later stages where the emphasis is on the actualization of this human capacity for pretend in Sociodramatic Play together with other abilities at the service of basic intellectual social and emotional needs of young children.

2. Sociodramatic Play should be differentiated from other forms of fantasy behavior as well as from dramatization of stories or socio-drama. Little is known on the relationship between different types of fantasy, but there is an important distinction between dramatic and Sociodramatic Play and other forms that should not be overlooked The dominant and unique elements of Sociodramatic Play seem to be the self-imposed restriction of adherence to real life behavior and events, a feature which in a way contrasts other forms of free-floating fantasy that come from within as well as different forms of dramatization and fantasy that are suggested from outside.

---

[1]Griffing (1983) presents an outline and useful suggestions for furthering Sociodramatic Play in the classroom, based on her experience in teacher training.

3. Observational and evaluation techniques should distinguish between the presence and level of elaboration of Sociodramatic Play and between other aspects of behavior manifested during play. The procedures presented in this book stress Sociodramatic Play per se, on it's own value. However, there are also many additional important dimensions—some of which were dealt with by other researchers—emotional climate, social standing and leadership styles, aggression, etc. All these are important issues, as long as the subject of interest is clearly defined.

4. At the intervention level, the most important distinction concerns the purpose of intervention. It is our belief that supported by many empirical studies, that Sociodramatic Play in itself is instrumental in promoting a variety of intellectual and socio-emotional targets. Therefore, the major aim should be to secure that the child's play repertoire contains all basic components (skills) of Sociodramatic Play as outlined in this book and he has plenty of opportunity to actualize them. Intervention in play is not an end in itself, it is a means for bringing the child to a point where he is able to develop and sustain an elaborated play theme, and then to let go.

However, in addition to promoting the child's Sociodramatic Play ability, intervention in play can be utilized as a mean for achieving a variety of specific and educational goals in a nonformal and enjoyable manner.

Teachers should be made aware of these possibilities and encouraged to experiment with different types of methods to achieve well defined goals. Sociodramatic Play can be a most effective way of promoting also exceptional and handicapped children.

According to our experience, even a short period of training is relatively effective with preschool teachers, especially since the dramatic change that takes place in the children's play behavior has a reinforcing effect. However, in order that the teacher be able to act autonomously and creatively much more is required at the theoretical as well as the practical level, in initial teacher education as well as in-service training and guidance in this field.

It is clear today, that without some kind of active intervention, a large proportion of children will not have the benefit of this type of play-experience, especially those children who did not benefit from intervention in their homes. Providing in the kindergarten equipment and encouragement to play "make-believe" is not going to cause substantial progress. Much more is needed, and it is time to do something without delay.

Appendix A:
A Criterion Referenced Scale for Assessing Dramatic and Sociodramatic Play
(Ages 3–8 years)

1. Introduction

There is much evidence that sociodramatic play behavior is of crucial significance for the child's cognitive, social and emotional development. Most children between the ages of three and seven (and even above) can be observed taking on roles and developing sociodramatic play-themes as a cooperative enterprise and enjoying intensive interaction centered around the play theme(s) over a long period of time.

However, it was found that there are individuals and groups of children—especially, although not exclusively, those from different cultural backgrounds and/or low socioeconomic status—who do not engage in sociodramatic play even if provided opportunities to do so in their preschool classes. Many of these children show interest in role-playing or in manipulating toys designed for make-believe play, but they seem unable to enact a role and develop a play-theme.

There are several research studies which demonstrate the effectiveness of educational intervention in terms of helping non-players to actualize their need for make-believe and thereby to profit from the developmental benefits of sociodramatic play behavior (as elaborated in Chapter 5).

The Smilansky Scale for Evaluation of Dramatic and Sociodramatic Play was designed to serve as a diagnostic tool for assessing the level of the child's dramatic and sociodramatic play. Such a scale can serve research purposes as well as provide a basis on which educational intervention can be determined and focused.

2. Rationale for Designing the Scale

Criteria and procedures for the evaluation of dramatic, symbolic, make-believe, or pretend play have been developed only for very early stages of infant play (Belsky and Most, 1981; Fenson and Ramsay, 1980; Nicolich, 1977). Dramatic and sociodramatic play for older age groups was assessed mainly in terms of the symbolic elements, such as imaginativeness (Singer, 1973; Tower, 1979), transcendence (Pulasky, 1973) or in terms of behavioral characteristics expressed during play, such as affect, mood, aggression, concentration, language, etc. (Freyberg, 1973; Marshall and Hahn, 1967; Singer, 1973).

Dramatic and sociodramatic play is indeed a multifaceted type of behavior which provides the observer an opportunity to assess a wide range of the child's behavioral repertoire. But none of the behavior traits mentioned above can provide us categories useful for diagnosing the child's level of play itself.

Our aim was to establish criteria for the assessment of those elements that define the unique aspects of sociodramatic play and constitute an integral part of such play behavior.

Six elements that characterize dramatic and sociodramatic play were derived on grounds of the descriptive definition of sociodramatic play behavior (as elaborated in chapters 1–6):

1. Imitative Role-Play. The child undertakes a make-believe role and expresses it in imitative action and/or verbalization.
2. Make-Believe objects, movements or verbal delarations are substituted for real objects.
3. Make-Believe in regard to actions and situations. Verbal descriptions are substituted for actions and situations.
4. Persistence in the play episode (for some period of time).

5. Interaction. There are at least two players interacting within the context of a play episode.
6. Verbal Communication. There is some verbal interaction related to the play episode.

The first four elements might be present in solitary play. The last two are, by definition, only found in sociodramatic play. We cannot state any order of importance in the six elements. It seems that each is essential for the development of such play and to some extent they are interdependent. The richness of the play, however, depends not only on the presence of all six elements, but also on the extent to which they are utilized and elaborated. For example, it is different if a child cooperates with a whole group or with only one other child; there is a difference if a child only occasionally uses make-believe in order to create and describe a nonexisting situation or if his play is full of such imaginative creations.

The Smilansky Scale for Evaluation of Dramatic and Sociodramatic Play provides guidelines for assessing the presence or absence of each category as well as the level of utilization.

3. Description of The Smilansky Scale for Evaluation of Dramatic and Sociodramatic Play

A. Procedures

Evaluation of the child's play level is based on written records of the child's verbalizations and activities during a certain period of time: (a 30-minute period divided into 6, five-minute units; or a 20-minute period divided into 4, five-minute units; etc). The observations can be conducted in the play areas of the preschool class as well as in a more structured setting. For research purposes the structured procedure is imperative and one observer is assigned to each of the four children playing. For educational diagnosis the natural setting is adequate. In both situations the children are invited to play make-believe (the teacher refers to this explicitly, using whatever terms are familiar to the children) and are encouraged to continue playing for half an hour. Following is a list of play materials that were available to the children during our observation sessions.

Equipment Available During Observation of Sociodramatic Play

Housekeeping:

Stove, sink, refrigerator
Toy dishes, pots and pans
Table, 3–4 chairs
Telephone
Magazine (on table)

Doll bed
Two dolls
Doll blanket
Doll mattress

Dress-up Clothes:

Hats, purses for girls
Hats, jacket, sweater for boys

Tool Kit; Accessories:

Tools: screwdriver, pliers,
    hammer
    flashlight
Toolbox, 2–3 pieces of wood

Lunchbox, thermos
Wheel

Unstructured equipment:

Cardboard tubes, assorted sizes
Length of plastic rope
Assorted blocks, pieces of wood
    (scattered around in the room)

Newspaper
Scissors
Some crayons
2–3 large cardboard
boxes

Grocery store:

Cash register

Table, chair, table or shelves for
    grocery items
"STORE" sign

Large assortment of
    empty boxes,
    tin cans, etc.
    (with label)
Bags to put the
groceries in

Nurse-Doctor area:

Assorted Nurses' hats, apron	Stethoscope, ear instrument
Doctor's headband (light), coat	Telephone
Nurse Kit: First-Aid box, pill bottles, pieces of white cloth	Table, chair
	"DOCTOR" sign

B. Play Observation and Scoring

Scoring of the child's play level is based on the six categories that are considered integral elements of good sociodramatic play behavior. Ratings of 0, 1, 2, or 3 are assigned to each element.

0 = the element is not present

1 = the element is present but to a limited degree

2 = the element is present to a moderate degree

3 = the element is present consistently and in many situations during the child's play.

Each element is rated according to the above system for each five-minute observation unit and then an overall summary score is calculated.

a. Sample Form for Observation and Scoring

Observer's Name: _____ Place: play-ground classroom laboratory Date: _____

Names of children playing: 1) Linda 2) Tommy 3) Mary
Subject of this scoring: <u>LINDA</u>

PLAY ELEMENTS: **RATING:**   **OBSERVATIONS:**

PLAY ELEMENTS:	0	1	2	3	1st 5 minute Interval
a. Takes on a role					The teacher invited three children to the play-corner & said: *"Play here together any way you want."* Linda looks at the clothes in the box, puts them in another box, selects a dress and tries it on. Puts on another dress & hat and says to Tommy: *"I will be mommy, will you be the daddy?"* Tommy: *"Yeah!"* Linda gives Tommy a man's jacket: *"Here daddy, I will help you put it on."* Tommy takes a hat & puts it on his head: *"I am the daddy."* Linda sets the table: *"Are you ready to eat, honey?"* Tommy: *"Yeah!"*
b. Make-believe with objects					
c. Make-believe w/actions & situations					
d. Persistence					
e. Interaction					
f. Verbalization					

PLAY ELEMENTS:	RATING:				OBSERVATIONS:
	0	1	2	3	2nd 5 minute Interval
a. Takes on a role					Linda: *"Do you like bacon & eggs?"* Tommy: *"Just bacon."* (Sits down and pretends to eat.) Linda: (To baby doll) *"Sally, you want some eggs?"* (Takes from Tommy's plate & feeds the doll.) Tommy pretends to eat. He uses the toy-bottle. He pours it until it looks like empty: *"Hey! We need more syrup. I want more pancakes too."* Linda: *"Oh!"* (gives him the doll): *"I will make some more, you feed Sally."* Tommy looks at the doll, then pretends to feed her. Puts her down.
b. Make-believe with objects					
c. Make-believe w/actions & situations					
d. Persistence					
e. Interaction					
f. Verbalization					
	0	1	2	3	3rd 5 minute Interval
a. Takes on a role					Linda: *"I can't find anymore pancakes. Can you, Tommy, get some in the store?"* Tommy: *"O.K."* Linda: *"Put on the hat & coat, it's cold. Use the car, it will take you fast."* Tommy takes the steering wheel, touches the chair: *"Pretend this is my car."* Sits on chair (car) and makes *"Vroom! Vroom!"* sounds. Linda: *"Don't forget to put your seat belt on."* Tommy: *"I won't."*
b. Make-believe with objects					
c. Make-believe w/actions & situations					
d. Persistence					
e. Interaction					
f. Verbalization					
	0	1	2	3	4th 5 minute Interval
a. Takes on a role					Tommy pretends to drive and he comes to the store. Mary arranges the boxes, sits in the store and plays with the cash register. Tommy: *"I want to buy a pancake."* Mary gives Tommy a box and says: *"We have a special on birthday cakes. You buy one?"* Tommy: *"Umm. Yeah! How much?"* Mary: *"3 dollars."* Tommy: *"Here."* (gives pretend money). Linda: *"Did you get the pancakes?"* Tommy gives more pretend money to Mary. Mary puts the money in the cash register.
b. Make-believe with objects					
c. Make-believe w/actions & situations					
d. Persistence					
e. Interaction					
f. Verbalization					
	0	1	2	3	5th 5 minute Interval
					play continues . . . .

b. Summary—Diagnostic—Record of Child's Socio Dramatic Play During 30 Minutes

Child's Name _____ Age _____ Sex _____

Observer _____ Date _____ Teacher _____

CHILD'S SCORE IN EVERY PLAY ELEMENT DURING TIME INTERVAL

DRAMATIC SOCIO-DRAMATIC ELEMENTS	I Imitative Role-Play	II Make-Believe w/Objects	III Make-Believe w/action-situtations	IV Persistence in Role-Playing	V Interaction w/Others	VI Verbal Communication	Total Score for each Interval	Kind of Role Child Plays (mother, doctor, etc.)
POSSIBLE SCORE	0 – 3	0 – 3	0 – 3	0 – 3	0 – 3	0 – 3	0 – 18	
child's scores								
1st 5 min. play interval								
2nd 5 min. play interval								
3rd 5 min. play interval								
4th 5 min. play interval								
5th 5 min. play interval								
6th 5 min. play interval								
TOTAL SCORE—POSSIBLE								
for 30 minutes play	0 – 18	0 – 18	0 – 18	0 – 18	0 – 18	0 – 18	0 – 108	
child's total score								
MEAN SCORE—POSSIBLE								
for 30 minutes play	0 – 3	0 – 3	0 – 3	0 – 3	0 – 3	0 – 3	0 – 18	
child's mean score								

c. Graph—Child's Mean Score in Each Socio Dramatic Play Element During 30 Minutes

Childs' Name _____   Observers' Name _____

Dramatic & Socio-dramatic play elements	I Imitative Role-Play	II Make-Believe w/Objects	III Make-Believe w/actions & situations	IV Persistence in Role-Play	V Interaction w/others in S.D.P.	VI Verbal Communication
Child's Mean Score 3						
2						
1						
0						

d. Evaluation Categories and Rating Guidelines

I. Imitative Role-Play

The child undertakes a make-believe role and expresses it in imitative action and/or verbalization. He enacts the character of a person (or animal) or other than himself in another context.

Rating Guidelines

3 Role-play is highly elaborated. Carries out many different ideas; imitation of voices, gestures, posture.
2 Role-play to a moderate degree. Child enacts one or more roles with some elaboration within the five-minute period.
1 Role-play is present but there is little or no elaboration.
0 Role-play is not present.

Notes

The dimensions of role-play are primarily those of elaboration, involvement and the amount of role-play. A child who does a great deal of role-play in five minutes can get a score of 2 although he may not be persistent in any one role. Persistence is scored separately. At least 1 is scored for the presence of role-play: it is considered to be present when there is a (brief) sequence of acts indicating the enactment of a theme; i.e., there is one or more of the following factors:

a. Child announces role and carries out at least one act associated with that role.
b. Child wears a garment or carries equipment associated with the role and performs at least one action associated with that role; i.e., puts on the stethoscope and doctor's hat and listens to own, doll's or another child's heart.
c. Child carries out at least two role-associated actions other than role announcement or wearing garments; i.e., picks up wheel, turns it and says "car."
d. Observer interpretation of behavior as role-play is inserted in the body of the protocol.

Role announcement alone, wearing a garment alone, and single imitative acts, such as pretending to listen or call on the telephone or pretending to hammer two blocks together or listening to a doll's heart with a stethoscope are not considered imitative role-play for our purposes.

In order to rate role-play as 1 or more there must be *some* involvement or real intention to play. A child "sits at the cash register, asks Ray if he wants groceries. . . . They laugh, get up and start to chase each other around." This is not role play. However, if children really carry out a play episode sequence, they can be silly and still get 1 or 2 for role-play.

II. Make-Believe with Objects

Toys, unstructured material, gestures, verbal declarations are substituted for real objects. A toy being used in a way other than intended (a cash register is used as a typewriter or a screwdriver is used as a nail) is also make-believe with objects.

Rating Guidelines

3 The child employs some combination of the actions described above extensively while enacting a role or roles. The child uses words and actions referring to or substituting for objects. The use of toys alone, no matter how extensive cannot be rated 3.

2 The child uses some gestures or words as a substitute, either with or without toys, but usually in addition to toys. The use of toys and one pretend action is usually rated 1; the use of toys and a few pretend actions would be 2.

1 Slight use of one or more of the actions listed above. This need not be within an episodic context, i.e., the child makes an imaginary phone call to someone present (or not).

0 No use of any of the actions listed above (no make-believe with objects).

Notes

Simple labelling of objects (store items, for example) is not make-believe with objects. If a child takes groceries to the cash register to check them out or otherwise uses them in enacting a scene, then it is make-believe with objects. Using clothing is not make-believe with objects.

III. Make-Believe with Actions and Situations

Verbal descriptions are substituted for actions and situations. This refers to verbal behavior only.

Rating Guidelines

3 Extensive and very imaginative use of make-believe ("Let's have a picnic. You pack the lunch. We have to go in the car. Be careful! The eggs will break.")
2 Moderate. Two or three different situations are referred to verbally or there is some elaboration of a single situation.
1 Slight or simply there. One or two related statements. All of these would be rated as 1: *"I'm going to the doctor." "I'm going to cook dinner." "Let's go to the store."*
0 No make-believe with actions and situations.

Notes

Role announcement and assigning of roles counts as long as that is not the only thing going on. Statements which are primarily object-centered are scored as make-believe with objects (I'm drinking coffee." "I'm driving a car."). A statement like "I'm driving my car to work." is both make-believe with objects and situations.

Make believe with actions and situations applies to all speech, whether it is part of an interaction or not. It should be recorded as "MBA" and "MBS" (Make-believe with Actions; Make-believe with Situations) since it also refers to actions. However, most of the make-believe refers to situations: a sick baby, a broken arm, a picnic, going to work, robbing the bank, saving a drowning child, visiting grandma, going to the market or the store, cooking breakfast or dinner, fixing the (broken) stove. Make-believe with situations is the *verbalization* of these situations and often, as in "I'm driving to work," refers to actions as well. The action thus verbalized may or may not be actually carried out.

IV. Persistence in Role-Play

The child persists in a play episode for at least five minutes.

Rating Guidelines

3 Extensive. The child stays with a single role or related roles for all of the five-minute period. The play can be repetitious or elaborated. There may be a brief interruption as long as the child returns to the main theme. A child can get a low score on role-play and a high score on persistence. Role involvement is considered; if he stays with the role but is not involved, he cannot get more than a 2.

2 Moderate. The child undertakes one or two roles with some elaboration or repeats activities of the roles to a moderate extent. Some interruption activity can take place. The child definitely has a theme around which he plays.

1 The child undertakes three or more roles with slight elaboration or repetition. The child follows through on some role-play; i.e., he goes to the store, gets groceries and takes the groceries home.

0 There is no persistence in role-play.

V. Interaction

There are at least two players interacting in the context of the sociodramatic play episode. Interaction means that the child directs an action or words to another child. He intends for the other child to respond at least by listening. A child waiting at the cash register to check out is an example of interaction whether or not the other child responds.

Rating Guidelines

3 Truly reciprocal role-play (doctor, nurse; husband, wife; worker, boss) is an integral feature of the play behavior for

most of the five-minute period. This category includes two children who interact with each other as two mothers ("We need groceries" or "Your baby is sick.").

2 Moderate degree of interaction. The child does interact but his play does not require or reflect the presence of a partner to the same extent as that rated as 3. As soon as play activity occurring during the five-minute period is predominantly interaction with another child, the rating is 2. A 2 means interaction is more than minimal but not necessarily integral.

1 Slight interaction, verbal or non-verbal. We would not consider a child with interaction scores of 1 to be one who engages in sociodramatic play. To receive a 2 or more the child must evidence some reciprocal cooperative role-play. A 1 means interaction is present but play activity is predominantly solitary or parallel.

0 No interaction with another child.

Notes

A child who is merely submitting to a doctor's examination is not considered to be role-playing. If he opens his mouth, groans, etc. it is role-play.

VI. Verbal Communication

There is some verbal interaction related to a sociodramatic play episode.

Rating Guidelines

3 Extensive and integral to play.
2 Moderate verbal interaction.
1 Present but slight. Verbal interaction exists, but only just.
0 No verbal communication or verbal interaction.

Notes

Role announcement alone is not verbal communication. Be careful to distinguish between a monologue and a communication addressed to another child. A child reported talking with another child during a sociodramatic play episode is counted as communication unless otherwise specified. "Give me" "That's mine" etc. is not verbal communication in the framework of a sociodramatic play episode.

Discussing roles alone is usually not considered verbal interaction. If the role discussion is related to an episode which preceded or followed, then it may be considered.

If a child has received a score for verbal communication, he must also be rated for interaction. The score a child receives for interaction may be higher than that for verbal communication but the score for verbal communication may not be higher than that for interaction.

e. Information on the Development of the Smilansky Scale and it's Psychometric Characteristics

A preliminary version of the evaluation scale served for assessing socioeconomic status differences in play behavior as well as for the evaluation of an experimental intervention for study promoting development of sociodramatic play in children from lower socioeconomic backgrounds (Smilansky 1968). In these studies sociodramatic play was evaluated globally, determining the presence or absence of each of the six elements of sociodramatic play. Thus, it was possible to determine whether the children had the skills necessary to engage in dramatic and sociodramatic play at their disposal. For the purpose of quantitative evaluation the following checklist was used and filled in during the observation periods as well as for post factum analysis of the detailed play-records by both observers and non-observers.

A more elaborate procedure for evaluating each of the six play elements was developed during a seminar on sociodramatic play in which preschool supervisors participated while taking an inservice courses in the School of Education at Tel Aviv University (1967–1969). During the Ohio seminar (1970–1971) the scale was elaborated further by a group of graduate students under the guidance of Sara Smilansky.

Each of the six elements were defined in more detail as four level scales: from the total absence of the element to its full utilization. The participants in the Ohio seminar varied only slightly in terms of certain details in the definition of each element. The version presented here is recommended on the basis of its correspondence to our concept of sociodramatic play and its usefulness as a reliable measure. This scale was translated, reevaluated and used during a graduate seminar in the Department of Psychology at Tel Aviv University (1977–1979).

The *inter-rater reliability* of the final scale was established in the United States by Griffing (1974), a participant in the Ohio seminar on sociodramatic play, working in cooperation with the other members of the seminar group. Subjects used in the reliability study were 169 randomly selected black preschoolers, half of them from higher socioeconomic backgrounds and half from lower socioeconomic backgrounds.

Consistency of scoring among different raters was determined by pairwise correlations. Independently derived scores for pairs of raters scoring the same children on each of the six play elements were correlated with those of two other raters. Each correlation coefficient involved 60 pairs of data: the scores of ten randomly chosen children for each of six five-minute intervals. The findings are presented in Table 25.

Correlations between pairs of raters are consistently high for all play criteria. The correlations for total play scores are .88 and .89 for two pairs of raters respectively. Griffing concludes that the raters appeared to be scoring in a qualitatively consistent manner not only with regard to the total play scores, but also with regard to each component of play behavior. Griffing made further analyses, aimed at establishing the consistency of

Table 25: Pairwise Correlation Coefficients between Evaluations of Different Raters, by Play Variables

Play Elements	Rater 1 vs. 2	Rater 1 vs. 3
1. Imitative Role-Play	.92	.88
2. Make-Believe with Objects	.84	.91
3. Make-Believe with Situations	.90	.87
4. Persistence in Role-Play	.83	.92
5. Interaction	.86	.73
6. Verbal Communication	.89	.89
Total Play Score	.88	.88

scores given by different observers as well as establishing the differentiating power of the assessment device across children and play criteria. Therefore, a three-way analysis of variance was carried out (raters by children by play variables). There were strong and significant children and play variables effects as well as less strong but still significant interaction between the two. There was, however, no rater effect at all. Griffing summarizes the findings by stating that different children exhibit different patterns of play and that the raters are not differentially influencing the scoring of children's play.

The data presented by Griffing points to the usefulness of the Smilansky scale as a sensitive and reliable tool for evaluating sociodramatic play.

High *inter-rater reliability* was also obtained with the Hebrew version of the scale. Three observers recorded the activities and behavior of 15 nursery school children (age 3–4), 15 kindergarten children (5–6), and 15 primary school children (7–8). The content of the protocols was compared and there was great agreement with regard to the observed behavior. Thereafter, protocols for each child were scored separately by the three observers. Correlations of total play scores between pairs of three observers were .84, .85, and .87.

Test-retest reliability was established for 20 out of these 45 children, after a three-week period without intervention. Total scores correlated .84, despite considerable differences in the play content.

Cross-situational consistency of the American children's play behavior is indicated by the findings of Soiberg (1972). Correlations in the sociodramatic play level in structured situations of 45 children against their sociodramatic play level in the usual preschool setting was .85 (45 black children, some from lower and some from higher socioeconomic backgrounds). *Cross-situational consistency* of the Israeli children's play behavior is indicated by the findings of Smilansky & Feldman (1980). Correlations in the sociodramatic play level in the usual preschool settings of 40 children (ages 4–7), against their sociodramatic play level, when observed (playing in groups of four children) in a structured laboratory situation, was .87.

With regard to the *validity* of the scale it should be emphasized that the categories of evaluation were directly derived from the definition of sociodramatic play and the description of its elements. The *construct validity* of the device is demonstrated also by the fact that training for sociodramatic play activity (based on the same six elements) results in considerable improvement in performing that type of play behavior, as measured by the scale.

Additional evidence for the scale's validity is provided by studies that show *concurrent relationships* between the level of sociodramatic play as measured by the Smilansky scale and related characteristics of the child. In the United States Lewis' study of 78 children from low socioeconomic background (1972) showed high correlations between several variables in picture reading with total play scores as well as with some of the subscores. In Israel Taler (1976) used the scale with 96 kindergarten children (half of which were from low and half were from high socioeconomic backgrounds) and found a strong relationship between total sociodramatic play scores and two independently derived measures of social adjustment: teacher rating and sociometric standing.

Evidence for the scale's *predictive validity* with regard to school achievement was found in Smilansky Feldman's study of 49 children of whom 17 were from high and 32 from low socioeconomic backgrounds (see Table 26). There was considerable correlation between second grade reading comprehension and arithmetic test scores and scores for the six sociodramatic play elements.

There are *no norms* in the Smilansky scale since it is meant to be a criterion referenced assessment tool. There is no need for norms if it is to be used for research purposes and for educational intervention. The aim of the teacher should be to ascertain that each child has the ability to engage in sustained, well-developed sociodramatic play activities.

4. Uses for the Scale

As already noted the Smilansky scale for evaluating sociodramatic play is designed as a tool to assess the dramatic and

Table 26: Correlations Between Sociodramatic Play Scores in Kindergarten and Achievement in Reading Comprehension and Arithmetic in Second Grade

Scores for Six Elements	Reading	Arithmetic
Total Play Score	.40**	.45**
Imitative Role-Play	.38**	.34**
Make-Believe with Objects	.41**	.41**
Make-Believe with Actions & Situations	.32**	.38**
Persistence in Role-Play	.22	.33**
Interaction with Co-players	.31*	.34**
Verbal Communication Within a Role	.27*	.30*

*p<.05
**p<.01

sociodramatic play of young children both qualitatively and quantitatively. It has been established as reliable and valid mainly as regards preschool-attending children from the age range of 3–8. It is hoped that research and studies will provide data concerning its reliability and validity for younger aged children as well, age range 1–3 years.

It should be emphasized that the reliability of the scale depends on the conditions of data collection. The reliability studies mentioned were conducted according to the procedures described earlier. For research purposes these procedures should be adhered to.

Since the Smilansky scale was found to be effective for diagnosing play behavior in non-structured settings as well—in the kindergarten play corners and even on the playground—it would seem unnecessary to control conditions, such as space, equipment, one-to-one observer rate and detailed record-keeping of the activities strictly, when being used by teachers for purposes other than research. Scoring of the six elements of play for the purpose of non-structured evaluation can be based on the recording sheet: *Attainments in Sociodramatic Play*. This provides a quick and efficient evaluation method. However, its reliability is not established.

ATTAINMENTS IN SOCIODRAMATIC PLAY

Name of preschool
Address

Name of Preschool Teacher
Date

No.	Names of Children	Whether Engaged in Dramatic Play during Observation	Factors Existing and Missing from Sociodramatic Play — Play Elements																Teacher's Remarks
			a			b			c			d			e			f		
			+	?	0	+	?	0	+	?	0	+	?	0	+	?	0	+	?	0	
1.	Dan	P	x					x			x	x				x				x	
2.	Shoshana	NP			x			x			x			x			x			x	
3.	Hanna	P	x				x		x			x					x	x			
4.																					
5.																					
6.																					
7.																					
8.																					
9.																					
10.																					
11.																					
12.																					

Appendix B:
A Survey of Sociodramatic Play in the Preschool Curriculum and Teacher Attitudes

Realizing the growing awareness of early childhood educators that sociodramatic play has significance for the child's cognitive as well as emotional development, we conducted a survey to clarify the actual status accorded sociodramatic play within the preschool curriculum in the United States and in Israel.

A. Procedure

Sixty kindergarten and preschool teachers from the United States (Boston Mass., Columbus Ohio, and Washington D.C.) and sixty from Israel (the Tel Aviv area) responded to the following questionnaire before beginning a workshop on sociodramatic play.

B. Questionnaire on Dramatic and Sociodramatic Play in the Classroom

Name of Teacher:
Number of boys: girls: in class. Ages:

1. Is there a "house" corner in your classroom?
   ☐ Yes   ☐ No

2. List the type and quantity of equipment in the "house" corner:

_____

_____

_____

_____

3. Time(s) of day when the children play in the "house" corner:

_____

4. Number of boys: girls: who played in the "house" corner during the past three weeks.

5. Do you expect all the children in your class to play in the "house" corner at some time during the day or week? Why or why not? (please explain)

_____

_____

_____

_____

6. Do you think teachers should help children learn how to play? Why or why not? If so, how?

_____

_____

_____

_____

7. Do you think that the play activities of children in the "house" corner help prepare them to succeed in school? Why or why not? If so, in what way?

_____

_____

_____

_____

8. During your training to become a teacher, did any of the courses you took deal with the importance of playing in the "house" corner?

_____

9. During your training to become a teacher, did you learn how to develop a child's ability to engage in dramatic or sociodramatic play activity while in the "house" corner?

_____

10. During your education to become a teacher did you learn how to assess or evaluate a child's play ability? _____

_____

C. Findings

The questionnaire was designed to provide information on five basic issues. The findings are summarized accordingly.
1. <u>Equipment for Sociodramatic Play available in the Classroom.</u>
   a. All 120 teachers, without exception, reported that there is a "house" corner in the classroom.
   b. There were no significant differences between the countries or classrooms in terms of the type of toys and equipment which was available in the play-house. The major differences between the classrooms were in

terms of the quantity and quality of the toys. For example, in some classrooms there were only one or two shabby, overused dolls, and in others there were 16, mostly new, high quality dolls of all sizes and shapes. Toys found in all the classrooms included: a sink, cabinets, a stove, a table and chairs, pots and pans, a broom, a doll bed, clothing, an ironing board and iron, a doctor's bag, a telephone, purses and pocketbooks, some toy animals, empty food boxes, toy knives and forks, plates and cups.

2. The Attitude of Teachers toward Sociodramatic Play as Part of the Curriculum

   a. 60% of the teachers reported that the children could play in the "house" corner at any time during the school-day: during the free play period or after finishing the directed work. 40% reported that children could play in the "house" corner during a 30-minute period.

   b. When considered according to sex, 10–25% of the boys and 25–50% of the girls played in the "house" corner.

   c. 80% of the teachers did not expect all of the children to play in the "house" corner; 15% expected only certain of the children to play in the "house" corner and 5% expected all of the children to play in the "house" corner at some point during the week. Some of the comments were: "I like them to play there only when they like to." "Some children are not comfortable there." "The children have other options available." "If he/she doesn't feel like playing, it should be up to the child." "Some children (mainly boys) are not interested in that type of playing."

Thus we can see that preschool teachers from both the United States and Israel do not include dramatic and sociodramatic play as part of their conscious curriculum. Although they maintain an environment which would be suitable for such play, they do not devote specific time to such play nor do they expect all the children to make use of the equipment, which they would in terms of other areas of the curriculum.

3. The Teachers' Awareness of the Relevance of Sociodramatic Play for School Success
   a. 90% of the teachers did not consider sociodramatic play as contributing to future school success.
   b. 10% regarded it significant in terms of contributing to the child's emotional well-being.

Reasons given for not considering sociodramatic play to be useful in terms of future school behavior were: "Play only helps develop the personality" "Play helps emotional well-being" "Play makes children happy" "Play gives children satisfaction, joy, provides a relaxed atmosphere" etc.

4. The Teachers' Attitude toward Intervention in Sociodramatic Play
   a. 50% of the teachers reacted negatively to the idea of intervening in sociodramatic play
   b. 30% declared that teachers might encourage and demonstrate, but should not help or facilitate
   c. 20% said that teachers should help and intervene to promote the ability of children to engage in sociodramatic play.

The following represent responses to the question of why or how the teacher should/should not facilitate such play ability:

"The teacher may show the toys and equipment to the children, but the children must develop the skill to play with them on their own; teachers may show the children how to play with the equipment, how to excel in play, how to use new toys and equipment appropriate for the different seasons, how to use the dress-up clothes; the teacher may indicate which toys are available."

"Children will learn by watching other children."

"They will learn by themselves after a time"

"They should create their own play"

"They will learn by exploring the toys"

"They will learn by exposure to the toys at home"

"Play is a highly emotional experience; therefore, the children should make their own choices—a teacher could harm the child by trying to 'help' him" etc.

5. <u>Training Teachers Received: Assessing and Enhancing</u>
   <u>Sociodramatic Play Behavior</u>
   a. None of the 120 teachers had had a course during their
      teacher-training period which dealt with facilitating,
      developing and assessing play activities in the "house"
      corner. Only four Israeli teachers noted that they had
      observed such activity during their practice teaching
      and had learned a small amount about developing more
      effective play activities.
   b. None of the teachers knew how to evaluate their chil-
      dren's sociodramatic play and what assessment tools
      or criteria are available. Some applied occasional anec-
      dotal and impressionistic reporting.

It is important to note here that there were no significant
differences between the training experiences of American and
Israeli teachers in terms of sociodramatic play.

D. Summary

It is clear that all preschool and kindergarten teachers had
the equipment and facilities in their classrooms which were
appropriate for sociodramatic play. However, such play was
not part of the conscious curriculum. The teachers did not expect
all children to engage in such play during the school day or
even during the school week; they did not feel that they should
intervene in order to encourage or develop such play. They
assumed that children would learn to play on their own. The
teachers were neither taught about the significance of sociodramatic play nor were they taught how to intervene, facilitate or
assess such play. The teachers did not see sociodramatic play
as preparation for future school performance.

Bibliography

Ariel, S., Carel, C.A. & Tyrano, S. (1985) Uses of children's make-believe play in family therapy. *Journal of Marriage and Family Therapy*, 11: 47–60.

Ausubel, D.P. (1952) *Ego Development and the Personality Disorders*. New York: Grune & Stratton.

Axline, V.M. (1955) Play therapy procedures and results. *American Journal of Orthopsychiatry*, 25: 618–626.

Belsky, J. & Most, R.K. (1981) From exploration to play: A cross-sectional study of infant free play behavior. *Developmental Psychology*, 17: 630–639.

Bowman, B. 1990 Play in Teacher Education, In E. Klugman and S. Smilansky (eds.) *Children's Play and Learning*. Columbia University Press, N.Y.

Borke, H. (1971) Interpersonal perception of young children. *Developmental Psychology*, 5: 263–269.

Borman, K. (1979) Children's interactions on the playgrounds. *Theory Into Practice*, 18: 251–257.

Brainlrol, C.J. (1982) Effects of group and individual dramatic play training on cognitive development. In D. Pepler and K.H. Rubur (Eds.) *The Play of Children*. Basel, Switzerland: Kayer.

Bretherton, I. (1984) Event representation in symbolic play: Reality and fantasy. In I. Bretherton (Ed.) *Symbolic play: The representation of social understanding*. N.Y. Academic.

Buhler, C. (1935) From Birth to Maturity. London: Kegan Paul.

Burns, S.M. & Brainerd, C.J. (1979) Effects of constructive and dramatic play on perspective taking in very young children. *Developmental Psychology*, 15: 512–521.

Cartwright, S. (1988) Play can be the building blocks of learning. *Young children*, 43(5): 44–47.

Chaille, C. (1978) The child's conceptions of play, pretending, and toys, *Human Development*, 21: 201–210.

Cheyne, J.A. (1982) Object play and problem solving. In D.J. Pepler & K.H. Rubin (eds.) *The play of children: current theory and research*. Basel, Switzerland: Karger.

Christie, J.F. and Johnsen, E.P. (1983) The role of play in social-intellectual development. *Review of Educational Research*, 53: 93–115.

263

Christman, M.L. (1979) A look at socio-dramatic play among Mexican-American children. *Childhood Education*, 56: 106–110.

Clune, C., Paolella, J. & Foley, J. (1979) Free play behavior in atypical children: An approach to assessment. *Journal of Autism and Developmental Disorders*, 9: 61–72.

Cole, D. and LaVoie J.C. (1985) Fantasy play and related cognitive development in 2–6 years old. *Developmental Psychology*, 21: 233–240.

Connolly, J., & Doyle, A. Ceschin, F. (1983) Forms and functions of social fantasy play in preschoolers. In M.B. Liss (ed.) *Social and Cognitive Skills & Children's Play*. N.Y. Academic: 71–92.

Connolly, J. and Doyle, A.B. (1984) Relation of social fantasy play to social competence in preschoolers. *Developmental Psychology*, 20: 297–806.

Corsaro, W.A. and Tomlinson, G. (1980) Spontaneous play and social learning in the nursery school. In H.B. Schwartzman (Ed.) *Play and Culture*. West point, N.Y. Leisure Press.

Dansky, J.L. (1980) Cognitive consequences of sociodramatic play and exploration training for economically disadvantaged preschoolers. *Journal of Child Psychology and Psychiatry*, 21: 47–58.

Dansky, J.L. (1980a) Make believe: A mediator of the relationship between play and associative fluency. *Child Development*, 51: 576–579.

Dewey, J. (1902) *The Child and the Curriculum*. Chicago: The University of Chicago Press.

Dewey, J. (1934) *Art as Experience*. New York: Minton, Balch & Co.

Doyle, A.B. (1980) The effect of playmate familiarity on the social interaction of young children. *Child Development*, 51: 217–223.

Dunn, J. & Dale N. (1984). I a daddy: 2-year olds' collaboration in joint pretend with sibling & mother. In I. Bretherton (Ed.) Symbolic Play: *The Representation of Social Understanding*. N.Y. Academic.

Dunn, J. & Wooding, M. (1979) Play in the home and its implications for learning. In B. Tizard & D. Harvey (Eds.) *Biology of Play*. Philadelphia: Lippincott.

Elder, J.L. & Pederson, D.R. (1978) Preschool children's use of objects in symbolic play. *Child Development*, 49: 500–504.

Elkind, D. (1988) *Play in Young Children.*

El-Konin, D. (1966) Symbolics and it's function in the play of children. *Soviet Education*, 8(2), no. 9: 35–41.

Erickson, F.H. (1958) Play interview of 4 year old hospitalized children. *Monographs of the Society for Research in Child Development*, 23(3), no. 69.

Fein, G. (1984) The self building potential of pretend play. In T.D. Yowey & A.D. Pellegrini (Eds.) *Child's Play: Developmental & Applied*. Hillsdale, N.J. Erlbaum.

Fein, G.G. (1979) Echoes from the nursery: Piaget, Vygotsky, and the relationship between language and play. *New Directions for Child Development*, 6: 1–14.

Fein, G.G. (1981) Pretend play in childhood: An integrative review. *Child Development*, 52: 1095–1118.

Fein, G.G. & Apfel, N. (1979) Some preliminary observations on knowing and pretending. In, M. Smith & M.B. Franklin (Eds.), *Symbolic Functioning in Childhood.* Hillsdale, N.J.: Erlbaum.

Fein, G. (1986) Pretend play: Creativity and consciousness. In D. Gorlitz & J. Wohwill (Eds.) *Curiosity, imagination and play.* Hillsdale, NJ.

Fein, G. & S. Schwartz (1986) The social coordination of pretense in preschool children. In G. Fein & M. Rivkin *The Young Child at Play.* N.A.E.Y.C.

Fein, G. & Stork, L. (1981) Sociodramatic play: Social class effects in integrated preschool classrooms. *Journal of Applied Developmental Psychology,* 2: 267–279.

Feitelson, D. & Ross, G.S. (1973) The neglected factor—play. *Human Development,* 16: 202–223.

Fenson, K. & Ramsey, D.S. (1980) Decentration and integration of the child's play in the second year. *Child Development,* 51: 171–178.

Fenson, L. (1978) Sequence and pretense in play in the second year. Paper presented at the Eighth Annual International Conference on Piagetian Theory and the Helping Professions, Los Angeles.

Fenson, L., Kagan, J., Kearsley, R.B. & Zelazo, P.R. (1976) The developmental progression of manipulative play in the first two years. *Child Development,* 47: 232–235.

Fenson, L. & Ramsay, I. (1981) Effects of modeling action on the play of young children. *Child Development,* 52: 1028–1036.

Field, T. DeStefano, L. & Koewler, J. (1982) Fantasy play of toddlers and preschoolers. *Developmental Psychology,* 18: 503–508.

Fink, R.S. (1976) Role of imaginative play in cognitive development. *Psychological Reports,* 39: 895–906.

Freud, A. (1946) *The psychoanalytical treatment of children.* London, Imago.

Freud, S. (1949) *An outline of psychoanalysis.* New York: Norton & Co.

Freud, S. (1899, 1928) *The Interpretation of Dreams.* London: Allen.

Freyberg, J.T. (1973) Increasing the imaginative play of urban disadvantaged children through systematic training. In L.S. Singer (Ed.), *The Child's World of Make-believe.* New York: Academic Press.

Froebel, F. (1947) *Theories des Spiels.* Weimar Thuringer Verlagsanstalt.

Frost, J.L. & Sunderlin, S. (Eds.) (1985) *When Children Play.* Wheaton, MD.

Glaubman, R. (1990). Play in teacher education. The Israeli Perspective. In E. Klugman and S. Smilansky (Eds.) *Children's Play and Learning.* Columbia University Press, N.Y.

Golomb, C. & Bonen, S. (1981) Playing games of make-believe: The effectiveness of symbolic play training with children who failed to benefit from early conservation training. *Genetic Psychology Monographs,* 104: 137–159.

Golomb, C. & Cornelius C.B. (1977) Symbolic play and its cognitive significance. *Developmental Psychology,* 13: 246–252.

Gottfried, A. & Brown C. (1986) *Play Interactions: The Contribution of Play Materials & Parental Involvement to Child Development.* Lexington, MA: Health.

Griffin, H. (1984) The coordination of meaning in the creation of a shared make-believe reality. In I. Bretherton (Ed.) *Symbolic Play: The Development of Social Understanding,* N.Y. Academic.

Griffing, P. (1980) The relationship between socioeconomic status and socio-dramatic play among black kindergarten children. *Genetic Psychology Monographs*, 101, 3–34.

Griffing, P. (1983) Encouraging dramatic play in early childhood. *Young children*, 38, (2): 13–22.

Griffing, P.S. (1974) The Relationship Between SES and Sociodramatic Play Among Black Kindergarten Children. Ph.D. Dissertation, Ohio State University.

Groos, K. (1922) *Das Spiel*. Jena, Fischer.

Guthrie, K. & Hudson, L.M. (1979) Training conservation through symbolic play. *Child Development*, 50, 1269–1271.

Halloway, S.D. Reichhart-Erickson, M. (1988) The relationship of day care quality to children's free-play behavior and social problem-solving skills. *Early Childhood Research Quarterly*, 3(1): 39–53.

Holliday, J. & McNaughton, S. (1982) Sex differences in play at kindergarten. *New Zealand Journal of Educational Studies*, 17: 161–170.

Isaacs, S. (1933) *Social Development in Young Children:* A Study of Beginnings. London, Routledge & Sons.

Isaacs, S. (1935) *Intellectual Growth in Children*. London: Routledge & Sons.

Johnson, J.E. (1976) Relations of divergent thinking and intelligence test scores with social and non-social make-believe play of preschool children. *Child Development*, 47: 1200–1203.

Johnson, J.E. & Ershler, J. (1982) Intellective correlates of preschooler's spontaneous play. *Journal of General Psychology*, 106: 115–122.

Johnson, J.E. & Roopnarine, J.L. (1983) The preschool classroom and sex differences in children's play. In M.B. Liss (Ed.) *Social and cognitive skills: sex roles & children's play*, N.Y. Academic.

Kagan, J., Kearsley, R.B. & Zelazo, P.R. (1978) *Infancy: Its Place in Human Development*. Cambridge, Mass: Harvard University Press.

Kelly-Byrne, D. (1983) Play: The child-adult connection. In B. Sutton-Smith & D. Kelly-Byrne (Eds.) *The Masks of Play*. West Point, N.Y. Leisure Press.

King, N.R. (1979) Play: the kindergartners' perspective, *The Elementary School Journal*, 80: 81–87.

Klein, M. (1955) The psychoanalytic play technique. *American Journal of Orthopsychiatry*, 25: 223–237.

Klein, P. (1985) Mediated learning experience. In, P. Tamir, T.B. Brazelton & A. Russell (Eds.), *Intervention and Stimulation in Infant Development*. London: Freund Publ.

Levy, A.K. (1986) Increasing preschool effectiveness through planned socio-dramatic play. *Early Childhood* Research Quarterly, Vol. 1 (2): 133–140.

Lieberman, J.N. (1979) *Playfulness: Its Relationship to Imagination and Creativity*, N.Y.: Academic.

Liss, M.B. (1983) Learning gender-related skills through play in M.B. Liss (Ed.) *Social Cognitive Skills: Sex Roles and Children's Play*. N.Y. Academic.

Liss, M. (1986) Play of Boys & Girls. In G. Fein & M. Rivkin (Eds.) *The Young Child at Play*, NAEYC.

Lovinger, S.L. (1974) Sociodramatic play and language development in pre-school disadvantaged children. *Psychology in the Schools*, 11: 313–320.

Lowe, M. (1975) Trends in the development of representational play in infants from one to three years: An observational study. *Journal of Child Psychology and Psychiatry*, 16: 33–47.

Lowenfeld, M. (1935) *Play in Childhood*. London: Gollancy.

Lynn, D.B. (1961) Sex differences in identification development. *Sociometry*, 24: 372–383.

Marshall, H.R. (1961) Relations between home experiences and children's use of language in play interaction with peers. *Psychological Monographs*, 75(5), no. 509.

Marshall, H.R. & Doshi, R. (1965) Aspects of experience revealed through doll play of preschool children. *Journal of Psychology*, 61: 47–57.

Marshall, H.R. & Hahn, S. (1967) Experimental modification of dramatic play. *Journal of Personality and Social Psychology*, 5: 119–122.

Maun, B.L. (1984). Effects of realistic & unrealistic props on symbolic play. In I.D. Yowke and A.D. Pellegrini (Eds.) *Child's Play: Developmental and Applied*, Hillsdale, N.J.

McCune-Nicolich (1977) Beyond sensory-motor intelligence: Assessment of symbolic maturity through analysis of pretend play. *Merrill-Palmer Quarterly*, 23: 89–99.

McCune-Nicolich, L. (1981) Toward symbolic functioning: Structure of early pretend games and potential parallels with language. *Child Development*, 52: 785–797.

McLoyed, V. (1986) Scaffolds or Shackles? The role of toys in preschool children's pretend play, in G. Fein and M. Rivkin (Eds.) *The Young Child at Play*, N.A.E.Y.C.

Miller, N.E. & Dollard, J. (1941) *Social learning and imitation*. New Haven, Yale University Press.

Miller, P. and Garvey C. (1984) Mother-baby role play. In Bretherton, I. (Ed.) *Symbolic Play: The Representation of Social Understanding*, N.Y. Academic.

Miller, S.N. (1974) The playful, the crazy & the nature of pretense. *Rice University Studies*, 60: 31–51.

Mooney, R.L. & Smilansky, S. (1973) An experiment in the use of drawing to promote cognitive development in disadvantaged preschool children in Israel and the United States. Final report, U.S. Department of Health Education & Welfare, Office of Education, NCERD, project no. 2-0137.

Mowrer, O.H. (1950) Identification: A link between learning theory and psychotherapy. In, *Learning Theory and Personality Dynamics, Selected Papers*. New York: Ronald Press.

Murphy, G. (1946) *Personality: A Biosocial Approach to Origins and Structure*. New York: Basic Books.

Murphy, L. (1956) *Methods for the Study of Personality in Young Children*. New York: Basic Books.

Mussen, P. & Distler, L. (1959) Masculinity, identification and father-son relationship. *Journal of Abnormal and Social Psychology*, 59: 350–356.

Nicolich, L.M. (1977) Beyond Sensory-motor Intelligence: Assessment of Symbolic Maturity through Analysis of Pretend Play. *Merrill-Palmer Quarterly,* 23: 89–99.

Parsons, T. & Bales, R.F. (1956) *Family Socialization and Interaction Process.* New York: MacMillan.

Pellegrini, A.D. (1980) The relationship between kindergartner's play and achievement in prereading & writing. *Psychology in the schools,* 17, 530–555.

Pellegrini, A.D. (1986) The effect of play centers on preschooler's explicit language. In G. Fein and M. Rivkin (Eds.) *The Young Child at Play.* N.A.E.Y.C.

Pellegrini, A.D. and Perlmutter, J.C. (1982) A reexamination of the Smilansky-Porter matrix of play behavior. *Journal of Research in Childhood Education,* (2): 89–96.

Pestalozzi, J.H. (1801, translated 1915) *How Gertrud Teaches her Children.* Syracuse, N.Y.: W. Bardeen.

Phyfe-Perkins, E. and J. Shoemaker (1986) Indoor play environments. In G. Fein and M. Rivkin (Eds.) *The Young Child at Play.* N.A.E.Y.C.

Piaget, J. (1962) *Play, Dreams and Imitation in Childhood.* New York: Norton & Co.

Piaget, J. (1966) Need and significance of cross-cultural studies in genetic psychology. *Journal of Psychology,* 1: 3–13.

Piaget, J. (1971) Response to Brian Sutton-Smith. *Psychological Review,* 73(1): 111–112, republished in R.E. Herron & B. Sutton-Smith (1971) (Eds.), Child's Play. New York: Wiley & Sons, pages 337–339.

Piaget, J. & Inhelder, B. (1956) *The Child's Conception of Space.* London, Routledge & Kegan Paul.

Piaget, J. & Inhelder, B. (1971) *Mental Imagery in the Child.* New York: Basic Books.

Power, T. and Lynn Chapieski (1985) Assessment of individual differences in infant exploration and play. *Developmental Psychology,* 21(6): 974–981.

Pulasky, M.A. (1973) Toys and imaginative play. In, L.S. Singer (Ed.) *The Child's World of Make-believe.* New York: Academic Press.

Rivkin, M. (1986) The Educator's place in children's play. In G. Fein and M. Rivkin (Eds.) *The Young Child at Play.* N.A.E.Y.C.

Rosen, C.E. (1974) The effects of sociodramatic play on problem-solving behavior among culturally disadvantaged preschool children. *Child Development,* 45: 920–927.

Rubin, K.H. & Maioni, T.L. (1975) Play preference and it's relation to egocentrism, popularity and classification skills in preschool. *Merrill-Palmer Quarterly,* 21: 171–179.

Rubin, K.H. and Seibel, C.G. (1979 March) The effects of ecological setting on cognitive and social play behaviors of preschoolers. Paper presented at the annual meeting of American Educational Research Association, San Francisco.

Rubin, K.S. & Pepler, D.J. (1982) Children's Play: Piaget's views reconsidered. *Contemporary Educational Psychology,* 7: 289–299.

Saltz, E. & Brodie, J. (1982) Pretend play training in childhood: A review and critique. In D.J. Pepler and K. Rubin (Eds.) *The Play of Children: Current Theory and Research*, Basel, Switzerland: Karger.

Saltz, E., Dixon, D. & Johnson, J. (1977) Training disadvantaged preschoolers on various fantasy activities: Effects on cognitive functioning and impulse control. *Child Development*, 48: 367–380.

Saltz, R. and E. Satz (1986) Pretend Play and its outcomes in G. Fein and M. Rivkin (Eds.) *The Young Child at play*. N.A.E.Y.C.

Sancho-Olivia N. (1984) Construction and validation of the play rating scale. *Early Child Development and Care*.

Schiller, F.V. (1795) Briefe uber die Aesthetische Erziehung des Menschen. (English ed. On Aesthetic Education of Man, 1967, Oxford, Clavendon Press.

Sears, P.S. (1953) Child rearing factors related to playing of sex-typed roles. *American Psychologist*, 8: 431.

Sears, R.R. (1957) Identification as a form of behavioral development. In, D.B. Harris (Ed.) *The Concept of Development: An issue in the Study of Human Behavior*. Minneapolis University of Minnesotta Press.

Shefatya, L. (1988) Formative Evaluation of Project "Parents". The Henrietta Szold Institute, Jerusalem.

Sigel, I. & McBane, B. (1967) Cognitive competence and level of symbolization among five-year old children. In, J. Hellmuth (Ed.), *The Disadvantaged Child*. Seattle, Washington: Special Child Publications.

Singer, L.S. (1973) *The Child's World of Make-believe—Experimental Studies of Imaginative Play*. New York: Academic Press.

Slade, A (1987) Quality of attachment and early symbolic play. *Developmental Psychology*, 23,(1) 78–85.

Slater, P.E. (1961) Toward a dualistic theory of identification. *Merrill-Palmer Quarterly*, 7: 113–126.

Smilansky, S. (1968) *The Effects of Socio-dramatic Play on Disadvantaged Preschool Children*. New York: Wiley & Sons.

Smilansky, S., Hagan, J. & Lewis, H. (1988) *Clay in the Classroom—Helping Children Develop Cognitive and Affective Skills for Learning*. N.Y. Teachers College Press, Columbia University.

Smilansky, S. & Shefatya, L. (1976) Diagnosis by the Kindergarten Teacher: Construction of an Adjustment Rating-Scale—It's Validation as Predictor of Achievement in Grades 1 & 2. Jerusalem, The Henriette Szold Institute.

Smilansky, S. & Shefatya, L. (1979) Narrowing socio-economic gaps in achievement through kindergarten reading instruction. *University of Haifa, Studies in Education*, 21: 41–68.

Smilansky, S., Shefatya, L. & Frenkel, E. (1976) Mental Development of Infants from Two Ethnic Groups: Findings from the Jerusalem Study of Growth and Development. The Henrietta Szold Institute, Jerusalem.

Smith, P.K. (1983) Training in fantasy play. *Early Child Development and Care*, 11: 217–226.

Smith, P.K., Dalgleish, M. & Herzmark, G. (1981) A comparison of the effects of fantasy play tutoring and skills, tutoring in nursery classes. *International Journal of Behavioral Development*, 4: 421–441.

Smith, P.K. & Dodsworth, C. (1977) Social-class differences in the fantasy play of preschool children. *Journal of Genetic Psychology*, 133: 183–190.

Smith, P.K. & Syddal, S. (1978) Play and non-play tutoring in preschool children: Is it play or tutoring which matters? *British Journal of Educational Psychology*, 48: 315–325.

Spencer, H. (1872) *The Principles of Psychology*. London. Williams & Norgate.

Stoke, S.M. (1950) An inquiry into the concept of identification. *Journal of Genetic Psychology*, 76: 163–189.

Sutton-Smith, B. (1977) Piaget on Play: A Critique. In, Herron, R.E. & Sutton-Smith B. (Eds.), *Child's Play*. New-York: Wiley & Sons.

Taler, I. (1976) Social status of kindergarten children and their level of sociodramatic play. M.A. thesis, Department of Psychology, Tel-Aviv University.

Tizard, B., Phils, J. & Plewis, J. (1976) Play in preschool centers, II. Effects on play of the child's social class and of the educational orientation of the centre. *Journal of Child Psychology & Psychiatry*, 17: 265–274.

Tower, R.B., Singer, D.G., Singer, J.L. & Biggs, A. (1979) *American Journal of Orthopsychiatry*, 49: 265–281.

Udwin, O. (1983) Imaginative play training as an intervention method with institutionalized preschool children. *British Journal of Educational Psychology*, 53: 32–39.

Udwin, O. & Shmukler, D. (1981) The influence of sociocultural, economic and home background factors on children's ability to engage in imaginative play. *Developmental Psychology*, 17: 66–72.

Valentine, C.W. (1942) *The Psychology of Early Childhood*. London: Methuen.

Vygotsky, L.S. (1967) Play and it's role in the mental development of the child. *Soviet Psychology*, 5: 6–18.

Wagner, B.S. and Frost, J.L. (1986) Assessing play and behaviors of infants and toddlers. *Journal of Research in Childhood Education*, 1(1): 27–36.